EMBRACING ARMS

EMBRACING ARMS

Cultural Representation of
Slavic and Balkan Women in War

Edited by
HELENA GOSCILO
with
YANA HASHAMOVA

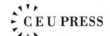

C E U PRESS

Central European University Press
Budapest–New York

Published in 2012 by

Central European University Press

An imprint of the
Central European University Limited Liability Company
Nádor utca 11, H-1051 Budapest, Hungary
Tel: +36-1-327-3138 or 327-3000
Fax: +36-1-327-3183
E-mail: ceupress@ceu.hu
Website: www.ceupress.com

400 West 59th Street, New York NY 10019, USA
Tel: +1-212-547-6932
Fax: +1-646-557-2416
E-mail: mgreenwald@sorosny.org

ISBN 978-615-5225-09-3 cloth

LIBRARY OF CONGRESS CATALOGING-IN-PUBLICATION DATA

Embracing arms : cultural representation of Slavic and Balkan women in war /
[edited by] Helena Goscilo & Yana Hashamova.
    Includes bibliographical references and index.
    ISBN 978-6155225093 (hbk.)
1. War in mass media. 2. Women in mass media. 3. Women and war—Slavic countries. 4. Women and war—Balkan Peninsula. I. Goscilo, Helena, 1945– II. Hashamova, Yana.
    P96.W352E8524 2012
    355.02082--dc23
                            2012019490

Printed in Hungary by
Prime Rate Kft., Budapest

На майка ми, чиято мъдрост
продължава да ме вдъхновява.

To my mother, whose wisdom
continues to inspire me.

YANA

In memoriam:
To David Lowe, a much-loved
brother in all but blood.

HELENA

Table of Contents

Preface and Acknowledgments

Embracing Arms examines the cultural representations of women in war across geographical and generic boundaries. The chapters treat Polish and Russian film and television, Russian graphics, literature, song, and journalism, as well as Balkan film and literature. Given the breadth of the volume's purview, we envision a readership of academics from various disciplines, ranging from Slavists and Balkanists to historians, political scientists, and specialists in gender studies and feminism.

Our respective home institutions responded with alacrity and generosity to our appeal for financial sponsorship of the bi-partite conference titled *Women in War* (2007) at The Ohio State University (OSU) and the University of Pittsburgh (Pitt), which served as the basis for this volume. We are therefore most happy to express our gratitude to the following institutional entities for underwriting our enterprise:

At OSU, the Center for Slavic and East European Studies (CSEES), the Mershon Center for International Security Studies, the Office of International Affairs; the Departments of Slavic and East European Languages and Literatures (DSEELL), Comparative Studies, Film Studies, Women's Studies, and Near Eastern Languages and Cultures; the Centers for Folklore Studies and the Study of Religions; Women in Development, and the College of Humanities.

At Pitt, the Office of A&S Deans, which awarded us a substantial A&S FRSP (Faculty Research and Scholarship Program) grant, the Office of the Provost of Research, the European Union Center, and programs in Cultural Studies, Film Studies, Women's Studies;

the Center for Russian and East European Studies (CREES); and the Department of Slavic Languages and Literatures.

Our profound thanks to all conference participants, including our capable, sometimes inspired, discussants. Andrew Chapman's design of the poster at Pitt and his invaluable aid in the practical organization of the conference made him the Hero of the Hour, and if I (HG) had the appropriate medal to award him, I would pin it on his...chest.

Finally, for enabling the success of the conference on the Pitt campus, HG wishes to acknowledge the largesse of George Klinzing—a far-seeing and committed supporter of the Stalinka website housed at Pitt's DRL—and Alberta Sbragia, a source of sagacious counsel and intellectual energy.

Our appreciation to all those involved for contributing to the intellectual vitality and collegial pleasures of both conferences and the dialogues that followed.

Finally, we extend gratitude to OSU's College of Arts and Sciences and its Dean of Research, Sebastian Knowles, for the grant that defrayed the costs incurred in preparing the book for publication; to Alex Trotter, professional extraordinaire; and to Virág Illés, an exemplar of editorial grace and efficiency at the Central European University Press. For invaluable information regarding copyright, HG is indebted to Aleksandr Vislyi, current Director of the Russian National Library in Moscow.

Introduction

Helena Goscilo

"Only the dead have seen the end of war."
Plato[1]

"Women should not die this way. War is a man's affair."
Razman, member of Russian OMON troops in Chechnya[2]

"I say with Euripides that I would rather go through three
wars than through a single childbirth."
Søren Kierkegaard, *The Diary of a Seducer*[3]

War as Litmus Test of Masculinity

Regardless of stirring legends about the military prowess of Boadicea, Penthesilea, and other Amazons, historically, war has been a quintessentially male preserve.[4] For millennia, men's capacity and readiness to kill or

---

[1] I could not find this axiom, attributed to Plato on a wall of the Imperial War Museum in London, as well as by George Santayana and General Douglas MacArthur, in any of Plato's dialogues.

[2] Quoted in Ferreira-Marques (2003).

[3] Søren Kierkegaard, *The Diary of a Seducer* (Ithaca, NY: The Dragon Press, 1932), 157.

[4] Notable dissenting voices that detect nothing redemptive in war have included Aristophanes, Voltaire, Tolstoi, and Remarque in literature, and Stanley Kubrick, among an increasing number of directors, in film. Joseph

die in battle served not only as a rite of passage into full-fledged masculinity, but also as a prerequisite for the status of hero and the mythologiza-
tion that such a reputation automatically entails. Until recently, conquest
and colonization through armed conflict have constituted the very stuff
of "history"—and "his story." According to Melissa Stockdale, "A new
stereotype of modern masculinity was created and widely diffused" in late
eighteenth-century Europe, whereby "heroism, discipline, and sacrifice
of one's life on behalf of a higher purpose became the set attributes of
ideal masculinity" (Stockdale). Though mortal combat was indisputably a
gendered prerogative, that ideal, in fact, already existed in ancient Rome,
implicitly summed up in the renowned lines from one of Horace's *Odes*,
"Dulce et decorum est / Pro patria mori." Modern masculinity merely sys-
tematized and consolidated the normative stereotype (Mosse 1996, 5). As
Nancy Huston argues, "Hunting and warring have been institutionalized
as the *sacred privilege* of the male," rooted in the actualization of the mythical "mutual exclusiveness between war [...] and motherhood" that the
above epigraph borrowed from Kierkegaard obliquely references (Huston
1986, 130, 129, emphasis in the original). This symmetrical binary proceeds by a flawed syllogism: men make war, whereas women make babies;
men biologically cannot give birth; therefore women biologically cannot
wage war. Such a dichotomous bent of mind partly accounts for the
imputation of lesbianism to women in the military.[5]

Normally distanced from this troubling but widely accepted
formula for masculinity by virtue of their gender, women during World
War I nonetheless proved receptive to the notion of warfare as a reliable measure of heroic manhood and patriotism—a stance at odds with
Samuel Johnson's moral depreciation of patriotism as "the last refuge of
the scoundrel," Oscar Wilde's equally disdainful gloss on it as "the virtue
of the vicious," and George Bernard Shaw's dismissal of it as "a perni-
cious, psychopathic form of idiocy." In a flag-waving *volte-face*, feminists

---

Heller's antic, inspired *Catch-22* (1961) impresses many (myself included)
as the ultimate artistic anti-war statement in the twentieth century. For a historical survey of female combatants, see Goldstein 59–127.

[5] As Leisa Meyer notes, "Public assumptions that military women would be
mannish, when joined with the cultural equation of mannishness with lesbianism, meant that women joining the Army during World War II were popu-
larly perceived as having the potential to be lesbians" (Meyer 1996, 6).

on both sides who earlier had advocated peace "in transnational women's solidarity" reacted to the outbreak of war with patriotic fervor in the hope of enhanced prospects for women's suffrage once peace returned (Goldstein 2001, 318). Uncompromising in their endorsement of the national imperative, countless British women participated in the officially organized White Feather campaign—deplored by Shaw and others— that publicly stigmatized men whose reluctance or refusal to enlist was equated with cowardice, symbolized by the feather awarded them.

In a more radical vein, various Russian women's impassioned requests to enlist led the Russian government in 1915 to adopt a policy that accepted them into the regular army on a case-by-case basis (Stockdale). Some women's determination to see action firsthand took a more aggressive and original form: in 1917, the Russian peasant Maria Bochkareva, who in 1914 had joined the 25th Reserve Battalion of the Russian Army and had been decorated for bravery in battle, mobilized a short-lived Women's Death Battalion. Partly designed to shame exhausted Russian male troops into renewed efforts on the battlefield, under Bochkareva's "draconian discipline," the original subscription of 2000 women shrank to 300 recruits (Stites 296). Other female battalions modeled on hers, however, formed in quick succession, totaling approximately 5,000 women soldiers, who may have lacked adequate combat training, but not stoicism and courage under fire (Stockdale).[6] Male troops' mixed reactions to these battalions and their failure as propaganda—they provoked more resentment than shame—resulted in their disbandment by year's end. The precedent for female military collectives nonetheless was established.

Frequently proclaimed a "watershed" in gender politics,[7] the First World War, as Nicole Ann Dombrowski accurately observes,

---

[6] Stockdale's article offers a penetrating, comprehensive overview of female active military service in World War I, as well as the conditions enabling women's inclusion on the battlefield.

[7] Joan Scott's thoughtful essay "Rewriting History" proposes jettisoning the conventional notion of war as a watershed for gender equity, instead asking whether "the gender system [was] transformed or reproduced in the course of the extraordinary conditions generated by wartime" and examining "metaphoric uses of gender representation" (Scott, 1987, 26). Oleg Riabov's studies undertake precisely such an investigation. See Oleg Riabov, *"Rossiia-Matushka": Natsionalizm, gender i voina v Rossii XX veka*. Stuttgart: ibidem-Verlag, 2007.

"marked women's definitive entry into the war machine" and "demonstrated that blind patriotism seduced women as well as men" (Dombrowski 1999a, 7). Variously spurred by the incentives of anticipated political enfranchisement and economic autonomy, the desire to "do their bit" for family and country or to escape the drudgery of their private lives, droves of women in Great Britain, the United States, and Eastern and Western Europe rushed to answer their countries' clarion call for aid. They volunteered for work in auxiliary units, nursed the wounded, served as telephone operators, and filled the vacancies left by enlisted soldiers in traditionally male spheres of employment, including industrial production, and above all the munitions plants crucial to the war. Yet these jobs proved stop-gap measures, for the reinstatement of "normalcy" after the war and male survivors' demobilization required women's retreat to their "proper" domain—domesticity—and their "appropriate" functions of wives and mothers. As temporary replacements, they were expected to resume their peacetime lives as if their contributions to the war effort and support of their families through remunerated labor outside the home had never been. As Joshua Goldstein notes, "The 'reconstruction of gender' in Britain after World War I constrained women's roles and reinvigorated the ideology of motherhood" (2001, 320). In short, peace restored an all too familiar binary gender model.

Expectations of women's access to full-fledged citizenship nevertheless were realized when Denmark, Iceland (both in 1915), Finland, the Netherlands, the Soviet Union (all in 1917), Great Britain, Sweden, Germany, Austria, Poland (1918), and the United States (1920), among others, finally extended voting rights to women (Dombrowski 1999a, 32–33). To ascribe that belated milestone straightforwardly to the war, however, is to embrace the fallacy of *post hoc ergo propter hoc*, mistaking sequence for causation, especially in the case of Russia, where a series of revolutions played a decisive role in the new gender egalitarianism that would distinguish the Soviet Union from other parts of Europe during the ensuing years. Unlike any other World War I belligerents, from 1914 until 1920 Russia was racked by the upheaval of not only the World War, but also the two Revolutions of 1917 and the Civil War, with women participating in all three as volunteer-combatants, resistance fighters, and partisans. These events endlessly complicate the myth of the mutually exclusive nature of war and motherhood discussed by Stockdale, which Aleksandr Askol'dov's film *Commissar* [*Kommissar,* 1967] problematizes.[8]

Based on a story by Vasilii Grossman, Askol'dov's sole feature-length film dramatizes the heart-wrenching dilemma of a pregnant female commissar ("an 'oxymoron' made flesh," to borrow Joe Andrew's felicitous phrase [2007, 40]) who gives birth during the Civil War, but leaves her baby son with a Jewish family so as to rejoin the Bolshevik troops. Examining the film's reliance on binary archetypes, Andrew tellingly maintains that the protagonist must choose between "two ways of being: a masculine persona of the ruthless political army officer, and a feminine identity as a mother" (2007, 29). Whereas Askol'dov presents a final choice that is simultaneously personal and ideological, other films emphasize emotional motivations for crossing the line between traditionally gendered categories. In Fridrikh Ermler's *She Defends the Motherland* [*Ona zashchishchaet rodinu,* 1943], what transmogrifies the cheerful tractor-driving protagonist into a violent, vengeful partisan leader is the barbarous murder of her child by a Nazi. Her merciless execution of the killer simultaneously constitutes an act of "justice" and a sacred maternal duty. Both films address the complex issue of maternity intertwined with the allegedly male-specific capacity to kill in combat, a twinning that "impossibly" unites the ostensibly contradictory categories of giving and taking life—a dual power traditionally attributed solely to the divine.

Though the exigencies of universal war destabilized time-honored gender roles, however briefly, the concept of woman as soldier generally remained an anomaly, a symptom of deviance. Why? As Leisa Meyer remarks, "the most resilient and entrenched images of female soldiers are those of the camp follower and cross-dresser" (L. Meyer 6)—with Nadezhda Durova (1783–1866), who adopted the name Aleksandr Aleksandrov, as the most famous Russian instance in the latter category, during the Napoleonic campaign.[9] Inspired by her ingenuity, a small number of Russian women, such as Anna Krasil'nikova

---

[8] For an astute analysis of *The Commissar* from the perspective of gender, see Andrew (2007).

[9] For a reliable translation of Durova's memoirs, see Nadezhda Durova, *The Cavalry Maiden,* translated by Mary Fleming Zirin. Bloomington: Indiana University Press, 1988, which also supplies a valuable introduction.

and Marfa Marko, successfully adopted the same strategy of disguise in World War I (Stockdale).[10] By the outbreak of the Second World War, however, such military masquerades were unnecessary.

The vast scholarship on the two World Wars has analyzed the major critical differences between them. Fueled by idealism and the misguided belief that the First would be "the last war," belligerents in the 1910s fought primarily in the trenches, remote from the home front. By 1939, advances in technology and particularly aeronautics had transformed the terms of warfare, rendering it more mobile. Bombings capable of reducing entire cities to rubble extended war to the home front. At war's end civilian casualties exceeded those within the armed forces. If earlier the mothballed construction of womanhood as passive, nurturing, dependent, and devoted to love, domesticity, and maternity had largely precluded the presence of women on the battlefield other than as nurses, the realities of World War II shattered that image, and nowhere more forcefully than on the Eastern Front.[11]

Women on the Eastern Front (1941–1945)

While all Allies annually commemorate World War II, Victory Day has special resonance in Russia, as it did in the Soviet Union, which experienced by far the greatest losses—more than 26 million out of an approximate total of 59–60 million fatalities.[12] Today Russians continue to view the defeat of Nazism as a national rather than interna-

---

[10] On the negative reputation of the *soldatka* (soldier's wife), often 'bracketed' with the prostitute, see Stites (1990), 305.

[11] For a clear exposition of the 1939 Soviet Law on Universal Conscription and the government's subsequent (1941) mobilization of women volunteers to the front through such bureaucratic structures as the Komsomol Central Committee, see Krylova (2010), 120–43.

[12] Shortly before Victory Day in 2010, a Russian commission especially established in October 2009 to determine the total Soviet losses suffered between 1941 and 1945 submitted the official figure of 26.6 million, 8.7 of them soldiers (Kononova 2010).

tional achievement and commemorate it accordingly.[13] Celebrations on the 65th anniversary (9 May 2010) cost an estimated $40 million and included "the most impressive military parade on Red Square since the collapse of the Soviet Union" (Kononova 2010). Women's contribution to the outcome of the prolonged, wrenching struggle was significant, though subsequently undervalued or largely forgotten. Even in "democratic" America, the women who served as WASPs (Women Airborne Service Pilots),[14] flying noncombat missions to free male pilots for overseas flights, received recognition only in 2010: "No flags were draped over their coffins when they died on duty" (as 38 did), and funeral expenses were partly paid by their fellow female aviators. When the women's service ended, "they had to pay their own bus fare home" (Hefling 2010).[15]

While most Allies assigned noncombat responsibilities to women in the military, in occupied Poland women not only participated in the resistance as scouts, couriers, and medics, but also bore arms in the Warsaw Uprising of 1944. Of all warring countries, however, the Soviet Union deployed female militants most broadly and boldly, the majority of its 800,000-plus enlisted women serving on the front lines, approximately 200,000 of them in the air defense forces, with thousands fighting as "rank-and-file soldiers, as machine gunners, as snipers, as sappers, and as driver-mechanics in tank units" (Engel 1999, 139).[16] Their most innovative deployment was in aviation units: of the Allies,

---

[13] A recent poll shows that 63 percent of respondents believe that "the Soviet Union could have defeated Nazi Germany alone" and 91 percent view its contribution to the final victory as decisive. Tellingly, 58 percent think that the war started in 1941 (Kononova 2010).

[14] Hefling estimates 200 members, whereas Goldstein cites a figure of 1,000 (Goldstein 2001, 91).

[15] Tellingly, it was female senators and House representatives who spearheaded the push in Congress to acknowledge the women's wartime activities (Hefling 2010).

[16] Different historians cite different figures. According to Krylova, "During the war, 520,000 Soviet women [...] served in the Red Army's regular troops and another 300,000 in combat and home front antiaircraft formations—a level of female participation far surpassing that in the British, American, and German armed forces" (Krylova 2010, 3).

only the Soviet Union permitted women to fly combat missions and bomb crucial enemy targets.[17]

Shortly after the Nazi invasion, Stalin granted Marina Raskova, then a major in the Soviet Air Force, permission to organize three all-female air regiments selected from volunteers and grouped into separate fighter, dive bomber, and night bomber units. Their pilots distinguished themselves, particularly Lidiia Litvak (nicknamed White Lily of Stalingrad), Ekaterina Budanova, and Ol'ga Iamshchikova—the highest scoring female aces of all time. Their implacable pursuit of the enemy was matched by their daring and accuracy in bringing down German aircrafts. The success of the 588th Night Bomber Aviation Regiment (one of the three assembled by Raskova and placed under the command of Evdokiia Bershanskaia), which specialized in precision and harassment bombing over German territory, earned Evgeniia Zhigulenko, Natal'ia Meklin, Irina Sebrova, Nadezhda Popova, and the other aviators the German nickname *Nachthexen* (Night witches).[18] Germany's concept of women's unsuitability for armed aggression explains why one of its commanders reportedly confessed, "We simply couldn't grasp that the Soviet airmen that caused us the greatest trouble were in fact women. They came night after night in their very slow biplanes" ("Night Witches" 2005). Comprising approximately 4,000 women, the Night Witches may have decorated their planes with flowers and used their navigation pencils to color their lips and eyebrows, but they reportedly flew a total of 24,000 missions—often unarmed and without parachutes ("Night Witches" 2005; Goldstein 2001, 67). Such edifying and poignant accounts of young women's perilous feats in defense of their country (Raskova perished during the war at 31 years of age, Budanova at 26, Litvak at 21)[19] should not be

---

[17] For a detailed study of airwomen during the war, see Pennington (2001).

[18] Now a great grandmother who every 2 May joins the surviving members of the Night Bomber group outside the Bolshoi Theater to reminisce about their raids Nadezhda Popova told an interviewer: "The Germans [...] spread a rumor that we had been injected with some unknown chemicals that enabled us to see so clearly in the pitch dark!" Reportedly their daring inspired tributes from American airwomen, comic book artists such as writer Garth Ennis and penciller Russ Braun, creators of *Battlefields: The Night Witches,* and a Dutch heavy metal band ("Night Witches" 2009).

[19] Litvak's death was presumed, though her body was never recovered.

generalized onto the Soviet female population at large, however, for they represented a small, extraordinary minority. Yet their tireless dedication to eradicating the enemy forces and their proficiency as bomber pilots, as well as armed female partisans' direct involvement in repelling the Nazis, laid to rest the myth of women's biologically defined inability to engage in combat.

After the Second World War, as after the First, gender relations largely reverted to peacetime paradigms. Stalin's policies favored the consolidation of families and increased reproduction, not only to compensate for a drastically reduced population (especially its male contingent) but also to ensure expansion of the labor force. Once the initial euphoria at victory abated, Soviets confronted the daunting task of rebuilding a ravaged country, integrating traumatized or disabled veterans into society, and coping with thousands of homeless orphans (*besprizornye*) as well as colossal shortages of basic goods.[20] As people attempted to assimilate and appraise the experience of war in retrospect, state propaganda began codifying the official version of recent history—a narrative of Soviets' triumphant, self-sacrificial heroism under the infallible leadership of Stalin. *Kulturarbeiter* likewise strove to represent and interpret the war years, sometimes in ways that diverged from state propaganda, with its agenda of self-congratulatory exceptionalism. Meanwhile, owing to the cynicism of the three dominant powers at the Yalta Conference in February 1945, for Poland, Allied "victory" meant loss of territory and independence.[21] The traditional image of Poland as a martyred nation flagellated by its neighboring states became an immutable self-identity for decades to come.

---

[20] Similarly, after the War, there was an estimated 1 million Polish orphans. See http://histclo.com/essay/war/ww2/dc/cou/pol/no-orp.html (last accessed 29 November 2010).

[21] On Poland's continuing tensions with Russia about the legacy of the war, see Roland Oliphant, "The Long Shadow of 1939," *Russia Profile*, 3 September 2009. Available at http://www.russiaprofile.org/page.php?pageid=International&articleid=a1251997618 (last accessed 3 September 2009).

World War II in Cultural Production:
Gender and Genre

Representations of the War unavoidably vary according to period, geographical area, and genre. Under wartime conditions, lack of adequate resources, the need for rapid production, and shifting developments at the front affected some cultural genres (graphics, film, literature) more than others, such as songs. Subsequent depictions of the War, and specifically of gender disposition during the years of conflict, came under different pressures, exerted by age-old conventions as well as state ideology.

As Elżbieta Ostrowska argues in chapter 1, postwar films by the Polish Film School (1955–early 1960s) acknowledge the reality of women's share in the armed resistance during the Nazi occupation, and especially in the Warsaw Uprising of 1944. Yet, while such prominent directors as Andrzej Wajda and Tadeusz Konwicki gave women's endurance and bravery their cinematic due, female deaths are conspicuous in their onscreen absence in their war films. These lacunae are gender-specific, contrasting starkly with the extended, almost operatic sequences of heroic men expiring in solitude, among comrades, or before "spectators," exemplified by Maciek's death in *Ashes and Diamonds* [*Popiół i Diament* 1958]. The younger and more experimental Andrzej Żuławski opted for a different stratagem to erase the palpable nature of women's individual deaths by a kind of substitute "replay" that metamorphoses female fatalities into resurrection. Why did Polish directors elect to register female deaths off screen or to negate them while treating male deaths as visual spectacle? Ostrowska suggests that the discrepancy results from an insistence on the vulnerability of the male subject in postwar Poland, on the one hand, and, on the other, the importance of preserving intact the concept of an eternal Poland traditionally personified by the woman as symbol of nationhood. Thus the antinomic dyad of masculine-as-historical and feminine-as-mythical visually privileges the former, with the latter rendered invisible, disembodied or shrouded in darkness—an image, as Ostrowska puts it, "fabricated by [... male] subjectivity."

Women's allegorical function as mother-nation likewise provided the conceptual linchpin for Soviet films of the 1940s, above all the genre of melodrama and narratives featuring female partisans as protagonists.[22] As Alexander Prokhorov (chapter 2) maintains, in prize-winning films by Ermler (*She Defends the Motherland*) and Mark Donskoi (*The Rainbow* [*Raduga* 1943]), female partisans' bodies trope the Russian and Soviet people's indestructible regenerative powers and draw on the iconography of war posters for maximum visual impact while sidelining narrative continuity. The nation's plenitude materialized in the maternal body recalls the stacking dolls (*matryoshki*) pioneered in the 1890s during the concerted drive to forge a specifically Russian national identity. While motherhood defends and protects "its own," the moralized polarization intrinsic to melodrama dictates that female collaborators appear as Westernized "camp followers," self-centered, addicted to luxury, devoid of maternal traits, and mired in perverse relationships with the enemy. Though criticized for their excesses as melodramas, with objections focused mainly on the feminization of what ideally should have been the exemplary masculine discourse of socialist realism, upon completion both films were released chiefly because of the country's need for a steady stream of celluloid propaganda. Unlike Soviet officials, audiences—who during the war comprised primarily women and children—responded enthusiastically to these gynocentric screen stories of intrepid women's agency, which also enjoyed popularity abroad.

Though the reestablishment of peace eliminated the immediate need to reassure the population and agitate for its support, films that deviated markedly from the official line on Soviet wartime action as an epic of unwavering, heroic patriotism ran afoul of censorship. Proscribed or discouraged phenomena included depictions of collaboration and sexual intimacy with the enemy, humorous or light-hearted treatments of the national struggle, and the image of women as lethal warriors instead of faithful wives and caring mothers. In such a context, the films of Larisa Shepit'ko—a rare instance of a successful female director in a male-dominated profession—stand out as revisionist. Both her first post-diploma film, *Wings* [*Kryl'ia* 1966], and her last, *The Ascent* [*Voskhozhdenie* 1976, based on a novella by Vasilii

---

[22] For a thorough treatment of Russian and Soviet war films spanning a period of ninety years and of women's roles in them, see Youngblood (2007), *passim*.

Bykov], courted disapprobation, the latter by its unflinching, complex treatment of wartime collaboration in occupied Belorussia, the former by its nuanced examination of a female aviator's socio-psychological displacement and anomie after the War.

Kryl'ia raises a host of gender-marked issues through its protagonist, whose divided self exemplifies the dilemma of demobilized women in postwar civilian life. As a former fighter pilot and now school principal and single woman with an adopted daughter, Petrukhina violates two hardy notions of Soviet womanhood: she yearns for the days when she assumed the "masculine" role of killing, and she fails to perform the duty touted as women's supreme fulfillment—biological reproduction. The school performance, in which she as the chief *matryoshka* requires physical support at each step, indexes her failure at maternity: in a realized metaphor, she needs to be carried onto the stage by her male students. Whereas the Night Witches merely recalled their risky war missions as an unforgettable, exhilarating challenge, Petrukhina cannot adjust to her "normalized" peacetime role, so at odds with her death-dealing, hence "masculine" wartime activities. Stranded between a memorable but irretrievably lost past and an arid present, between action and stasis, decision and compliance, she suffocates in alienation from her surroundings, her daughter, and the pupils to whom she feels incapable of giving the surrogate-mother nurturing sympathy expected of a female pedagogue-administrator. "Petrukhina's power and freedom as a woman," Tatiana Mikhailova and Mark Lipovetsky conclude, "cannot manifest themselves outside of war conditions, outside the realm of death" (chapter 3). That insight informs their persuasive interpretation of the film's highly controversial conclusion.

Given the colossal mortality rate and unimaginable ordeals on the Eastern Front, neither Poland nor the Soviet Union favored screen treatments of World War II leavened by humor, frivolity, and intimations of sexuality, even if mediated by sublimating codes. A noteworthy exception in this regard, Konrad Nałęcki's *Four Tank Men and a Dog* [*Czterej pancerni i pies* 1966, 1969–70], a Polish TV series based on a novel by Janusz Przymanowski, enjoyed huge success in Poland and the Soviet Union. Essentially an adventure narrative set during the War, the series depicts military threat, victims of a concentration camp, Polish-Soviet alliances on a personal and political level, and other aspects of canonical war representation, but laces it with a heady brew of youthful camaraderie, romance, and playfulness. Its approach to gender relations is notable for its lightheartedness, not subversive interrogation; ultimately the series affirms gender stereotypes as well as wartime derring-do without dogmatically belaboring either. The series verges on a slightly more mature version of the British writer Enid Blyton's *Famous Five* series of children's novels, which depict the group dynamic of four adolescents and their mongrel dog, Timmy, in encounters with mysterious places and colorful characters. Though the protagonists' youth permits the Polish series to adopt a frequently blithe tone atypical for the war genre, Elena Prokhorova (chapter 4) shows how the concluding segments, dramatizing the Allies' triumphant entry into Berlin, opt for a conservative plot resolution and coda: they spotlight specifically Soviet valor, the chief protagonist's maturation into adulthood, marriage within a patriarchal structure, and a vision of the future that accords with the precepts of socialist realism. Play has ended, yielding to the serious business of rebuilding the nation and producing offspring as guarantors of the future.

It is difficult to imagine a text that contrasts more with *Four Tank Men and a Dog* than Lidiia Ginzburg's searing account of the Leningrad Siege (*Blockade Diary* 1984 [*Chelovek za pis'mennym stolom*]), which she endured firsthand. Hers is a chronicle of embattled survival amid degradation and despair that describes the horrors of the Siege in dispassionate detail without ever lapsing into the official glorification of the fortitude purportedly demonstrated by the city's entire population. *Blockade Diary* probes individual and collective coping mechanisms primarily along gender lines.

Focusing on women's "speaking bodies" in Ginzburg's account, Irina Sandomirskaja (chapter 5) elaborates on the psychologically motivated stratagems that women adopted in a frantic attempt to retain feminine identity and establish a gendered social hierarchy even as their bodies gradually lost external markers of femininity and the biological processes that define their sex. According to Sandomirskaja, government documents and medical records testify to sexual discrimination by the authorities as they struggled to contain mortality during the Siege. Doctors' and administrators' "more pronounced interest in males accorded both with the tradition of medical knowledge and with the authorities' apparently greater investment in the survival of men,

who were considered more valuable [...] for the purposes of resisting
the siege." The priority given to men's rescue originated in the pre-
supposition that women had greater intrinsic resources for recovery—a
perception that, on the one hand, contravened the proselytized image
of males as hardy defenders of "the weaker sex," and, on the other,
coincided with the literary icon of "the strong Russian woman" popularized by nineteenth-century novels and such modern women's texts
as I. Grekova's *Ship of Widows* [*Vdovii parokhod* 1981].

For self-evident reasons, Ginzburg's bleak, retrospective rumina-
tions about Leningrad's tragedy have little in common with wartime
works intended to kindle hatred of the aggressors, and especially with
graphics. A major force in galvanizing the populace into action, the
genre of Soviet war posters employed a visual rhetoric congruent with
state codification of gender. Graphics in the USSR, as elsewhere, cast
the global conflict in the ennobling terms of chivalry, whereby men
sallied forth to protect imperiled women and children. Helena Goscilo
(chapter 6) contends that the very function of posters—recruitment
and reassurance in the midst of havoc—required that they sanitize the
grim realities of combat while cheering the population on to renewed
effort with optimistic promises of eventual victory. One could hardly
rally Soviet citizens to the common cause by referencing male vulnerability, citizens' collaboration with the enemy, and colossal loss of lives.
These facets of the War belonged to the Unsaid. Similarly, poster-
women appeared not as pilots or ground combatants, but as workers
in fields and factories, occasionally as nurses, as mothers hugging
children to their chests or grannies imploring soldiers to save them,
and as symbols of Mother Russia, rousing men to arms or crowning
them with laurels.[23] If omission of unpalatable facts characterized war
graphics from 1941–1943, once the Red Army went on the offensive,
the tone shifted to jubilation that proliferated a conventional iconography—of liberation (chiefly of women and children), repatriation (of
male soldiers), and reconstruction (frequently by smiling female enthu-
siasts).

---

[23] Newspapers, however, included images of female combatants, such as the
agitational sketch in *Komsomol'skaia pravda* dated November 1942, which
included a female sniper in a six-member team, reproduced in Krylova,
219. For other visuals of this nature, see Krylova, *passim*.

Whereas Soviet war graphics fell under state supervision and reflected official policies, Soviet war songs benefited from greater diversity partly owing to their provenance. The overwhelming majority of Soviet poets and professional lyricists sentimentalized traditional gender roles, but anonymous soldiers created lesser-known, down-to-earth works that reportedly circulated in *samizdat* or *magnitizdat* and more accurately reflected the realities of war. Robert Rothstein argues (chapter 7) that lyrics identifying women with home and mother-land, such as the canonized "Dark Night" ["Temnaia noch" 1943], existed alongside less predictable songs about female soldiers, pilots, and guerilla fighters. Moreover, though women as keepers of the hearth patiently awaiting their men's safe return dominated various wartime genres—poetry, film, graphics, and song—a handful of films and several songs composed mainly by non-professionals touched on women's infidelity. As Petr Bogatyrëv and Roman Jakobson main-tained many decades ago, an oral genre by definition not only under-goes variation according to its performers, but also eludes the kind of vertical censorship imposed upon genres that depend on paper, canvas, and celluloid.[24] Songs about women's involvement in combat, however, presented scant challenge to gender binarism, for, Rothstein notes, they were few in number and, moreover, implied the "unnatu-ralness" of deploying armed women on the battlefield.

Despite the Soviet Union's pragmatic reliance on female com-batants in the Second World War, the Russian military remains a male domain in a society indentured to a rhetoric that essentializes femininity and dismisses feminism as political correctness *tout court*. Military service is obligatory only for men, who continue to occupy top positions in government, business, and the armed forces. Women's "duties" primarily consist of cultivating physical allure and bearing children, though demographics indicate a sufficient drop in Russian birthrates to warrant concern about population decline. In 2006, then President Vladimir Putin called Russia's radically shrinking population

---

[24] See Peter Bogatyrëv and Roman Jakobson, "Folklore as a Special Form of Creativity" (1929), in *The Prague School: Selected Writings, 1929–1946*, edited by Peter Steiner, translated by Manfred Jacobson (Austin: University of Texas, 1982), 32–46. Revised version in Roman Jakobson, *Selected Writings* 4 (The Hague: Mouton, 1966), 1–15.

"the most acute problem of contemporary Russia," for since the 1990s the population has diminished by five million people (Rosenberg).

Embattled Chechen and Balkan Women Today

Unlike the two global World Wars, Russia's protracted war with Chechnya and the Balkan conflict are "domestic," inasmuch as the battling sides in each case involve two antagonistic entities fighting in a smaller geographical area within previously demarcated national or republican borders. Until the Soviet Union crumbled, traditionally Muslim Chechnya did not particularly stand out from the rest of the Caucasus, which Russian culture since the late eighteenth century has constructed as a hotbed of passions and violence, with submissive women wholly subordinated to men, just as the region was subordinated to the political center by Russian and Soviet imperialist aspirations.[25] A division of Russia during the Soviet era, Chechnya sought and achieved independence after the dissolution of the Soviet Union in 1991. Subsequent hostilities surrounding its secession led to the First Chechen War (1994–1996), which ended with a ceasefire treaty signed by Boris Yeltsin, only to be threatened by repeated kidnappings, mainly but not solely of Russians in the area. Tensions finally erupted in the Second Chechen War (1999–2009).

The wars have left a poisonous residue in Russia, where the government and part of the population harbor intractable antipathy toward Chechens, stirred or strengthened by a series of alleged and corroborated terrorist attacks by Chechen separatists and articulated in racial slurs against "dark-skinned Caucasians." What initially shocked Russians, as well as Western observers, was Chechen women's participation in this seemingly indiscriminate violence and bloodshed, especially in light of their pliancy and recessiveness within Chechen society. A fiercely patriarchal enclave, Chechnya advocates segregation by gender at social gatherings, as well as women's exclusive responsibility for children and housework; customs dictate that they deferentially rise when

---

[25] For the most recent and comprehensive survey of Russia's relations with the Caucasus, particularly as reflected in Russian and Soviet culture, see Bruce Grant, *The Captive and the Gift: Cultural Histories of Sovereignty in Russia and the Caucasus* (Ithaca, NY: Cornell University Press, 2010).

a man enters a room, and express modesty in men's presence through silence and lowered eyes. Yet these normally submissive women, given the sobriquet of Black Widows owing to their husbands' (as well as other family members') deaths at the hands of Russian soldiers, have figured prominently in a number of high-profile suicidal terrorist acts—inside a school and a theater, on the subway, outside the entrance to the capital's National Hotel, and on Moscow's streets (Murphy 2004).

Russian officials, Western journalists, and several Chechen interviewees ascribe the women's part in kamikaze bombings to their victimization by their fellow countrymen, who manipulate them with the aid of drugs, hypnosis, and threats (Myers 2003). Trina Mamoon (chapter 8), however, contends that many factors may motivate the women's actions, a view that takes into account Kheda Iusupova's narrower diagnosis: namely, that grief drives their susceptibility to "recruitment" by male militants (Ferreira-Marques 2003). According to hostages at the Dubrovka Theater siege in 2002, which took the lives of 129 Russians and 40 Chechens, most of the Chechen women with explosives strapped to their bodies had lost menfolk in the war. Attributing their suicidal missions to a single cause is simplistic, Mamoon concludes, for "[t]o varying degrees their actions are rooted in political conflict, nationalist ideology, patriotism, trauma, coercion, and personal revenge, but it is impossible to determine which motive predominates."

If the Second Chechen War evidences women's untraditional adoption of radically violent "male" stratagems against random civilians to further the Chechen separatist cause, the Bosnian War of 1992–1995, which pitted Serbs against Bosniaks, demonstrated, on a startling scale, a more familiar scenario: wartime rape of women as a weapon against the enemy. Violation of German women primarily by the occupying Red Army at the end of World War II was never prosecuted at the Nuremberg trials and received no mention in Soviet historical accounts. Serbian militants' officially condoned, systematic sexual assault of anywhere from 20,000 to 50,000 female Bosniaks as part of the ethnic cleansing designed to drive the Bosniak population out of Bosnia, however, prompted the first international trial "focusing on rape as a war crime and a crime against humanity" (Socolovsky 2000). Given the magnitude of this ethnic campaign, calculated to impregnate Bosnian women so as to ensure future generations of half-Serbs in the region, a majority of commentators have designated the sustained attacks as genocide. Such a label, Rhonda Copelon objects, downplays the gendered nature of rape, which "seeks to destroy a woman based on her identity as a woman" (Copelon 1999, 334), and therefore constitutes an atrocity separate from genocide.

In her analysis of German women's reactions to forced impregnation by Allied soldiers in the periods just before and after the Nazi capitulation, Atina Grossman reports that at least ninety percent of pregnancies were terminated, with the official approval of a hastily assembled health commission (Grossman 1999, 177, 172). Viewed and viewing themselves as helpless victims, the raped women relied on the abortion wards instituted "to eliminate unwanted Mongol and Slav offspring," thereby erasing the physical consequences of their experience (Grossman 1999, 172).

Projected against this historical background, Slavenka Drakulić's *S. A Novel about the Balkans* [*Kao da me nema* 1999] and Jasmila Žbanić's film *Grbavica: The Land of my Dreams* [*Grbavica* 2006] are remarkable for their sensitive depiction of raped Bosnian women who, unlike their earlier German counterparts, exercise agency and decide to bear and raise the progeny resulting from the violence perpetrated against them. Without minimizing the psychological trauma of either their protagonists' sexual assaults or the discovery of their pregnancies—initially experienced as imprisonment within their own bodies—Drakulić and Žbanić spotlight the women's freedom of choice. If opting for maternity on the basis of a unique, part-biological, part-mystical bond between mother and child appears bound by conservative patriarchal stereotypes, the circumstances of conception in both cases wrest the women's situations from any recognizable norm. Moreover, Drakulić and Žbanić chart a complex interior route to the women's hard-won and consequence-laden decision to deliver and rear children conceived in spasms of hatred amid the ravages of war. Neither work glosses over the unimaginable difficulty of preserving silence regarding paternity and the circumstances of conception. Žbanić's film traces in rich detail the mother's inevitably ineffectual solution of withholding from her daughter the real identity of her nameless father, which she shrouds in politically expedient lies. Yana Hashamova's trenchant reading (chapter 9) implicitly indicts the masculine-military mandates that censor history and illuminates the centrality of matrilineal memory in the case of Drakulić's novel and of female subjectivity in both works.

Memory in the Croatian writer Dubravka Ugrešić's episodic *Museum of Unconditional Surrender* [*Musej bezuvjetne predaje* 1994], which ruminates on the manifold consequences of the Yugoslav Wars, attains the status of an algorithm, one articulated through recollections, dreams, and the genre of museum. An impassioned anti-war critic of nationalism, the opinionated Ugrešić has voiced her stance with sufficient eloquence and frequency to provoke media harassment on home territory in the 1990s and such tags as "traitor," "public enemy," and "witch"—the last echoing the Nazis' derogatory name of "Night Witches" for Soviet female night-pilots during World War II. "Nationalism," Ugrešić asseverates, "is like a pesticide: its poison lasts longer than one season and it penetrates everywhere." She calls the new nationalistic myths constructed to underscore differences among Bosniaks, Croats, and Serbs a "collective psychotherapy" to rationalize the wars (Zelenko).

Two years after the outbreak of armed hostilities (1993), Ugrešić moved to Berlin, a location inseparable from the specter of World War II and evocatively incorporated into what Jessica Wienhold-Brokish (chapter 10) pithily characterizes as Ugrešić's "textual war museum." Eschewing the conventions of narrative continuity and representation, Ugrešić operates in aleatory, disjunctive fashion, regularly resorting to a displacement of phenomena that parallels her own cultural displacement in exile. As Wienhold-Brokish proposes, her technique of sidestepping narrative stability and negotiating "between the contrary modes of preservation and surrender, absence and presence, enabl[es] her to address the war indirectly." Consistently gynocentric, Ugrešić's text exemplifies the departure from linearity that Gayle Greene and others have posited as a constituent feature of feminist writing (Greene 1991, 14–20). And, as in Drakulić's novel, in *The Museum of Unconditional Surrender* matrilineality forges historical and spiritual connections threatened and sundered by the entrenched patrilineal genre of war.

Female Infiltration

Since the rise of feminism in the late 1960s, women in the West gradually have invaded previously impregnable bastions of all-male camaraderie: clubs, "tough" sports such as football and wrestling, professions long deemed unfeminine, and the military. In the U.S., especially working-class women have joined the armed forces in increasing numbers, partly as a route to upward mobility and for the perquisite of a funded college education. By 1989, they represented more than ten percent of the armed services personnel, and by 1991 they made up approximately seven percent of the forces assigned to "Operations Desert Shield and Desert Storm" (Dombrowski, 1999b, 14). No worse than their male counterparts in all military spheres except those demanding sheer physical strength, they took part in the Gulf War and in America's intervention in Iraq.[26] In contrast to the White Feather campaign of World War I, the Gulf War inspired "the pervasive phenomenon of 'yellow-ribbonism' and the belligerent demand to 'love our boys' [sic] that the ribbons and the American flag displays encoded." The association of ribbons with femininity "enabled the construction of a rigid binary of gender," despite American women's historic presence at the combat front (Boose 1993, 76–77), which received extensive coverage by the media (Cooke and Woollacott 1993a, 320).

The pace of women's integration into the army and navy elsewhere lags behind America's. For instance, according to a NATO report, women in Poland constituted only 1.45 percent of the total armed forces in 2008. Though reliable information about gender percentages in the Russian military is scant, a BBC commentary estimated the number of female members at 90,000 in 2002, though two years earlier figures ranged from 115,000–160,000. Women are not conscripted and serve primarily in the standard support roles of nurses and engineers ("Russian Ground Forces"), albeit the nature of contemporary wars places those in non-combat roles at considerable risk, as attested by various lists of war fatalities (Goldstein 2001, 95).

These developments have come at a cost, however. During the last two decades, rape—historically a concomitant of war and often invoked as a metaphor for it (Goldstein 2001, 369, 371)—not only continues to figure in invading soldiers' behavior,[27] but also has complicated women's integration into the American military community. In 2007,

---

[26] That women's performance in the military is not inferior to men's is a major motif in Goldstein's wide-ranging monograph.

[27] A rapid perusal of verbal and visual material on the Internet offers access to items documenting blood-chilling attacks against women by Russian soldiers in Chechnya and American soldiers in Iraq.

"Nearly 1,400 women reported being assaulted and raped by their fellow soldiers, in some cases by their commanding officers. [...] Since NOW first aired its investigation, [...] the Pentagon has released new reports in which one-third of military women" claim to have been sexually harassed ("Rape in..." 2008). According to the Pentagon, nearly 3,000 women were sexually assaulted in 2008, and official inquiries confirm that the figure is substantially larger among those serving in Iraq and Afghanistan, even though the Pentagon believes that 80–90 percent of such attacks remain unreported. The fact that approximately eighty percent of soldiers convicted of sex crimes receive an honorable [sic] discharge attests the military's failure at meaningful discipline and validates the widespread perception of military culture as "intrinsically violent and hypermasculine" (Gibbs 1000). Democratic House Representative Jane Harman, though a supporter of the war in Iraq, has declared that "a female soldier is more likely to be raped by a fellow soldier than killed by enemy fire" (quoted in Gibbs 2010). Publications of these and similar data give the lie to unexamined propagandistic clichés of war as men's noble defense of women and children.

In light of such revelations, female veterans' testimonies, and annual surveys issued by the US government, Russia's recent tactics for stimulating army conscription appear nothing short of grotesque. To counter the Russian military's reputation for brutal hazing rituals and pitiful pay, as well as its deterioration of morale and prestige, in 2003 officials launched a Miss Russian Army competition in Moscow's Russian Army Theater. Reprised in 2005 under the rubric "Beauties in Shoulder Straps," the beauty pageant, replete with patriotic songs and performing children, attracted nineteen contestants, with Lieutenant Kseniia Agarkova crowned the winner. Whereas one of the women forthrightly admitted that the competition's goal was to encourage more conscript-age males to join the army's ranks, Nikolai Burbyga, the major general who chaired the jury, identified the contest as simply a means of relieving the monotony of soldiers' lives (Bigg 2005). Both interpretations ignore or condone the potential for violence against enlisted Russian women by their male counterparts.

While generally the military no longer excludes female volunteers from its forces, violence and war remain masculine strongholds. As in countless other areas of culture, Alphonse Karr's maxim "plus ça change, plus c'est la même chose" has not lost its relevance. What does testify to evolution, modifications, and diverse perspectives, however, is the portrayal of gender under wartime conditions by sundry genres within culture across geographical and temporal boundaries, as collectively suggested by the following chapters.

REFERENCES

Andrew, Joe. 2007. "Birth equals rebirth? Space, narrative, and gender in *The Commissar.*" *Studies in Russian and Soviet Cinema* 1, no. I: 27–44.

Bigg, Claire. 2005. "Russia: Army Puts on a Pretty Face." *RFE/RL*, 22 June. http://www.rferl.org/articleprintview/1059432.html (last accessed 29 September 2007).

Boose, Lynda E. 1993. "Techno-Muscularity and the 'Boy Eternal': From the Quagmire to the Gulf." In *Gendering War Talk*, edited by Miriam Cooke and Angela Woollacott, 67–106. Princeton: Princeton University Press.

Cooke, Miriam and Angela Woollacott. 1993a. "Postscript." In *Gendering War Talk*, edited by Miriam Cooke and Angela Woollacott, 317–25. Princeton: Princeton University Press.

———, eds. 1993b. *Gendering War Talk*. Princeton: Princeton University Press.

Copelon, Rhonda. 1999. "Surfacing Gender: Reengraving Crimes against Women in Humanitarian Law." In *Women and War in the Twentieth Century: Enlisted with and without Consent*, edited by Nicole Ann Dombrowski, 332–59. New York and London: Garland Pub. Co.

Dombrowski, Nicole Ann. 1999a. "Soldiers, Saints, or Sacrificial Lambs?: Women's Relationship to Combat and the Fortification of the Home Front in the Twentieth Century." In *Women and War in the Twentieth Century: Enlisted with and without Consent*, edited by Nicole Ann Dombrowski, 2–41. New York and London: Garland Pub. Co.

———, ed. 1999b. *Women and War in the Twentieth Century: Enlisted with and without Consent*. New York and London: Garland Pub. Co.

Elshtain, Jean Bethke. 1987. *Women and War*. New York: Basic Books. Inc.

Engel, Barbara Alpern. 1999. "The Womanly Face of War: Soviet Women Remember World War II." In *Women and War in the Twentieth Century: Enlisted with and without Consent*, edited by Nicole Ann Dombrowski, 138–59. New York and London: Garland Pub. Co.

Ferreira-Marques, Clara. 2003. "Chechnya's suicide widows are new threat for Russia." *Reuters*, 27 May. http://www.reuters.com/newsArticle.jhtml?type=ourWorldNews&storyID=2845583 (last accessed 2 July 2003).

Fussell, Paul. 1975. *The Great War and Modern Memory*. London, Oxford, New York: Oxford University Press.

Garrard, John and Carol Garrard, eds. 1993. *World War 2 and the Soviet People: Selected Papers from the Fourth World Congress for Soviet and East European Studies*. New York: St. Martin's Press.

Gibbs, Nancy 2010. "Sexual Assaults on Female Soldiers: Don't Ask, Don't Tell." *Time*, 8 March. http://www.time.com/time/printout/0,8816, 1968110,00.html (last accessed 29 October 2011).

Goldstein, Joshua S. 2001. *War and Gender: How Gender Shapes the War System and Vice Versa*. Cambridge: Cambridge University Press.

Greene, Gayle. 1991. *Changing the Story: Feminist Fiction and Tradition*. Bloomington: Indiana University Press.

Grossman, Atina. 1991. "A Question of Silence: The Rape of German Women by Soviet Occupation Soldiers." In *Women and War in the Twentieth Century: Enlisted with and without Consent*, edited by Nicole Ann Dombrowski, 162–83. New York and London: Garland Pub. Co.

Hefling, Kimberly. 2010. "Female WWII aviators honored with gold medal." *AP*, 6 May. http://www.google.com/hostednews/ap/article/ALeqM5iMdYRUedjmyrD-nnbULYjPI5ALswD9EC0J680 (last accessed 10 October 2010).

Higate, Paul and John Hopton. 2005. "War, Militarism, and Masculinities." In *Handbook of Studies in Men and Masculinities*, edited by Michael S. Kimmel, Jeff Hearn, and R.W. Connell, 432–47. Thousand Oaks, CA, London, and New Delhi: Sage Publications.

Huston, Nancy. 1986. "The Matrix of War: Mothers and Heroes." In *The Female Body In Western Culture: Contemporary Perspectives*, edited by Susan Rubin Suleiman, 119–36. Cambridge, MA, and London: Harvard University Press.

Juergensmeyer, Mark. 2003. "Why Guys Throw Bombs." In *Terror in the Mind of God: The Global Rise of Religious Violence*, 3rd edition. Berkeley: University of California Press. Available at http://web.fuberlin.de/gpo/pdf/juergensmeyer/juergensmeyer_e.pdf, 1-10 (last accessed 15 July 2011).

Kimmel, Michael S., Jeff Hearn, and R.W. Connell, eds. 2005. *Handbook of Studies in Men and Masculinities*. Thousand Oaks, CA, London, New Delhi: Sage Publications.

Kononova, Svetlana. 2010. "A Restless War." *Russia Profile*, 11 May. http://www.russiaprofile.org/page.php?/pageid=Politics&articleid=a1273603729 (last accessed 13 May 2010).

Krylova, Anna. 2010. *Soviet Women in Combat: A History of Violence on the Eastern Front*. Cambridge: Cambridge University Press.

Meyer, Alfred G. 1991. "The Impact of World War I on Russian Women's Lives." In *Russia's Women: Accommodation, Resistance, Transformation*, edited by Barbara Evans Clements, Barbara Alpern Engel, and Christine D. Worobec, 208–24. Berkeley, Los Angeles, Oxford: California University Press.

Meyer, Leisa D. 1996. *Creating GI Jane: Sexuality and Power in the Women's Army Corps During World War II*. New York: Columbia University Press.

Mosse, George L. 1996/1998. *The Image of Man: The Creation of Modern Masculinity*. New York and Oxford: Oxford University Press.

Murphy, Kim. 2004. "'Black widows' caught up in web of Chechen war." *Los Angeles Times*, 7 February. http://www.rickross.com/reference/rs/rs43.html (last accessed 6 January 2011).

Myers, Steven Lee. 2003. "Female Suicide Bombers Unnerve Russians." *New York Times*, 7 August. http://www.nytimes.com/2003/08/07/world/female-suicide-bombers-unnerve-russians.html (last accessed 2 March 2004).

"Night Witches." 2009. *BBC World Service*, 2 November. http://www.bbc.co.uk/world service/documentaries/2009/11/091102night.witches.shtml (last accessed 4 April 2010).

"The Night Witches—Russian Combat Pilots of World War Two." 2005. *BBC*, 2 December. http://www.bbc.co.uk/dna/h2g2/A5849076 (last accessed 24 November 2008).

Pennington, Reina. 2001. *Wings, Women, and War: Soviet Airwomen in World War II Combat*. Lawrence, KS: University Press of Kansas.

"Rape in the Military." 2008. *NOW*, 23 May. http://www.pbs.org/now/shows/421/index.html (last accessed 5 January 2010).

Rosenberg, Matt. 2010. "Population Decline in Russia." 17 November. http://geography.about.com/od/obtainpopulationdata/a/russiapop.htm (last accessed 2 December 2010).

"Russian Ground Forces." No date. *WorldLingo*. http://www.worldlingo.com/ma/enwiki/en/Russian_Ground_Forces#Personnel (last accessed 6 January 2010).

Scott, Joan W. 1987. "Rewriting History." In *Behind the Lines: Gender and the Two World Wars*, edited by Margaret Randolph Higonnet, Jane Jenson, et al., 19–30. New Haven and London: Yale University Press.

Socolovsky, Jerome. 2000. "Bosnian 'Rape Camp' Survivors Testify in The Hague." *WEnews*, 19 July. http://www.womensenews.org/story/rape/000719/bosnian-rape-camp-survivors-testify-the-hague (last accessed 28 December 2010).

Stites, Richard. 1990. *The Women's Liberation Movement in Russia*. Princeton: Princeton University Press.

Stockdale, Melissa K. No date. "'My Death for the Motherland Is Happiness': Women, Patriotism, and Soldiering in Russia's Great War, 1914–1917." http://www.historycooperative.org/journals/ahr/109.1/stockdale.html (last accessed 22 December 2010).

Vinogradova, Luba. 2003. "Deadly secret of the black widows." *The Times*, 22 October.

Youngblood, Denise J. 2007. *Russian War Films: On the Cinema Front, 1914–2005*. Lawrence, KS: University Press of Kansas.

Zelenko, Michael. No date. "Dubravka Ugresic on the Danube in *The Rumpus*." *The Rumpus*. http://therumpus.net/2010/01/the-rumpus-international-rivers-interview-2-dubravka-ugresic-on-the-danube/ (last accessed 12 January 2011) [Interview with Dubravka Ugrešić].

WORLD WAR II

Film and Television

CHAPTER 1

Invisible Deaths: Polish Cinema's Representation of Women in World War II

Elżbieta Ostrowska

Entering the "Forbidden Zone"

In her essay "Women in the Forbidden Zone: War, Women, and Death," Margaret R. Higonnet notes that "death, it seems, is indeed what differentiates men from women in wartime [...] war and death are understood to define manhood" (1993, 193). For women, she argues, war and war death constitute a forbidden zone. This symbolic exclusion seems to operate not only within real life experience but is also worked through in cultural representations, though recently films have offered images of female war heroism that attract serious critical attention.[1] The discursive dichotomy of war experience and its cultural representations described by Higonnet can also be applied to the Polish experience of the Second World War.

While direct military confrontation between Poland and Germany in 1939 lasted less than two months, the beginning of the Nazi occupation marked the immediate development of an underground movement on Polish soil. Women entered the "forbidden zone" of armed resistance against the Nazis soon after Germany became the occupying

---

[1] As, for example, in *Courage Under Fire* (Edward Zwick 1996), in which a heroic female death is initially denied to save the masculine notion of honor and bravery (see Tasker 2005, 172–89).

power.[2] The climactic point in breaking with the traditional gendering of war was the Warsaw Uprising of 1944, the iconography of which ushered women into "the forbidden zone." Many Polish films representing the Second World War and Nazi occupation offer images of courageous women and girls, often shown as holding significant positions within underground formations and performing heroic deeds. Contrary to Higgonet's binary model, they also die. Their deaths, however, rarely occur on screen.

Despite their entry into the masculine zone of war and death in actual historical experience, Polish women's participation has not been adequately represented within Polish cinema, evidenced by the virtual absence of on-screen images of their deaths, probably motivated by ideological considerations. It is my contention that this unrepresented death serves as a "structuring absence" that governs the systematic signifying practices of Polish cinema. This absent female death assumes greater significance if juxtaposed with the abundant images of male death, usually represented as a lavish visual spectacle. Whereas the

---

[2] In her introduction to the non-fiction book *Girls from "Umbrella"* [*Dziewczęta z "Parasola"*], documenting Polish women's contribution to the fight against the Nazi occupier during the Second World War, Danuta Kaczyńska, herself a member of the resistance movement, writes: "Bullets did not spare us, we got injured, we got shot as often as our male fellows, if not more often" (5). The content of the book confirms this introductory statement, giving numerous examples of female bravery in acts that frequently resulted in death. Polish society tends to be fairly ignorant of such facts, for although it is common knowledge that women were involved in the resistance movement and participated in the Warsaw Uprising, they are usually perceived as merely supporting their male fellows in the fight. Kaczyńska's book does not by any means offers a revisionist perspective on wartime femininity; nor does it attempt to equate female fighters with the masculine model of wartime heroism. On the contrary, the author presents material that expands the concept of war heroism. She foregrounds the significance of ordinary everyday activities that are usually absent in cultural representations of the Second World War, as they do not easily lend themselves to the processes of mythmaking. She provides readers with material that helps them to see heroism beyond the framework of the familiar ruling myths. Interestingly, she often draws on male testimonies to enhance the ordinary heroism of female conspirators. For example, she includes Eugeniusz Schielberg's account of his experience of the illegal transport of weapons, which was most often a female job:

masculine body is often displayed for the viewer's gaze as vulnerable and damaged—especially in Andrzej Wajda's war films—the female body is largely kept intact even when lifeless. Most frequently, the death of female characters is overwhelmingly marked by their disappearance.

My chapter examines various narrative and visual strategies employed by major Polish filmmakers to render the female wounded body or female death invisible within the celluloid fictional world. Such an examination will reveal the ideological underpinnings of these structural absences, which, in denying female characters access to a traditional notion of heroism, render the war experience as masculine. No director demonstrates this tendency more clearly than the internationally acclaimed Wajda. Furthermore, disembodied female deaths manifestly exile the female characters from history into the realm of a universal myth of femininity. To explore these issues in detail, I analyze selected scenes from Wajda's *Generation* [*Pokolenie* 1955] and *Kanal* [*Kanał* 1958], Tadeusz Konwicki's *All Souls Day* [*Zaduszki* 1961], and

---

> I learned what one feels while doing these seemingly simple things. I gained more respect for the bleak, dull, and seemingly unimportant work of female liaisons, storewomen, and distributors. We [male soldiers] ... would experience hard moments for a very brief time, just before and during the action that happened very rarely. They [women] had to struggle with fear every single day ... A soldier with a weapon in his hand had an opportunity to defend himself ... what were the chances of a girl smuggling a weapon when caught by a Nazi soldier? (1993, 153)

Kaczyńska not only devotes much attention to these everyday struggles, but also provides the reader with numerous descriptions of women getting injured and dying. There is no single stylistic convention in these accounts, which stems from the simple fact that these stories belong to the memories of different individuals. These images range from the most intimate, like the one of a girl who, while dying, asked for a bar of chocolate and hugged her doll, to the ones that Rikke reports with a directness devoid of any emotionality (e.g., "She died on the second or third day after she got wounded. She was conscious all the time and wanted to survive very much" [250]). By and large, Kaczyńska's account of wartime womanhood does not easily fit into any collective myth of the national war. Nor does she attempt to create a myth of feminine war heroism. What she offers is a fragmentary and incomplete account of Polish women's war experience as a heroicism of the mundane.

Andrzej Żuławski's *Third Part of the Night* [*Trzecia część nocy* 1972]. All of these films belong to the tradition of the Polish Film School, still regarded as a vehicle for providing the most significant account of the Polish war experience and indissolubly connected to the national tradition as codified by Polish Romanticism.

The Gendered Zones of Polish Romanticism

Wajda's films are commonly regarded as "quintessentially Polish," invariably entangled with issues of Polish history and deeply rooted in the vernacular cultural tradition, Romanticism in particular. Though frequently acknowledged, Wajda's affinities with Polish Romanticism are insufficiently analyzed. Above all, his more or less explicit references to the Romantic tradition are customarily interpreted as a consciously chosen alignment with a particular strand within the national cultural tradition. Countering this view, Marcin Król claims that for almost two centuries Polish Romanticism was the only available project for collective consciousness and culture. Król also notes that the most significant strand of Polish culture that emerged after 1956 developed in proximity to this singular and Romantic paradigm (1998, 33, 40). The diversity of Polish Romanticism notwithstanding, the strand that seems to be particularly relevant to Wajda's films is that best represented by Adam Mickiewicz's canonical poetic drama *Forefathers' Eve* [*Dziady* 1823–32]. In the third part of this openly messianic work, which presents a group of young male conspirators in a Russian prison, the dramatic situation develops along two main lines: The first unfolds through brotherly bonds that connect the men to one another, whereas the second concerns their common suffering. The only woman in this part of the play is Mrs. Rollison, the mother of one of the male protagonists; her chief function is to mourn him after he dies under torture by the Czarist oppressors. In terms of gender discourse, Mickiewicz's work defines masculinity through homosocial bonds, whereas femininity is embodied in the phantasmatic figure of motherhood. Translated into the vocabulary of national discourse, this gender dichotomy equates suffering men with the whole nation in its historical experience, while the iconic mother figure stands for an equally suffering motherland, remarkable for its ahistorical and consequently allegorical dimension. This pattern of representation in Polish culture is not unique and inscribes itself into the larger paradigm of allegorical or metaphorical representations of women in culture. As Marina Warner argues in her seminal book *Monuments and Maidens: The Allegory of the Female Form*:

> The female form metamorphoses from one sign into another, and this flux of signs, each succeeding generation's variation on the ancient topic, is accepted as a sequence of statements of the truth. The body is still the map on which we mark our meanings; it is chief among metaphors used to see and present ourselves […]. Meanings of all kinds flow through the figures of women, and they often do not include who she herself is. (2000, 331)

When located within national discourses Woman serves most often as an allegorical embodiment of nationhood. In consequence, as Helena Goscilo argues in her essay on women as the embodiment of nation/hood, "[t]he immemorial diffusion of women as generalized symbols erases them as living beings" (2004, 32). Wajda's films, especially those of the Polish Film School, follow this representational dichotomy in presenting male heroes as national subjects and female characters as allegorical embodiments of the motherland. Most frequently, these films feature a young male character who serves as a canonical Polish tragic hero embodying the collective experience of the Polish nation. Maciek Chełmicki in *Ashes and Diamonds* [*Popiół i diament* 1958] is the supreme iconic example. All of these heroes die in sadomasochistic spectacles, yet they usually do not perish on a battlefield, which would locate them comfortably within the realm of the traditional masculine pattern of heroism. Rather, their deaths occur elsewhere and conform to a different iconography. In *A Generation*, Jasio Krone, facing Nazi soldiers, commits suicide; in *Kanal*, Korab dies in a woman's arms; and, finally, in *Ashes and Diamonds*, Maciek, after being shot, expires on a waste heap, curled up in a fetal position. Invariably, these images of a wounded and vulnerable body express an endangered masculinity. Female bodies remain intact in these films, including that of Dorota in *A Generation*, whose arrest and presumed death are one of the crucial moments in the narrative.

An indestructible female body in Wajda's iconic films seems to be both complicit and at odds with a dominant tendency in Polish cultural signifying practices—one in which the allegory of Poland as a woman occupies a central position. The "logic" of the national cultural discourse dictates that a female body represent the motherland's suffering.[3] Hence, in such allegorical representations, the female body appears violated and tormented, but significantly, its suffering never results in visible death. In this context it is useful here to pay closer attention to the motif of a grave, present in many Polish paintings, drawings, and prints,[4] which invariably place the female figure symbolizing Poland next to the grave, waiting to be interred or resurrected. This Christian iconography reinforces the national allegory of Poland as an everlasting idea, endangered yet indestructible. Wajda's films rely on this representational pattern in a selective way. He renders female characters indestructible, while dissociating them from physical suffering. Only vulnerable male bodies—the site of genuine suffering, invariably doomed to perish—are given this iconic and ideological privilege.

There are several possible explanations for Wajda's decision to focus on male death. To begin with, Wajda's films belong to a general trend in post-Thaw Eastern European cinema that replaced the officially promoted paradigm of the infallible hero of Socialist Realism (repeatedly depicted in Soviet cinema) of that era with a weak and vulnerable man. Secondly, although these films purported to depict the Polish war experience, they actually spoke to the situation in which Polish men found themselves in postwar reality. Central to this situation was the fact that soldiers in the Home Army were deprived of any recognition for their

---

[3] A tormented and suffering female figure as an allegory of Poland can be found in numerous nineteenth-century paintings, prints, and drawings, e.g., *Polonia* by Ary Scheffer (1831), and *Polonia* by Artur Grottger (1863), which were cultural responses to Poland's loss of independence. Both World Wars caused further dissemination of this imagery, e.g., *I wojna światowa* [First World War] by Józef Rapacki (after 1918), and interestingly, also in popular culture associated with World War II (see the Polish caricatures on the web site Stalinka at http://images.library.pitt.edu/cgi-bin/i/image/image-idx?c=stalinka). Finally, martial law (introduced in Poland in 1981) revived the female allegory of Poland, e.g., *Polonia '82* by Leszek Sobocki (1982).

[4] For example, *Motherland's Grave* by Franciszek Smuglewicz (1794), *Motherland's Grave* by Henryka Wentzl (1838), *Polonia in the Grave* by Stanisław Kaczor-Batowski (c. 1907), *Polonia Resurrected* by Stanisław Kaczor-Batowski (c. 1907).

decisive role in wartime resistance. They not only suffered a final defeat in the Warsaw Uprising, but were also considered "criminals" by the Communist government. There were two options for Polish men in this postwar reality: collaboration with the Communists or withdrawal from the realm of socio-political activity. Both options significantly limited male subjectivity in the postwar years. Wajda's images of the vulnerable male body effectively convey this endangered subjectivity.

For a third explanation we need to turn again to the tradition of Polish Romanticism, where Poland did not always take a female form. As Dorota Siwicka writes in her essay on the metaphorical images of the Motherland in Polish romantic poetry:

Love for the Motherland disrupts [...] the traditional gender dichotomy. [...] For it is possible to be a Pole and a man and feel like a woman, suffer and love like her, be pregnant like her. [...] A romanticist becomes a woman, because his love makes him internalize the Motherland. Poland, which ceases to exist on the outside, moves into the inside of Poles. [...] For romantic Polish men become women not only because they absorb the Motherland but also because they want to give birth to her. (1993, 71)[5]

In the post-Romantic age, this disrupted gender metaphor transformed into a female allegory, which had become a linchpin in Polish national ideology for the preceding two hundred years. In his films, Wajda refers to the original Romantic multivalent metaphor of the moth-

---

[5] This is expressed in Adam Mickiewicz's *Forefathers*, most conspicuously in the protagonist's Improvisation:
Now my soul is incarnate in my land;
My body has absorbed *her* soul.
I and my country – [together] one whole!
My name is "Million" – since, for millions, oh, alack!
I love, and suffer the rack,
I gaze on my poor land and feel
Like a son whose father is bound on a wheel –
I feel for the whole nation's doom,
Like a mother for the pains of the fruit of her womb ... (my emphasis) (1968, 174–5)

erland, at the same time questioning the ossified cultural icon of the female representation of Poland. He positions suffering male characters in proximity to metaphorical female images of the motherland and he privileges their suffering with a spectacular individual death confirming their prime importance. In short, he presents a male figure and exhibits his suffering as a trope of the nation as an imagined community of individual subjects, as defined by Benedict Anderson (1991, 6–7). Indeed, Christopher Caes claims, "The exhibitionist quality of many of the heroes of Wajda's cinema can be linked to the necessity of producing spectacle in order to become a (national) subject" (2003, 117). Therefore, privileging masculine deaths and rendering female deaths invisible leads to the emergence of a masculine national subject and a female national allegory. The former inhabits the realm of history, the latter that of myth. This dominant narrative and visual strategy discernible in Wajda's war films forms the focus of my scrutiny, which also registers the presence of some textual deviations from this binary opposition of the masculine/historical and the female/allegorical.

(In)visible Female Death as Rebellion

The character of Halinka in *Kanal* radically undermines stability in gender politics. She occupies neither the position of a national subject nor that of female allegory of the motherland. What is perhaps even more interesting is that she is the only female character in Wajda's War Trilogy whose death is represented on screen.[6] She perishes in the sewers

---

[6] It is worth mentioning here another film by Wajda in which there is a graphic and spectacular female death: *Landscape after Battle* [*Krajobraz po bitwie* 1970]. The action of the film takes place in a DP camp, where former prisoners of a concentration camp and refugees from Poland are waiting to return to Poland or to emigrate to the West. Among them is a Jewish woman, Nina, who is accidentally shot by an American soldier. Her death is shown as a lavish visual spectacle, as are male deaths in other films by Wajda. However, as a Jewess, she occupies a marginal position within the national Polish discourse, not to mention that she is determined finally to escape from Poland by emigrating. This resistant attitude to the national discourse seems to be a factor that unites the characters of Nina and Halinka (see Ostrowska 2003).

through which the squad of insurgents flee. Whereas many of them die from exploding mines, wounds, and fatigue, Halinka, strikingly, commits suicide because of unhappy love. On first glance, this episode may appear as an openly misogynistic act of belittling a female character and excluding her from the collective historical experience. One can also argue that her deed slots Halinka into a stereotypical image of femininity governed by emotions or possibly even prone to hysterical reactions. Such a reading would solidify the familiar account of emotions/femininity as inferior to rationality/masculinity. Yet Halinka's behaviour contradicts any notion of hysteria. Upon learning that her lover, Wise, has a wife and child, she remains calm and steady, while he is the one who reacts hysterically to their entrapment, frantically yelling that he has somebody to live for. Halinka, as well as the viewer, witnesses the metamorphosis of Wise, idolized by her as a brave soldier and romantic lover, into a petty and cowardly husband unfaithful to both his wife and his lover.

Wajda breaks with traditional gender discourse in the scene of Halinka's suicide, which demolishes the stereotype of masculine war heroism and redefines femininity through the act of female suicide. Her decision to end her life offers confirmation of Elisabeth Bronfen's claim that a woman's suicide may be seen as a moment of power and control over her life:

> The choice of death emerges as a feminine strategy within which writing with the body is a way of getting rid of the oppression connected with the feminine body. Staging disembodiment as a form of escaping personal and social constraints serves to criticize those cultural attitudes that reduce the feminine body to the position of dependency and passivity, to the vulnerable object of sexual incursions. Feminine suicide can serve as trope, self-defeating as this seems, for a feminine writing strategy within the constraints of patriarchal culture. (1992, 142)

Indeed, the first part of the film casts Halinka as a young, naïve, and vulnerable woman who serves as an object of male desire. When Korab catches her and Wise in bed, she covers her face with a blanket, resorting to a conventional gesture of feminine modesty. Costume likewise codes her femininity, for the soldierly uniform she dons is much too big for her, as if she were pretending to be somebody else. One could argue that she performs a kind of a masquerade, playing the generic role of "a petite soldier." And in keeping with the logic of this masquerade, Wise provides her with a prop, a small toy-like pistol. Disappointed with it, she says to him: "So small?" Laughter, derision, and disparagement come as a response to her question. Given the age-old symbolic meaning of the gun as masculine potency, one can see the small toy-like pistol that Wise presents to Halinka as his refusal to give her a "real" symbol of masculine power. Simultaneously, this symbolic prop in his hand may be seen as foreshadowing the discovery that he himself does not possess "real" masculine power. However, it is Halinka who eventually seems to be able to access this power. In the sewers she decides to use this prop to subvert its semantic value, using the toy-like pistol to disrupt the textual regime of the male story. By turning the gun upon herself, thereby "taking over" what has traditionally been seen as a male prerogative, she usurps a symbolic masculinity.[7] Therefore, her suicidal death operates as an inscription of her subjectivity. As Bronfen notes:

> Suicide implies an authorship of one's own life, a form of writing the self and writing death that is ambivalently poised between self-construction and self-destruction; a confirmation that is also an annihilation of the self, and as such another kind of attempt to know the self as radically different and other from the consciously known self during life. (1992, 142)

Halinka's suicide, both a self-destructing and self-constructing manifestation of female subjectivity, destabilizes not only patriarchal but also national discourse. In particular, it is radically at odds with the sentimentalized version of Polish Romanticism that mandated the primacy of the Polish collective over the individual, whether male or female. Refusing to act within a national scenario of collective defeat, Halinka chooses to perform the "anti-Polish" role of a lover. Her deed, I maintain, may be seen as an act of rebellion against "the terror of the national cause" governing the national discourse.[8] Since in the specific

---

[7] I am indebted to Helena Goscilo for this insight.

[8] Grażyna Stachówna, in her essay on melodramatic motifs in Wajda's films, interprets this scene in a similar manner. She writes, "Halinka's suicide is thus a classic death because of 'unrequited love,' a melodramatic death of a

context the only way of escaping the dominant ideological discourse is self-annihilation, she commits suicide.

While exercising control over her own death, Halinka denies it visibility. She does not perform the act as an "aesthetically staged performance of death," which Bronfen sees as "a moment of control and power" (1992, 141). Just a moment before shooting herself, she asks her lover to switch off his torch. Why does she refuse to make her death a visual spectacle? Is this decision obedient to the logic of a national discourse according to which only a male hero can die a spectacular death? Or is it a radical attempt to escape this national scenario and the narrative of the film itself? When Wise complies with her request that he extinguish his torch she finally acquires control over him as well as his story. In a sense she also acquires control over the cinematic narrative. The screen turns dark, tearing apart the solid fabric of the continuous narrative. This black screen can be seen as a textual "black hole," the only space capable of containing this simultaneously self-destructing and self-constructing female subjectivity. Halinka's suicide discloses a significant contradiction between the narrative and the visual elements of the film, which itself may be seen as a symptom of Wajda's contradictory attitude toward national myths. In his films, these myths are simultaneously preserved and destroyed. In the episode of Halinka's death, the film's narrative appears to be a contestation of the patriotic master narrative, whereas the invisibility of her death signifies the film's complicity with it.

Patriarchal Adjustment

Wajda's ambiguous relationship with national myths as worked into particular gender roles is evident elsewhere in *Kanal*. Early in the film, immediately after the virtuoso tracking shot that introduces the char-

---

rejected and deeply disappointed girl, not the death of a soldier surrounded by enemies who commits suicide to save his honor. A suicide for personal and sentimental reasons becomes forbidden during wartime, as one can die only for the motherland. From this perspective one can see Halinka's love and her later death as a romantic, girlish rebellion against the 'tyrannical imperatives of a patriotic ethic'" (2003, 216).

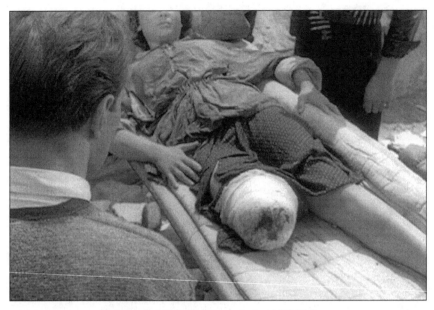

Figure 1.1. Image from Andrzej Wajda's
Kanal (Kanał, *1957) of a wounded female body*

acters, we see a young girl covered with a blanket lying on a stretcher.
A young man, Slim, approaches her, recognizing in her somebody he
met on the first day of the uprising. He asks jokingly, "I see that you
joined the uprising, then. What does your mother say to that?" The girl
answers calmly that she is dead. Confused, the man asks whether her
wound is bad. Equally calmly she replies, "Nothing much." A moment
later, the blanket moves and we see that she is an amputee [Figure
1.1]. Wajda keeps Slim's shocked face on screen for a significant
amount of time, encouraging viewers to share his extreme reaction.

   Certainly, Slim is not horrified by the sight of a wounded body, as
he has ample opportunity to see the many injured compatriots around
him. What horrifies him is that the wounded body is *female*. When he
approaches the girl, her calm and beautiful face evokes the notion of
tranquillity, domesticity, and family life. It is not surprising to hear
him ask about her mother, since he wants to transfer her, symbolically, into the domestic space—the Freudian *Heimlich*—as her mother's
"little daughter" belonging to a safer, pre-uprising life. The sudden
sight of her amputated leg radically blocks these efforts, revealing an

Figure 1.2. First appearance of Daisy in Andrzej
Wajda's Kanal *(Kanał, 1957)*

unheimlich aspect of femininity. This sequence undermines the boyish, often histrionic bravery typical of other male characters in *Kanal*, for, as Ricky Schubart points out, the image of the wounded female body "remind[s] the soldier of the repressed fact that his body, too, is soft, sensitive, and penetrable" (2007, 257).[9]

The masculine body as soft, sensitive, and penetrable occupies a central position in the second part of *Kanal*, which focuses on the wounded Lieutenant Korab and his unofficial nurse, Daisy, who initially is presented as a cynical, tough, and independent woman [Figure 1.2]. An efficient courier who bravely travels around the labyrinthine sewers, she exercises full control over her environment as well as her body

---

[9] This scene can also be seen as a reversal of a stereotypical gender reaction. The girl's response to the atrocious reality is controlled, if not tranquil (as later is Halinka's response to her discovery that Wise has a wife and child), whereas Slim reacts to it with horror and near-paralysis, conveyed by the prolonged static close-up of him. My thanks to Yana Hashamova for drawing my attention to this aspect of the scene.

Figure 1.3. Scene from Andrzej Wajda's
Kanał (Kanał, *1957) of Korab's death*

(numerous hints suggest her vigorous sexual activity). Hence, Korab's initial contradictory and stereotypical attitude to her: he desires yet scorns her. Daisy's troublesome femininity undergoes a process of "patriarchal adjustment" during the second part of the film. While taking care of the wounded Korab, she gradually metamorphoses into a maternal figure, a safe image of femininity. When the couple reaches a point in a sewer that proves a deadly trap, she says to him, "No, no, don't open your eyes because the sun's come out," thereby allowing him to return to the safe, dark warmth reminiscent of the maternal womb. Tellingly, the last image of them is of Korab dying in her arms. This Pieta-like configuration annihilates her previous incarnation of femininity—that of a promiscuous and independent woman—and returns her to the safe male fantasy of motherly femininity [Figure 1.3].[10] As a fantasy she needs to

---

[10] This patriarchal adjustment of Daisy's character is analogous to the transformation of Agnieszka's character from *Man of Marble* to its sequel, *Man of Iron*. See Ewa Mazierska (2006) and Elżbieta Ostrowska (2005).

Figure 1.4. Scene from Andrzej Wajda's A Generation
(Pokolenie, *1955*) *of Dorota's arresting*

be a timeless being and thus immortal, which is why there is no narrative closure in regard to her character. Whether she will die or survive is
immaterial, for life and death are inapplicable at this point of the film's
male fantasy.

Wajda uses a similar visual strategy in *A Generation*. Its heroine,
Dorota, is arrested by the Gestapo for her underground activity, but
the viewer is spared her execution, invited, instead, to hold on to
the bold and beautiful image of her as she is led away [Figure 1.4].
One could argue that her death is omitted because Stach, the male
protagonist who narrates the film, does not witness it. This explanation, however, fails to take into account that Stach does not witness
Jasio Krone's death either, yet this death is shown on screen, again
as a lavish visual spectacle. Therefore, the "horizon of the narrator's
knowledge" does not sufficiently explain the logic of the *siuzhet*, which
renders Dorota's death invisible. The sight of her death is withheld,
I maintain, because her character is also constructed as a male fantasy
rather than an individual female subject. Throughout the narrative

she appears as a combination of different myths and stereotypes of ideal femininity: the Romantic heroic woman-knight type (e.g., Emilia Plater); the figure of the "Superwoman" promulgated by Communist propaganda; and last but not least, the incarnation of a perfect "motherly" figure troping Motherland. All of these myths and stereotypes are necessary for a masculine subject for whom, as Eva Fedder Kittay proposes, women as metaphors serve as "vehicles for [...male] self-conception" (1997, 267). A female body wounded or in the process of decay would inevitably materialize the character and hamper the process of her idealized metaphorization. Thus the invisibility of Dorota's death confirms that even at the point of extinction she continues to function allegorically, abstracted into a Poland posited as indestructible.

Muted Death

A heroic female figure, similarly metaphorized, appears in *All Souls Day* by Tadeusz Konwicki, widely regarded as a representative of Polish *auteur* cinema. Though *All Souls Day* shares with the dominant stream of the Polish Film School an interest in the wartime past, its account of that past adopts not a national, but a universal perspective. With the action set several years after the war, the film examines the difficulties war survivors, both male and female, face in establishing a love relationship. The film consists of three flashbacks evoking the traumatic war experience. The male protagonist, Mężny, recollects two women with whom he was in love during that period. Both are invoked as myths rather than real women. What is of special significance is that before meeting them Mężny *heard* about them, through stories about a female lieutenant, Listek, and songs about a brave nurse, Katarzyna. Tellingly, in a voice-over commentary he says that he seriously doubted whether the latter actually existed or was simply a product of other soldiers' imaginations. Later we learn that Katarzyna was a real woman and survived the war, while Listek died solidifying her mythological status. Yet again, Mężny only *hears* about her death from his fellow soldiers.

I emphasize the act of hearing because it is of crucial importance here, particularly as it is contrasted with Mężny's earlier inability to hear Listek as she was delivering a speech to fellow soldiers. The ret-

rospective scene begins with a frontal long shot of the female protagonist addressing the group. Significantly, in this establishing shot over-
exposure undermines its potential realism. This partial disembodiment
of the female figure increases as the camera draws closer to her with
a slow tracking movement, to finally tighten on her in a choke shot.
Simultaneously, her voice gradually fades out, to be eventually replaced
by ambient music. All of these devices strive to create a male subjective vision—or, rather, a male fantasy. According to Kaja Silverman,
woman's "most ideal representation [is] when she is seen but not
heard [...] becoming [...] almost synonymous with the corporeal and
the specular" (1984, 134). In this case, however, cinematic devices
ensure that not much of the corporeal remains.

This disembodiment of the female protagonist finds its culmination later on, in the scene in which Listek's dead body is displayed for
the ceremony of mourning. Once again captured in a long shot, she is
surrounded by lamenting old women, her body entirely covered with
flowers, the symbolic *mise-en-scène* draining her image of any realism.
Flowers hide the corpse and its possible decay, allowing the male protagonist as well as the viewer to retain her earlier idealized image. That
image is facilitated by the lack of a close-up and by the presence of
the old women in mourning clothes, who transform the scene into a
kind of ancient ritual. For the second time in the film, the heroine is
expelled from history into mythical eternity.

The orchestration of Listek's deathbed image can be paralleled
with the canonical description of Emilia Plater's final image in Adam
Mickiewicz's poem *The Death of the Colonel*. As Halina Filipowicz
notes, Mickiewicz's idealizing strategy is to situate the expiring
national heroine "on her deathbed, not on a battlefield. She is cleansed
of carnality and glorified by death" (1996, 35), providing a model for
Listek in Konwicki's film. Interestingly, we also learn that Listek was
only wounded, not killed on the battlefield, and died in her soldiers'
arms while being carried to her quarters. Thus the viewer does not *see*
any of the situations that would link Listek's character with the idea
of military heroism. By withholding such scenes, Konwicki wholly
deprives her of "soldierly" glory and the identity of hero/ine in any traditional sense.

In considering the female protagonist's capacity to meet the
demands of male heroism, the semantics of male and female nick-

names used in Konwicki's film provide another interesting insight. The male protagonist is nicknamed "Mężny" which means "brave," "valiant," whereas the female protagonist's fellow soldiers call her "Listek," a diminutive form of "leaf" (recalling Daisy's nickname in *Kanał*). True to gender conventions, abstract virtues symbolize masculinity, whereas femininity is identified as an element of nature. The semantic valence of Listek's nickname is underscored in the scene of mourning, where flowers cover her body—a body, one can argue, that does not perish but undergoes a kind of mysterious transformation from one state of being into another. A tenable claim would be that she "returns to nature," where she belongs. This final image of Listek, along with the first shot of her as an almost translucent body, radically deprives her subjectivity of material substantiality and consequently puts this very subjectivity into question.

This unstable subjectivity is signaled earlier in the film, again through language. Initially all of the soldiers, Mężny included, speak about her as "him" or directly address her as Mister Lieutenant, which she neither protests nor corrects. Only when she dies do they start using a feminine form in talking about her. Activity can be expressed in language only through the pronoun "he," whereas passivity is expressed through the pronoun "she." It is as if the soldiers were demonstrating the incompatibility of linguistic structures with the notion of female heroism. This gap between the signified and signifier can be filled only when she is carried to her final rest by male soldiers, to lie silently as an inanimate object of their gaze. Now she no longer has to be admired and listened to, but is to be contemplated and adored. The soldier has died and the woman is born.

In Search of Death

Another disconcerting, albeit appreciatively different relationship between death and (re)birth can be found in Andrzej Żuławski's *Third Part of the Night* (1971). Since Żuławski (b. 1940) belongs to a later generation than Wajda and Konwicki, for him the Second World War was not a formative experience. Moreover, he spent the postwar years with his parents in Paris and Prague, which inevitably reduced his exposure to the national discourse. In 1959–60, he studied film directing in IDHEC[11] in Paris and philosophy at the Sorbonne. Interestingly enough, it was not the French New Wave that attracted the young film-maker, but Andrzej Wajda's war films, with their profuse visual flour-ishes, that captured his imagination. In an interview with Sergio Naitza many years later, Żuławski said that when he started his career, Wajda was the filmmaker he admired most as "a genuine master" (Naitza 2004,15). Upon returning to Poland, he started working with Wajda as his assistant and the director of a second unit. After completing three films with Wajda, he made his own directorial debut in 1971 with *The Third Part of the Night*, a visionary film re-enacting the experience of the Second World War as it has never been shown before.[12]

Often seen as a polemic against the Polish Film School, the film ended Żuławski's friendship with Wajda, who disliked the film's narra-tive structure and insisted on the elimination of its temporal ambiguities. Had Żuławski complied, the film would inevitably have lost its halluci-natory effect. Although Wajda's films often offer unrestrained visuals[13] that lead film critics to describe them as "baroque," this visual excess is always counterbalanced by well-ordered and almost classical narratives. Żuławski's style, however, embraces the principle of excess on both visual and narrative levels, which results in ambiguity and ontological uncer-tainty. The most disconcerting uncertainty in *The Third Part of the Night* concerns female death, which operates as a main narrative force.

The film begins with a female voice-over reciting fragments from the *Apocalypse* (Revelations in the Gospel of St. John) while the camera aimlessly wanders across a dark, gloomy landscape of fields and willow trees. This disembodied female narration radically breaks with the aesthetic strategy employed in the three films analyzed above, where a male voice-over establishes the textual regime of the fictional reali-

---

[11] Institut des hautes études cinématographiques (1944–85), the premier French film school.

[12] Many Polish film critics consider this film closely connected to the Polish Film School. For example, Aleksander Ledóchowski writes in his rather metaphorical review of the film that "*Third Part of the Night* is an aston-ishing renaissance of the Polish Film School. It is proof that a volcano active in 1956–60 erupted again, throwing out precious gold" (1971, 8).

[13] Aforementioned images of male deaths, such as Jasio Krone's suicidal jump from the top of a spiral staircase or Maciek Chełmicki's death at the waste heap, provide examples of the elaborated visuals in his films.

ties. *Kanal* begins with a standard "God-like" voice-over that sums up the current situation of the Warsaw Uprising and introduces the film's characters, requesting the audience to look at them carefully, as "these will be their last minutes before they die." This authoritative voice instantly displays its omniscience: "He" knows that Slim wants to be an airplane constructor after the war and that Halinka's mother asked her to wear warm underwear while fighting the Nazis. Thus, Wajda's film presents the uprising from the outset as a male narrative within which its participants are identified through traditional gender traits.

In *A Generation* and *All Souls Day* the voice-over narration proceeds from male characters within the films' diegesis. Consequently, the female characters of Dorota and Lt. Listek appear as male memories or phantasmatic images of the irrevocable past. Żuławski reverses this narrative strategy by introducing a female voice-over that emerges as almost literally "God-like," since its first words are those of the biblical text. However, the content of the narration undermines the seeming authority of the female voice, for this voice merely ventriloquizes a male-authored text—the apocalyptic ending of human civilization as it was revealed by God to St. John. Thus, the female serves as a messenger rather than a source of authority and authorial voice. Moreover, when the camera reaches a manor house and moves inside to show a woman reading a Bible, what initially seemed a bold break with the universal cinematic tradition of tabooing a disembodied female voice proves complicit with it. As Kaja Silverman notes, the rule of synchronization is more forcibly applied to women's voices than men's, and consequently women's voices are invariably tied to female bodies (1998, 45). In Żuławski's film, not only is the female voice attached to a body, thereby sealing up the uncomfortable gap between sound and image, but the owner of both is also located within a *heimlich* family structure that positions her as a wife and mother.

This solid socio-gendered fabric of patriarchal structure is torn apart in the next scene, when Michał (Leszek Teleszyński), the protagonist, goes for a walk with his father and son, Łukasz. A few minutes later, both Helena, his wife, and his mother, who have remained in the house, are attacked by a Nazi soldier, who rides a horse through an entrance door and into a room where Helena and her mother-in-law are sitting. He is filmed with a shaky hand-held camera in somewhat random shots that, curiously, exclude his "point of view" shot (POV)

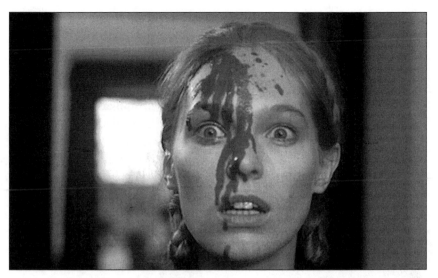

Figure 1.5. Scene of Helena's death from Andrzej Żuławski's
Third Part of the Night (Trzecia część nocy, *1971*)

of the interior and the two women. Rather, it is they who observe him. A close-up of Helena's face introduces in a highly conventionalized way her subjective look at the soldier, thus apparently empowering her gaze—an empowerment for which almost immediately she is severely punished. In response to her gaze, the soldier raises his rifle and hits her in her face, which we then see covered with blood, her eyes and mouth wide open [Figure 1.5]. The next moment we have her POV shot of her son running towards her, and when he reaches her, the soldiers encircle and shoot all three family members. The murder is observed from afar by Michał, who, after hearing the earlier shots, starts running back to the house.[14] Yet he does not actually see

---

[14] This image of Michał, while hiding and observing the death of his wife, might be paralleled to the scene from Wajda's *Generation* in which Stach observes Dorota's arrest as he hides from the enemy. These images of weak, vulnerable men who are forced to watch passively as women are tormented and assaulted by enemies are common in Polish cinema (e.g., *Hurricane* [Józef Lejtes, *Huragan* 1928], *Man of Iron* [Andrzej Wajda, *Człowiek z żelaza* 1981], Andrzej Wajda, *A Ring with a Crowned Eagle* [*Pierścionek z orłem w koronie* 1994]), and they invariably speak to the theme of a weakened and consequently endangered masculinity.

the soldiers kill his wife, son, and mother, for his father forcibly pulls him down the hill to hide them both from the invaders. Therefore, the final image of the opening sequence, a profile close-up of Helena's corpse, does not belong to Michał's subjective perspective. In the following sequence, Michał and his father stand over the dead bodies of two women and a little child, covered with white sheets, reversing the standard image of women mourning over dead male bodies. Here, it is Michał and his father who experience loss and mourn over it.[15]

Michał's mourning is the focus of later parts in the film that develop into an ambiguous narrative in which the past is intertwined with the present and the real is interlaced with Michał's hallucinations. After Helena's death, his first decision is to join the underground movement, for, as he says to his friend, he will have "plenty of time now to do lots of things." When he comes to a secret meeting, his fellow conspirator is shot by German soldiers and Michał is injured. While escaping, he finds shelter on the vast staircase of an apartment building—an intertextual reference to a scene from *A Generation* in which Jasio Krone dies in a suicidal jump from the top of a spiral staircase. Costume reinforces the parallel, for both protagonists wear a white coat. However, here costume turns out to be of even greater consequence for the rest of the story. While Michał hides in a dark spot, another man, likewise in a white coat, enters the building, only to be shot and taken away by the Germans, who mistake him for Michał. During the shooting a pregnant woman runs out from an apartment and hastily approaches the wounded man, who, we later learn, is her husband. Finally, when all quiets down, Michał goes to the woman's apartment. It is only when she lies on the floor in the throes of labor and asks Michał for help that her uncanny resemblance to his late wife, Helena, becomes evident. Tellingly, she is played by the same actress, Małgorzata Braunek. The following close-ups of her giving birth, with Michał's assistance, make this resemblance even more striking and disconcerting, as all of the shots of her [Figure 1.6] are almost identical in terms of camera work (close-up, frontal camera placement) to those of Helena's bleeding face and her death [Figure 1.5] In both instances,

---

[15] On the gendering of mourning rituals see Helena Goscilo, "Playing Dead: The Operatics of Celebrity Funerals, or, The Ultimate Silent Part" (2002, 313, n. 11).

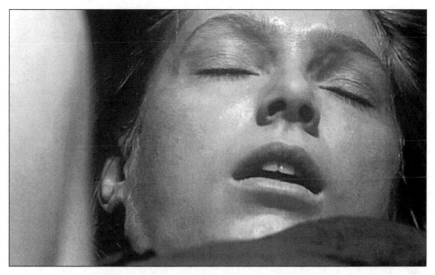

Figure 1.6. Image of Marta as Helena's double from Andrzej Żuławski's
Third Part of the Night (Trzecia część nocy, *1971*)

women's blood, overtly displayed in highly saturated color, signifies
female death as well as birth. This highlighted motif of blood suggests
a disturbing, inexplicable transformation of the two women into each
other as the blood accompanying female death converts into the blood
of a new life's beginning, in the process obliterating Helena's death as
if it never happened.

Elisabeth Bronfen devotes one of the chapters in *Over Her Dead
Body* to the cultural image of a male's dead beloved returning in the
body of a second woman. She examines this "risky resemblance," as
she calls it, in Edgar Allan Poe's *Ligeia*, Gustave Rodenbach's *Bruges-
la-Morte*, and Alfred Hitchcock's *Vertigo*. In the course of her analysis,
she writes:

> [T]he second beloved is ultimately to become an identical sub-
> stitute for her predecessor, yet such an achievement requires a
> blindness toward the singularity of both women. Regaining a lost
> amorous unity and denying the narcissistic wound induced by
> death, results in the repetition of the beloved as an image, but an
> image materialised over another body. Typical of the rhetoric of
> the uncanny, a fatal blurring of the distinction between the imag-

ined and the real occurs, in that the sublation of signifier into signified disaffects the difference between real materiality and semiosis. (1992, 327–8)

The "blindness toward the singularity of both women" in *The Third Part of the Night* is substantiated by the decision to cast Małgorzata Braunek in both female roles. The effect of "oversameness," though conspicuous, is ambiguous. Since Michał's character acts as the only narrative focalizer in later parts of the film, one could feasibly maintain that this act of substitution is simply a figment of his traumatized imagination. Yet the behavior of the second woman, Marta, feeds his imagination, reinforcing the process of sublation that takes place.

Shortly after giving birth to her son, Marta decides to leave her home for a shelter run by nuns, Michał's sister being one of them. The nuns place Marta and her baby in a room previously occupied by Michał and his late wife, Helena. When Michał decides to take a job as a lice-feeder at the Weigl Institute[16] that Helena had encouraged him to accept, Marta raises no objections and agrees that he should become a surrogate father for her child. Similarly she makes no protest when Michał states that the child is "his [Marta's husband], hers, and mine," and soon behaves as if Michał *is* a "third part" of her family. Apparently Michał attempts, in Bronfen's words, to "deny the narcissistic wound induced by [the] death" (1992, 327) of his wife and son, which is again conveyed in a line of dialogue: "When I look at you, I feel I've got another chance to experience what I've already experienced in a wrong way and what I didn't understand well." Michał's relationship with Marta, however, far from simply compensates for mistakes made in the past. It is by no means an act of redemption for the "sin" of not saving his wife and son; indeed, he relives the past through Marta, his wife's substitute and double. Therefore he denies the singularity of both women and their life

---

[16] The Rudolf Weigl Institute was the only Polish research center that legally functioned during the Nazi occupation owing to its production of the typhoid vaccine. It employed many Polish intellectuals, protecting them from death or deportation to Siberia. Żuławski's father, the renowned writer Mirosław Żuławski, was one of the institute's employees, working as a lice-feeder.

experience, including what is of particular importance here, Helena's death. His dead wife is retained as an image resurrected in the body of another woman. As Helena's exact match, Marta is protected and kept alive by Michał, thereby annihilating her predecessor's death and dispossessing it of its reality.

According to Bronfen, in the texts she analyzes, a "second killing" of the second beloved invariably takes place. As she claims:

> The second beloved is killed because she proves autonomous to the image of her lover's self, which she is meant to assure; because she enacts that misrecognition and difference is always inscribed in the illusion of finding a "lost" wholeness in and through another. The killing is meant to serve a denial of death's castrative threat to life as this threat shows itself whenever narcissism's stability and wholeness is wounded. Yet ironically the reproduced dead body of the second beloved confirms the irrevocable loss of prenatal unity. Though her death places the second woman outside the surviving lover's control, it also affirms his omnipotence of thought since he can mentally reanimate her, continue the sequence of refinding and killing her in further surrogate bodies. (1992, 329)

The narrative trajectory of *The Third Part of the Night*, however, does not follow this pattern. Marta is not killed and as such she does not affirm the male figure's omnipotence and his subjective wholeness. In fact, the opposite occurs.

Towards the film's ending, Michał searches for Marta's husband in the cellars of the Institute, passing by various emaciated naked bodies in separate cells before finally reaching the morgue, where a body lies covered with a white sheet. When he uncovers it, he sees his own face. Then the narrative loops back to the scene on the staircase, and this time it is Michał who is shot. Wounded, he frantically staggers around an unidentified space, primarily of corridors, to arrive at the manor house where the action began. We see a close-up of Michał's bloodied face before the camera tracks right down to show the three dead bodies covered with white sheets with which the opening sequence of the film ended, and then switches to a long shot of Małgorzata Braunek, who continues reciting the fragment of the Book of Revelation as she did at the film's beginning. Her image undergoes yet another transformation in the next shot, which shows her in contemporary attire, applying make-up. Thus she seems to escape the film's diegesis, to be associated with the mystical Biblical text, an abstract realm of the Word, transgressing any kind of historical reality.[17] In response to this image, Michał, his bloodied face substantiating his physical presence, halts at the threshold of the house as if incapable or unwilling to transgress this liminal space beyond which an abstract reality begins with yet another incarnation of a ghost-like figure in which Helena merges with Marta.

The female figure appearing in three different incarnations escapes the historical experience of the war. Instead, she emerges as an eternal image of an everlasting femininity, an allegory of Poland that may seem to perish yet is always resurrected. Her inscription into the biblical order of the Apocalypse as a disaster that precedes a revival substantiates the idea of an ultimate rebirth. For Michał, as a Polish male, this metaphorical order constitutes a vital dilemma: What should his role be? Is there anything he has to enact? The circular narrative signifies his futility in undertaking a subjective position within history. Unfortunately, his effort to be active in history finally takes the form of a vicious circle that brings him back to the point of departure in his journey.

Although in its visual and narrative strategies *The Third Part of the Night* radically differs from Wajda's and Konwicki's films and explicitly presents female death on screen, it shares their effort to de-substantiate female bodies, especially when dead—the image of Helena, once she is killed, becomes merged with her double, Marta. If the elliptical and ambiguous narrative of Żuławski's film is to be seen as a hallucinatory vision of the horror of war, it is still a male vision and, as such, expresses male subjectivity, even if it is a split subjectivity. A woman, whether alive or dead, can only function as an image fabricated by this subjectivity.

---

[17] One needs to remember the strong presence of this historical reality in the film, especially in all of the sequences in the Weigl Institute.

Conclusion

As mentioned earlier, Wajda's and Konwicki's films were made during the period of the Polish Film School that forms the core of Polish National Cinema. Commonly regarded as a polemic with the Polish Film School, Żuławski's film is to be located within the same paradigm. All three Polish films under analysis here operate within the framework of national cinema. In her examination of that cinema, Susan Hayward discusses the problem of "a gendered prescription of agency and power" that often takes the form of symbolic equations between violated motherland and violated woman, invasion by the enemy and rape of the mother-land/woman and rape and occupation (2000, 98). This symbolic imagery, which in Poland originated in the post-partition period, still permeates significant areas of the vernacular culture, including popular cinema,[18] which is why its virtual absence

---

[18] The TV mini-series *Columbuses* [*Kolumbowie* 1970] by Janusz Morgenstern serves as a perfect example of such symbolism. In consecutive episodes female bodies are shown as wounded, mutilated, and damaged. All of these images conform to the most conservative imagery of Polish culture, with an allegorical female form as its linchpin. It is this sentimentalized version of Polish Romanticism that underpins the iconography of Morgenstern's TV series and informs its visual rhetoric. According to its logic, a female character that suffers and dies signifies the suffering and tragedy of the motherland.

The death of one of the female characters, Niteczka (a diminutive of "thread"), is the final image of the series and is probably the most strongly allegorized. Before she dies we see her taking care of her injured boyfriend, Kolumb (a visible parallel to the characters of Daisy and Korab from Wajda's *Kanal*). When Nazis capture the building she does not resist the soldiers in the hope that she will be able to save her beloved. When she disappears with the soldier off screen, we see Kolumb struggling to help her, but he finally reaches her too late. The camera then slowly tracks right, exposing first her feet and bare thighs, then her crotch, with a broken bottle inside it, and finally her martyred face. The humiliated and destroyed female body serves here as an object of visual contemplation. The content of the scene and its stylization force its allegorical reading upon the viewer, who inevitably locates it within the wider cultural tradition. In an all too familiar scenario, s/he is the image of a martyred woman who symbolizes a martyred and defeated Poland. A woman dies, a national symbol is born.

in the World War II films by Wajda, Konwicki, and Żuławski is all the more intriguing.

What needs particular attention here, however, is the fact that all the female characters resist any form of annihilation. They either escape the diegesis without a definite resolution of their subplot (Dorota in *A Generation* and Daisy in *Kanal*), are visually swallowed by the blackness of the screen (Halinka in *Kanal*), return to the everlasting order of nature (Listek in *All Souls Day*), or revisit the fictional world as their doubles (Helena/Marta in *The Third Part of the Night*). All of these narrative and visual devices expel these characters from the realm of historical experience into the realm of the mythic. Their everlasting and indestructible femininity lends itself to symbolic identification with an equally eternal and imperishable idea of motherland. Yet to preserve this idea, a mortal sacrifice is indispensable, and that is a male task. Thus, the viewer is offered numerous images of violated and dead male bodies that stand for the violated and defeated nation protecting its motherland.

In his films, Wajda reworks the theme of Polish national identity across gender lines and thereby invokes a (perverse?) notion of beauty in his spectacles of male death. In this national scenario, a spectacular dying body conditions the emergence of a national subject. In Żuławski's film this theme is also present, although treated in a more ambiguous manner. Its protagonist's ghostly appearance in the final scene of the film seems to locate him in between the realms of life and death. Thus it speaks to the impossibility of a full and complete experience of one's death. If male death conditions the emergence of the national subject, one may contend that the central concern of Żuławski's film is that of the impossibility of the formation of a complete national subjectivity. Whether this model of masculine national subjectivity is more easily attainable, as in Wajda's and Konwicki's films, or less so, as in Żuławski's, it is inevitably linked to femininity. As such it interferes with the psychosexual aspect of masculinity (Coates 2005, 116–7). To resolve this dilemma a woman as Other is needed. Hence the strenuous efforts to purge wartime femininity from any traits of masculinity, to produce her image as an everlasting (maternal) femininity.

NOTES

My thanks to Helena Goscilo, Yana Hashamova, Beth Holmgren, Izabela
Kalinowska, and Michael Stevenson, who offered me insightful comments and
gave me generous assistance in writing this chapter.

REFERENCES

Anderson, Benedict. 1991. *Imagined Communities: Reflections on the Origin and
Spread of Nationalism*. London and New York: Verso.
Bronfen, Elisabeth. 1992. *Over Her Dead Body. Death, Femininity, and
Aesthetic*. Manchester: Manchester University Press.
Caes, Christopher J. 2003. "Catastrophic Spectacles: Historical Trauma and
the Masculine Subject in the Cinema of Andrzej Wajda." In *The Cinema
of Andrzej Wajda. The Art of Irony and Defiance*, edited by John Orr and
Elżbieta Ostrowska, 116–31. London: Wallflower Press.
Coates, Paul. 2005. *The Red and The White. The Cinema of People's Poland*.
London: Wallflower Press.
Filipowicz, Halina. 1996. "The Daughters of Emilia Plater." In *Engendering
Slavic Literatures*, edited by Pamela Chester and Sibelan Forrester, 34–58.
Bloomington and Indianapolis: Indiana University Press.
Goscilo, Helena. 2004. "Negotiating Gendered Rhetoric. Between Scylla and
Charybdis." In *Representing Gender in Culture*, edited by Elżbieta H. Oleksy
and Joanna Rydzewska, 19–37. Frankfurt am Main: Peter Lang.
———. 2002. "Playing Dead. The Operatics of Celebrity Funerals, or, The
Ultimate Silent Part." In *Imitations of Life: two centuries of melodrama in
Russia*, edited by Louise McReynolds and Joan Neuberger, 283–320.
Durham: Duke University Press.
Hayward, Susan. 2000. "Framing National Cinemas." In *Cinema and Nation*,
edited by Mette Hjort and Scott Mackenzie, 88–102. London and New
York: Routledge.
Higonnet, Margaret R. 1993. "Women in the Forbidden Zone: War, Women,
and Death." In *Death and Representation*, edited by Sarah Webster
Goodwin and Elisabeth Bronfen, 193–209. Baltimore and London: The
John Hopkins University Press.
Kaczyńska, Danuta. 1993. *Dziewczęta z "Parasola."* Warsaw: Oficyna Wydawnicza
Wiesław R. Kufirski.
Kittay, Eva Feder. 1997. "Woman as Metaphor." In *Feminist Social Thought:
A Reader*, edited by Diana T. Meyers, 265–85. New York and London:
Routledge.
Król, Marcin. 1998. *Romantyzm. Piekło i niebo Polaków*. Warsaw: Res Publica
Fundacja.

Ledóchowski, Aleksander. 1971. "Czas zatraty, czas odkupienia." *Kino* 10 (1971): 8, 4–12.

Mazierska, Ewa. 2006. "Agnieszka and Other Solidarity Heroines of Polish Cinema." In *Women in Polish Cinema*, edited by Ewa Mazierska and Elżbieta Ostrowska, 92–109. New York and Oxford: Berghahn Books.

Mickiewicz, Adam. 1968. *Forefathers' Eve*. Translated by Count Potocki of Montalk. London: The Polish Cultural Foundation.

Naita, Sergio. 2004. "Wywiad z Andrzejem Żuławskim." In *Opętanie. Ekstremalne kino i pisarstwo Andrzeja Żuławskiego*, edited by Sergio Naitza, 15–45. Warsaw: "Twój Styl" Wydawnictwo Książkowe.

Ostrowska, Elżbieta. 2006. "Krystyna Janda: The Contradictions of Polish Stardom." In *Poles Apart: Women in Modern Polish Culture*, Indiana Slavic Studies Vol. 15, edited by Helena Goscilo and Beth Holmgren, 37–64. Bloomington, Indiana: Indiana University Press.

———. 2003. "Dangerous Liaisons: Wajda's Discourse of Sex, Love, and Nation." In *The Cinema of Andrzej Wajda. The Art of Irony and Defiance*, edited by John Orr and Elżbieta Ostrowska, 46–63. London: Wallflower Press.

Schubart, Rikke. 2007. *Super Bitches and Action Babes. The Female Hero in Popular Cinema, 1970–2006*. Jefferson, North Carolina, and London: McFarland & Company, Inc. Publications.

Silverman, Kaja. 1998. *The Acoustic Mirror. The Female Voice in Psychoanalysis and Cinema*. Bloomington and Indianapolis: Indiana University Press.

———. 1984. "Dis-Embodying the Female Voice." In *Re-Vision. Essays in Feminist Film Criticism*, edited by Mary Ann Doane, et al., 131–49. Frederick: University Publication of America, Inc.

Siwicka, Dorota. 1993. "Ojczyzna intymna." *Res Publica Nowa* 7–8: 70–4.

Stachówna, Grażyna. 2003. "Kronika wypadków miłosnych według Andrzeja Wajdy." In *Filmowy świat Andrzeja Wajdy*, edited by Ewelina Nurczyńska-Fidelska and Piotr Sitarski, 211–31. Kraków: Universitas.

Tasker, Yvonne. 2005. "Soldiers' Stories: Women and Military Masculinities in *Courage Under Fire*." In *The War Film*, edited by Robert Eberwein, 172–89. New Brunswick, NJ and London: Rutgers University Press.

Warner, Marina. 2000. *Monuments and Maidens. The Allegory of the Female Form*. Berkeley and Los Angeles: University of California Press.

CHAPTER 2

She Defends His Motherland: The Myth of Mother Russia in Soviet Maternal Melodrama of the 1940s[1]

Alexander Prokhorov

In her discussion of the cult of maternity in Russian culture, Joanna Hubbs contends that the myth of Mother Russia, perceived as the divine spirit of the land and her children—the peasantry, the intelligentsia, and the nation's leader—played a central role in Russian culture and influenced its cultural and political institutions. Mother Russia's "dual nature as the fount of creativity and its limit assumes metaphysical as well as social and psychological dimensions, raising the question of the proper relationship of the individual to the whole" (Hubbs 1988, xv). Double-belief (*dvoeverie*)—the co-existence of paganism and Russian Orthodox beliefs introduced with the Christianization of Rus' in 988—indelibly marked the myth of Mother Russia. As Hans Günther notes, one can delineate two poles in Russian archetypes of the mother: the pagan values of spontaneity and fertility, and the Christian precepts of love, mercy, and suffering (Giunter 1997, 49).

During the 1930s, Stalinist culture articulated its own kinship myth, one that contested the myth of divine maternity: namely, the myth of a modern homosocial community, or what Katerina Clark calls the Great Soviet Family: "Like Germany and several other countries in this period, the Soviets focused on the primordial attachments of kinship and projected them as the dominant symbol for social allegiance. Soviet society's leaders became 'fathers' (with Stalin as the

---

[1] I owe thanks to Helena Goscilo, Yana Hashamova, and Lucy Fischer for generous advice on drafts of this essay.

patriarch); the national heroes, model 'sons'; the state, a 'family' or 'tribe'" (1981, 114). This homosocial family constituted the main ideological community of the socialist realist master-plot and emphasized the hierarchical structure of Stalinist society.

In Stalinist culture of the 1930s, the mother figure's role remained significant, but changed. She lost her grand symbolic status and power, but became important as a source of biological propagation, at least in the edicts issued during that period. The mother figure was relegated primarily to the small family, hence did not represent cultural capital of prime importance until the war required her allegorization. However, Günther notes that Stalinist culture continued to use the myth of Mother Russia for propaganda purposes, especially in the mass song. During the 1930s, the archetype of Mother Russia "underwent fundamental changes. Above all one can observe the trend toward the extrusion of the archetype's Christian content and the foregrounding of its folk-pagan aspects" (1997, 49; translation mine, AP). In the wake of the Nazi invasion, however, the myth of Mother Russia suddenly regained its earlier vitality, as evident in Stalinist iconography. With the beginning of the Great Patriotic War, Soviet propaganda employed the image of Russia as the Mother calling for her sons to defend her from the murderous enemy. The image of the maternal protagonist, victimized and resisting the invader, became central in the subgenre of maternal screen melodrama during the Great Patriotic War. On the example of Stalinist and early post-Stalinist maternal melodrama, I examine the interaction between the myth of Mother Russia and that of the Great Family in film during the Great Patriotic War (the traditional Soviet and Russian term for World War II) and the early postwar period.

I argue that during the Great Patriotic War, Stalinist cinema returned to the myth of a quasi-Christian Mother Russia for the purposes of mobilization and propaganda. Using as examples two critical films of the war era—Fridrikh Ermler's *Ona zashchishchaet Rodinu* [*She Defends her Motherland* 1943] and Mark Donskoi's *Raduga* [*Rainbow* 1943]—I analyze the instantiation of the myth of divine maternity in Russian cinema of the war period. Both films effectively combine the feminine mythology of love and self-sacrifice with the traditional masculine mythology of warrior in order to create the martyrdom story of the land struggling against the Nazis. In my discussion I focus on two critical aspects of these films' structure—(1) the narrative mode, and (2) the iconography of the maternal protagonist—as well as on the official reception of the films, above all on the conflicts surrounding the making of these films at the intermediate stages of production. For the purposes of basic survival, Stalinist culture temporarily had to abandon the myth of the homosocial Great Family and to appropriate the agrarian myth of divine maternity, which was more deep-rooted in Russian culture, as recognized in Nikolai Berdiaev's famous insight that the "fundamental category in Russia is motherhood" (1948, 6).

In her monograph on screen visions of the maternal, Lucy Fischer notes that the representations of maternity raise broader questions of the relationship between gender and genre (1996, 6). In the Soviet context, cinematic representations of motherhood are closely connected with the Soviet utopian project. In the 1920s, Vsevolod Pudovkin laid the foundation for the canon of revolutionary melodrama in his 1926 masterpiece, *Mother*. Experimental in form, Pudovkin's film embraced fairly traditional, if not to say retrograde, gender politics. As in Maksim Gor'kii's novel (1907), which Pudovkin adapted to the screen, the eponymous mother finds her way to the new ideology vicariously, via her biological capacity to reproduce: she helps her son in his revolutionary activity.[2]

During the same decade, Vertov made the rise of the new Soviet woman the center of his non-staged experiments in film truth, above all *Man with a Movie Camera* (1929). In this picture, maternity became a function of the city as the utopian modern machine, one that provides gender equality for men and women in labor and leisure. After all, two major cinematic machines in the picture, the camera and the editing machine, were operated by two equals, two co-workers and relatives of Vertov: his brother and his wife.

A significant shift occurred in the 1930s, however, when revolutionary gender equity yielded to Stalinist imperatives. Boris Shumiatskii, the head of the film industry, promoted the concept of "Red Hollywood," a genre-oriented self-sufficient film industry endorsing Stalinist ideology. According to Shumiatskii, two genres

---

[2] For a detailed feminist reading of Pudovkin's *Mother,* see Mayne (1989). See also Dobrenko 167–90.

had to dominate this new cinema: comedy and fairy tale.[3] Both of
these narrative models in their Stalinist inflection were renditions of
what Northrop Frye has designated as "the mythos of romance."[4]
As Günther points out, in such films the maternal is present as the
celebration of the cult of eternal fertility inherited from folk culture
and appearing through the vehicle of the mass song celebrating the
Motherland. In Stalinist comedy, maternity is not a site of conflict
between the forces of modernity and the forces binding together the
traditional nuclear family; rather, it is the site of a quasi-pagan celebration of eternal and infinite fertility: "The archetype of the mother in its
Soviet form manifests itself as the emotional-vegetative basis of life [...]
The vegetative aspect includes fecundity, communality, and spontaneity" (Günther, 50, translation mine, AP).[5] The celebration of Soviet
maternity as an allegory of the state's infinite ability to produce food
became the key theme of the Stalin-era collective-farm musical, with
Ivan Pyr'ev its major producer.[6] The male and female leads appeared
as the Motherland's children, whose romance developed parallel to
their harvesting of the inexhaustible fruit of Her earth.[7] Problematized
by modernity, motherhood was not part of Red Hollywood in the
1930s because it raised uncomfortable questions about the role of the

---

[3] See Shumiatskii (1935), chapter 6, "Bor'ba za novye zhanry" (234–63), and
Taylor (1994).

[4] Making his observations in the middle of the twentieth century, Frye noted:
"The romance is nearest of all literary forms to the wish-fulfillment dream,
and for that reason it has socially a curiously paradoxical role. In every age
the ruling social or intellectual class tends to project its ideals in some form
of romance, where the virtuous heroes and beautiful heroines represent the
ideals and the villains the threats to their ascendancy. This is the general
character of chivalric romance in the Middle Ages, aristocratic romance in
the Renaissance, bourgeois romance since the eighteenth century, and revolutionary romance in contemporary Russia" (186).

[5] "Arkhetip materi v ego sovetskoi forme predstavliaet soboi emotsional'no-
vegetativnuiu osnovu zhizni [...] Vegetativnyi aspekt vkliuchaet plodovitost',
kollektivnost' i stikhiinost'" (50).

[6] For a detailed discussion of Pyr'ev's musical see Taylor (1999).

[7] A special question is the role of maternity in Vertov's Lullaby (1937). I view
this picture as above all the celebration of the paternal leader, who provides
the possibility of happy Soviet maternity. For a detailed discussion of the
picture see Atwood (1993, 56–7), Deriabin (2001), MacKay (2007), and
Bogdanov (2007).

nuclear family in the Soviet state, about the gap between the rhetoric of gender equality and the return to the traditional family structure and gender roles in Stalinist society. Notably, the family melodrama, the most bourgeois film genre, was not at the center of 1930s Soviet cinema.

The Nazi invasion changed the USSR's cultural politics overnight, since the very survival of the regime was at stake. The initial devastating defeats of the Red Army and the urgent task of mobilizing the population to fight the common enemy prompted the authorities and filmmakers to look for narratives shared by the entire Soviet population, not only those who actively supported Soviet power. Denise Youngblood notes that from 1942–1944, "Pride of place was given to the exploits of the partisans, and especially the role of women in the partisan movement. Women were foregrounded in many of the important war films" (2007, 58).

While Soviet women participated actively in the war as pilots, snipers, and armor commanders, the official propaganda downplayed the role of women combatants in the Red Army in order to maintain the traditional gender hierarchy, in which masculinity was equated with military agency and femininity with domesticity, maternity, and vulnerability.[8] In this representational regime, however, the mother-partisan was an acceptable personage because she became a combatant spontaneously due to the extreme conditions of occupation and trauma caused by German atrocities. The mother combatant became the carnivalistic protagonist of the macabre world where all normal power relations were inverted by the occupation.

Most importantly, during the Great Patriotic War, melodrama figured prominently in Soviet cinema as an indispensable tool of the war effort. Ermler's *She Defends Her Motherland* and Donskoi's *Rainbow* reintroduced the domestic *mise en scène* and domesticity as the values that every Soviet citizen needed to defend. To the question "Why do we fight?" the Soviet film industry responded with films epitomizing the big and the small motherland in the image of the female protagonist, her family, and her rural household. One had to defend not some

---

[8] For the discussion of the role of Soviet women combatants in the Great Patriotic War see Cottam (1983) and Pennington (2001).

abstract USSR but one's own home, one's own wife, and one's own
children. Melodrama brought the state project of the war effort home,
into the domestic space.

Peter Brooks distinguishes the "moral occult" (a search for the
spiritual in the post-religious world) as a key feature of melodrama
represented via stylistic excess (53). In their war melodramas, Ermler
and Donskoi made the moral occult, including direct invocations of
Russian Othrodox iconography, an indispensable part of the female
protagonists' characterization. Youngblood points out that Ermler
incorporated religious imagery in the *mise en scène* and references to
God in the film's dialogue: "During the war, religious symbols, references, and allusions reentered public life, and we see a number of
examples in this movie. Pasha [the protagonist of *She Defends Her
Motherland* AP] helps an old woman carefully place her icon onto
an evacuation vehicle" (2007, 62). To be more precise, in this scene
Pasha helps the old woman save the icon of the Mother of God, and by
doing so enhances her image as the protagonist interceding on behalf
of Russia's sacred values. Beginning with the cinema of World War II,
melodramatic quasi-religiosity would remain an important part of the
representation of women in Soviet war films.[9]

From the Russian side, the war itself acquires quasi-religious motivation in Ermler's picture. When guerilla fighters led by Pasha fight
their first battle with the Germans, one of them kills the Nazis while
repeating the traditional Easter greeting "Christ is risen!" and the auto-
matic response, "Truly He is risen." The scene of the Russian counter-
attack combines brutal physical violence with verbal invocations of the
Christian Savior.

Both Ermler and Donskoi establish moral polarization, characteristic of the melodrama, along gender lines. Russians are primarily
women and children victimized by the male-dominated Nazi force.
Men—above all men serving in the Red Army—are conspicuously
absent from the diegesis. They appear only at the film's end to liberate
women. The action of the films takes place on occupied territories: the

---

[9] See the Thaw-era *Ballad of a Soldier* (dir. Chukhrai 1959) and *Clear Sky* (dir.
Chukhrai 1961), or the late-Soviet *Belorussia Station* (dir. Smirnov 1970),
in which World War II veterans find peace and comfort in the apartment of
their former nurse, who fulfills the function of their surrogate mother.

victims are the most vulnerable members of the population, and the villains butcher and torture them with little retribution in the first part of both pictures. In *She Defends Her Motherland*, Nazis kill wounded soldiers, beat Pasha, and finally throw the protagonist's little son under the tracks of a tank. In *Rainbow*, the invaders torture the pregnant peasant woman whom they suspect of having connections with anti-Nazi insurgents.

In her discussion of *She Defends Her Motherland*, Youngblood calls the protagonist "the avenging angel" (61). The designation accurately describes the transformation-education undergone by the female protagonist in the first part of the film. Having lost her husband and son, and having saved the icon of the Mother of God, the heroine turns into a female warrior inspired by the quasi-religious ideology of divine retribution evoking the Old Testament dictum, "Eye for eye, tooth for tooth, hand for hand, foot for foot, burn for burn, wound for wound, stripe for stripe,"[10] rather than Marxist ideology. Ermler carefully combines references to Orthodoxy and Soviet power in the ideology that boosts Pasha's warrior spirit, necessary to avenge the death of her family and the destruction of her country. Pasha's reeducation into a warrior is brief and almost miraculous. In the best tradition of melodramatic coincidences, Pasha meets her dying husband during the last moments of his life, loses her son, touches the Orthodox icon, and turns into a matriarch-warrior defending her country and avenging the loss of her men. The myth of Mother Russia and the myth of the Great Family intersect in the figure of the protagonist, simultaneously matriarch and warrior.

Ermler represents the war as the conflict of the German male world of technology and Russia's organic world revolving around the maternal figure of Pasha. Germans use machine guns, tanks, and trucks as their lethal tools, whereas God-fearing Russians appear as rural dwellers, close to nature and its rhythms. Before the war Pasha used to work as a tractor driver on the collective farm. With the outbreak of war, however, her tractor disappears and she retreats to more traditional peasant tools—above all, the ax—in her fight against the

---

[10] *Oremus Bible Browser*, Exodus 21, http://bible.oremus.org/?passage= Exodus+21.

Nazis. She and her friends use sticks, agricultural tools, bare fists, and teeth to kill the enemy. In the most memorable scene, Pasha starts her career as warrior by hacking the Nazis with an ax, thus inspiring her villagers to start a people's war against the invaders. In short, Ermler juxtaposes the Russian female protagonist, the allegory of land and tradition, and German males, aliens in thrall to the technology of a dubious modernity.

In *Rainbow*, Donskoi depicts the warfare as the story of two contrasting women. One, Olena, chooses the path of resistance against the Nazis, while the other, Pusia, becomes a Nazi officer's camp wife and collaborator. Olena is captured by the Nazis when she returns to her home village to give birth to her son, the child of a Red commander fighting at the front. Despite Nazi torture, starvation, and freezing weather, Olena delivers her son in a barn, evoking the architecture of the Gospel delivery ward. Nazis kill the newborn, however, and drag Olena to a mountain, where they shoot her. However, on route to her death, Olena and the villagers see a rainbow, which they interpret as a benign promise of their eventual delivery from the murderous enemy. Donskoi exploits patriarchy's favored image of the self-sacrificing mother to depict his protagonist-warrior, who represents an ideal.

Whereas Olena fights, suffers, and dies for her "love of country," her foil, Pusia the pragmatist, enjoys a comfortable life amid everyone's misery thanks to her intimacy with the Nazi commander, Kurt. Unusual for prudish Soviet cinema, Pusia is depicted as a woman of insatiable sexual appetite, spending most of her time in her bedroom, often in bed with her Nazi "sponsor." Donskoi depicts Pusia enjoying herself getting dressed in alluring urban clothes and putting stockings on her well-groomed, thin legs. The female antagonist is constructed in the repellent light of sexual desire against the background of her fellow villagers, who are preoccupied with fighting the enemy amidst starvation and ubiquitous death. Despite her active sexual life, and in eloquent contrast to Olena, Pusia is sterile. She cannot give birth because, according to Donskoi's disposition of moral values in the film, Nazis should not procreate: they are the agents of death, doomed to die, and inimical to all that is life-affirming.

Donskoi's *Rainbow* follows the conventions of World War II melodrama not only in its propagandistic slant, but also in its verbal excesses: its dialogue contains much more taboo vocabulary than audiences were accustomed to hearing in the typical Soviet film. For example, Pusia's maid Fedos'ia calls her "slut," and tells her that she cannot stand her "mug." Pusia's sister, who supports the partisans, calls her "Fritz's bitch." Stalinist censors usually kept film dialogue clean of dialect and substandard speech. All screen characters usually spoke in standard literary Russian. Even Stalin, whose Russian in real life had a heavy Georgian accent, appeared on screen as a model of pure literary Russian.[11] Since the Soviet Union's celluloid war against the Nazis called for another language, substandard vocabulary and curses became a legitimate weapon on screen. Thus villagers assault Nazi collaborators such as Pusia first verbally and then physically. Vulgarity, after all, was deemed excusable in the face of betrayal.

In her discussion of the melodramatic mode of representation, Linda Williams notes that melodrama, together with horror and pornography, is quintessentially a body film genre. Central to body genres is "the spectacle of a body caught in the grip of intense sensation of emotion" (Williams 2004, 729). Ermler and Donskoi placed the maternal body as the site of war-era crisis at the center of their films. Both filmmakers represent female characters' bodies as objects of physical violence, with the bodies of males slaughtered by the Nazis as quasi-extensions of mothers' bodies. As if the umbilical cord had never been severed, male deaths produce an immediate trauma in the bodies of maternal protagonists. In Ermler's picture, Pasha's hair turns gray when she observes the deaths of her husband and son, after which she appears only in black kerchief and dress—transformed into an iconic avenging spirit rather than a woman of flesh and blood.

Donskoi uses contrast as the main device of representing women's bodies. Olena possesses a carnivalistic pregnant body that, despite all tortures, is capable of regenerative power. Her body is clad in simple peasant clothing, emphasizing her folk origins, her connection with tradition and her people. Under her garb viewers can detect Olena's large breasts and protruding womb. In contrast, Pusia as the Nazi collaborator wears Western-style urban clothes. She is slim, almost boyish, with thin, presumably infertile, hips. Kurt gives Pusia black stock-

---

[11] In the late 1940s, Russian actor Aleksei Dikii, known for his impeccable Russian, was one of Stalin's favorite actors allowed to play the dictator.

ings, and when she puts them on they look like Germans' high boots [Plates 2.1, 2.2]. In this key sequence, Pusia both joins the Nazis by becoming somewhat similar to them in her outfit and stops being a traditional Russian woman by putting on black stockings resembling male boots. In the next sequence, Pusia takes a chocolate bar in her teeth and inserts this phallic object into Kurt's mouth [Plate 2.3]. I would argue that Donskoi makes Pusia's sexual identity similar to that of her Nazi lover (she acquires a surrogate penis and her legs start looking similar to the legs of her Nazi lover), thus representing their liaison as a relationship evoking a same-sex relationship. In his homophobic representation of the Nazis, Donskoi anticipates Roberto Rossellini's *Rome Open City* (1945), which depicts Nazis and their collaborators as same-sex partners, their perversity juxtaposed to the healthy, heterosexual, Catholic anti-fascists.[12]

Whereas in their narrative tone Ermler and Donskoi drew on the tradition of melodrama, in the construction of *mise en scène*, especially representing the female protagonist as the allegorical figure epitomizing the nation in need of defense and struggle, the filmmakers drew inspiration from the poster art of the era. In fact, the highly traditional allegorical representation of the nation as Mother Russia was used by Russian poster artists during World War I and in the months between the February and October Revolutions of 1917, but it did not resurface in political iconography until the Nazi invasion.[13] Victoria Bonnell points out that "between 1941 and 1945, a number of memorable posters were issued resurrecting the traditional image of Mother Russia in a new guise—a stately, matronly woman sometimes pictured with a small child in her arms" (1997, 72). In her analysis of images of the mother in Soviet cinema between 1941–45, Elena Baraban (2007) traces the cinematic iconography of the Soviet mother-warrior to the famous 1941 poster by Iraklii Toidze, *The Motherland Calls!* [Plate 2.4/6.3]. While I believe that melodramatic conventions are of

---

[12] Roberto Rossellini and Giuseppe De Santis considered Mark Donskoi's films, including *Rainbow*, their major inspiration (Zorkaia 2005, 265–6). For a detailed discussion of homophobic visions of fascism in Italian leftist cultural memory see Luca Prono's (2001) recent reading of *Rome Open City*.

[13] See Bonnell (1997, 71–2).

prime importance for Ermler and Donskoi's representations of women in their war-era classics, I contend that these films' generic memory of poster conventions, the art form relying more on display than narration, is not a coincidence, but rather a feature of war-era Soviet maternal melodrama. Whereas Stalinist cinema of the 1930s worked on establishing narrative continuity in Soviet films, with a prime emphasis on the socialist realist master plot, war-era melodrama sacrificed continuity for the display of extreme violence against the most vulnerable and the direct impact on the viewer in order to evoke pathos and the desire to avenge Soviet deaths and kill the enemy.

The representation of women in both films follows the allegorical logic of the propaganda poster rather than the logic of mimetic representation. In her analysis of the iconography of women in Soviet war-era posters, Helena Goscilo contends that "despite their surface diversity, female images largely reinforced the code of gender differentiation prevailing during peacetime [...] Women retained their timeless allegorical significance as the nation of homeland, a trope [...] that effectively short-circuited female subjectivity/agency in the socio-political sphere" (chapter 6). In these posters, Mother Russia appeared as a mature woman calling "young recruits, addressed as sons" to protect her, or as a mother with a child, threatened by the Nazi bayonet and calling for help (chapter 6) [Plates 2.5, 2.6 / 6.12]. Like these recruitment posters' artists, Ermler and Donskoi favored depicting female protagonists as allegorical figures symbolizing the country under attack by the bestial invader.

She Defends Her Motherland and *Rainbow* share with war-era posters highly traditional visual language used for depicting the female protagonist. Instead of emulating the posters and films of the late 1920s and early 1930s depicting the woman as a modern collective farmer embracing the new technology and ideology, Ermler and Donskoi followed the style of war-era posters depicting their protagonists as matronly women wearing peasant clothes and a kerchief tied in an old-fashioned way under their chins.[14] Like the heroines of war-era

---

[14] Bonnell notes that in the posters of the collectivization era the new woman "wears a red kerchief tied behind her head, in the style of women workers, rather than under the chin, as was formerly conventional in the representation of peasant women" (102). In contrast, war-era posters emphasize tradition as one of the inspirations for the war effort.

posters, the maternal protagonists of Ermler and Donskoi are corpulent and mature. They stand firmly on their native soil as though having grown directly from it.

Most importantly, Ermler and Donskoi—like the Soviet poster artists—abandoned the collectivization-era approach to representing the new Soviet woman modernized by ideology and technology, and went back to the prerevolutionary reliance on allegorical representations of the nation at war as the beleaguered woman. Bonnell notes that the image of Russia was the key female image in the late-tsarist iconography of power: "The visual representation of Russia as a woman corresponded to the word *rodina*, or motherland, etymologically connected to the word *rodit'*, to give birth" (71). The allegorical representations of Russia as a woman appeared on the posters recruiting Russians to support the tsarist government's imperial ventures [Plate 2.7].

Finally, as in the war-era posters, Donskoi, and to a lesser degree Ermler, uses perspectival disproportions to identify the heroic protagonist and contrast her with the enemy. Donskoi's peasant protagonist Olena appears bigger than her German tormentors. A similar function of contrast fulfills the poster-style device of visual alienation between human-looking Russians and bestial-looking enemies. Nazis harrassing Russian women appear subhuman and bestial, their bodies operating like poorly managed mechanisms. Though terrifying in their actions, Germans are at the same time ludicrous and disgusting in their appearance. They are small, primitive, and in Donskoi's picture wear rags and ridiculous square shoes as they desperately struggle to protect themselves from the Russian winter.[15] By rendering the enemy repellent yet pathetic, Donskoi ultimately diminishes them.

Cultural authorities found these filmmakers' emphasis on melodramatic pathos—rather than on the epic struggle with the enemy—

---

[15] Ironically, as in the case of *Alexander Nevsky*, in which the Russian winter was filmed in summer, both Ermler and Donskoi shot their films about the Russian winter in Central Asia during very warm weather. Because of the German invasion, the studios were evacuated from the Western regions of the USSR to Central Asian republics. Consequently, the Russian winter was filmed in the heat of Kazakh Alma Aty and Turkmen Ashkhabad. For a detailed account of these films' production, see Zorkaia (258–66).

problematic. The head of Agitprop (the Department of Agitation and Propaganda), Georgii Aleksandrov, reprimanded directors for creating female protagonists intended to evoke viewers' pity and sympathy instead of filming stalwart heroes and leaders devoid of human weakness:

> Conceived by the authors as the progressive Soviet woman, the protagonist Praskov'ia Ivanovna [in *She Defends Her Motherland*] over the course of the picture is depicted as a mother devastated by grief over losing her child and husband. She makes the viewer feel pity and compassion, rather than presenting him with an image of the ideologically conscious warrior who defends the freedom and independence of the Motherland. (2005, 352)[16]

The party functionary attacked Ermler for attempting to follow the dictates of melodrama, a genre that operates on audience affect, constructing scenes that cause viewers to cry and commiserate with the victimized protagonist. Instead, Ermler should have opted for an uplifting emphasis on the factors that explained why Praskov'ia was destined to lead the partisan detachment: "The film director didn't show convincingly enough why specifically Praskov'ia became head of the partisan detachment" (2005, 352).[17] According to Aleksandrov, her career as an exemplary tractor driver in the collective farm before the war prepared her for ideological leadership during the German invasion. In other words, the head of the Propaganda Department of the Central Committee demanded that the film's melodramatic narrative become a socialist realist tale.

Aleksandrov's list of the most problematic scenes in Ermler's film included those of emotional excess, where ideology gives way to an

---

[16] "Glavnaia geroinia fil'ma Praskov'ia Ivanovna, po zamyslu avtorov peredovaia sovetskaia zhenshchina, pokazyvaetsia na protiazhenii vsego fil'ma ubitoi gorem mater'iu, poteriavshei rebenka i muzha. U zritelia ona vyzyvaet skoree chuvstvo zhalosti i sostradaniia, chem predstavlenie o nei kak o soznatel'nom voine, zashchishchaiushchem svobodu i nezavisimost' Rodiny" (352).

[17] "Rezhisser fil'ma ne pokazal s dostatochnoi ubeditel'nost'iu, pochemu imenno Praskov'ia stala rukovoditelem partizanskogo otriada" (352).

overflow of human emotions. The party censor was outraged by the fact that in one sequence two partisans, a young woman and man, embarked on a flirtation while fulfilling their military assignment: "In the film several scenes are unrealistic. For example, the flirting between two young people during an important clandestine operation" (2005, 352).[18]

Aleksandrov especially criticized those scenes that revolved around the central narrative device of melodrama—a miraculous coincidence. During a clandestine operation, for example, lucky chance ensures that two lovers end up being assigned to fulfill the mission, which leads not only to the defeat of the Nazis, but also, and more importantly in the context of the film, to a serious relationship between them. In the final scene, partisans rescue Praskov'ia from seemingly inevitable death at the very last moment. Ermler uses the classic device of the last-minute rescue in the best traditions of Hollywood melodrama, which, unsur-prisingly, was ideologically unacceptable to a party ideologue.

Aleksandrov concluded his devastating ideological analysis of Ermler's melodrama on an unexpected note. Despite the numerous incorrigible flaws, it would be advisable, he stated, to release the film: "Part of the listed shortcomings can be fixed; the other part cannot be amended [...] It's expedient to release the picture" (2005, 352).[19] Limited resources as well as the urgency of the war effort led even such orthodox ideologues as Aleksandrov to compromise and release films that he considered ideologically problematic in their deviation from the rigid prescriptions of socialist realist cinema.

If the Agitprop Department attacked Ermler's film for its melo-dramatic aesthetics and lack of ideological rigor, Donskoi's *Rainbow* became the target of criticism by the Committee for Film Affairs (*Komitet po delam kinematografii*), led by Ivan Bol'shakov, for analogous reasons. A. Sazonov, senior editor of the Directorate in charge of the production of feature films, blasted Donskoi for his creative reworking of Wasilewska's film script, lack of understanding of the filmmaker's

---

[18] "V fil'me nekotorye stseny nepravdopodbny. Naprimer, flirt dvukh molo-dykh liudei v moment vypolneniia vazhnoi diversionnoi operatsii" (352).

[19] "Chast' iz otemechennykh nedostatkov mozhet byt' ustranena, druguiu chast' vypravit' nevozmozhno [...] Kartinu tselesoobrazno vypustit' na ekran" (352).

role in Soviet cinema, and, most importantly, for introducing various melodramatic devices: moral polarization, a focus on the heroine as victim, and the equations of her virtue with suffering, rather than with "inextinguishable faith in the rightness of her ideological cause" (2005, 456). Sazonov's memo did not include any final recommendation for the picture's release, but was followed by a meeting of the Committee on Film Affairs, during which party functionaries criticized Donskoi's *Rainbow* and a few courageous filmmakers tried to defend their colleague.

The special session of the Committee on Film Affairs discussed ways of ideologically improving literary and shooting scripts for Soviet films. Donskoi became the scapegoat at this meeting, for his shooting script for *Rainbow* strayed from the literary script and the original socialist realist novel—both written by Wanda Wasilewska.[20] Crucially, by producing a shooting script different from the literary script Donskoi violated the 1938 regulation of the Soviet of Peoples' Commissars prohibiting filmmakers from altering even a word in the approved literary script without an additional imprimatur by the Committee on Film Affairs ("Ob uluchshenii" 2007, 549). To make matters worse, Donskoi dared to introduce changes into a script based on a novel that had won the Stalin Prize.

Sazonov meticulously explained how Donskoi turned a socialist realist story into a melodrama, thereby feminizing a supremely masculine paradigm. In his shooting script, Donskoi included an opening scene of the Red Army's retreat, with the disheartening separation of women from their men. Moreover, Sazonov noted, Donskoi changed the goal-oriented motivation of a key scene: "The circumstances of Fedos'ia's appearance near the corpse of her son have been changed. In the literary script Fedos'ia went to get water and managed to get

---

[20] Like many communist writers, Wanda Wasilewska combined a political career with her literary work. After the Polish defeat in the Polish Defensive War in 1939, she moved to the Soviet Union and even became a member of the Supreme Soviet of the USSR in 1940. After the German invasion of the Soviet Union, she joined the Red Army and held the rank of a colonel. In 1944, Wasilewska became the deputy chief of the Polish Committee of National Liberation, the pro-Soviet Polish provisional Polish government. She advocated Poland's incorporation into the Soviet Union.

to her son's corpse despite the Germans' prohibition. In the shooting
script this is absent. Fedos'ia simply sits next to the corpse" (Sazonov
2005, 456).[21] If in Wasilewska's novel the mother's teleological motivation and her skill in outwitting the enemy are at the center of the narrative (she outsmarts the Germans so as to reach her son's body), in
the shooting script Donskoi emphasizes her grief at the loss of her son.
To the great disappointment of the cultural administrator, not active
Russian cleverness, but passive maternal sorrow holds center stage in a
narrative of victimization, not collective triumph.

Finally, Sazonov condemned the changes in the shooting script as
evidence of Donskoi's irresponsible attitude toward his role of Soviet
filmmaker: "The director treats irresponsibly his artistic duty to convey
to the full extent possible the value of the author's design when he
replaces her tale with his own invented scenes and characters" (456).
Given wartime priorities, it is perhaps predictable that the party bureaucrat would not allow the filmmaker any artistic freedom and would
view the scriptwriter as the film's sole true author. During the meeting,
Mikhail Romm rebutted Sazonov's attacks on Donskoi, arguing that the
Soviet filmmaker was the creative individual responsible for the picture,
with the right to interpret the script, thus defending Donskoi's redefini-
tion of *The Rainbow*'s narrative stance ("Iz stenogrammy" 2005, 458).
The immediate issue—the legitimacy of a melodramatic recasting of
the socialist realist script—turned into a far-reaching dispute about the
limits of permissible interpretations and artistic freedom within the rigid
ideological framework of the Soviet film industry.

Most importantly, war-era maternal melodrama, traditionally seen
as a women's genre, provided a disruption of the socialist realist male
mode of imagining war as an ideological confrontation of the Soviet
"us" versus the Nazi "them." In a discussion of Hollywood melodrama—above all, the films of Sirk, Minnelli, and Vidor—the Western
scholars Laura Mulvey (2005), Geoffrey Nowell-Smith (1991), and
Linda Williams (1998) identified melodrama with the domestic sphere
of powerless women and children protagonists whose agency is based

---

[21] "Izmeneny obstoiatel'stva poiavleniia Fedos'i u trupa syna. V literaturnom
stsenarii Fedos'ia khodila za vodoi i, nesmotria na zapreshchenie nemtsev,
probiralas' k turpu svoego syna. V rezhisserskom stsenarii etogo net.
Fedos'ia prosto sidit uu trupa" (456).

on the virtue of their suffering. The primary audience of such films, according to these critics, is women. The discussion focused primarily on the possibility of articulating a female point of view within the patriarchal order of Hollywood cinema. Similarly, Soviet war-era maternal melodramas made central the issue of female spectatorship. As in the West—with the men fighting at the front lines—the majority of viewers during the war would have been women and children. Owing to the urgency of the war effort, Soviet authorities allowed filmmakers to search for the artistic forms that would provide alternative regimes of spectatorship to Stalinist culture's repressive patriarchal gaze. The matriarch-led family fighting the male invader became one of such successful alternative forms of narration that not only worked for the war effort but also disrupted the coherence of Stalinist tropes, above all the trope of the homosocial Great Family. While the authorities viewed Ermler's and Donskoi's pictures as ideologically unsuccessful, the films had a great success not only with domestic audiences,[22] but also with audiences in the West.[23] From the end of World War II onward, the question of melodramatic narration in the Soviet Union inexorably became ideological, for it challenged the patriarchal regime of Stalinist cinema.

With the victorious end of the war, Stalinist cultural producers defused the importance of the myth of Mother Russia via two strategies: cult epics about Russian male warriors (*Admiral Nakhimov* [*Admiral Nakhimov* 1946, Pudovkin], *Admiral Ushakov* [*Admiral Ushakov* 1953, Romm]), Stalin above all (*Stalingradksaia bitva* [*The Battle of Stalingrad* 1949], *Padenie Berlina* [*The Fall of Berlin* 1949]), and comedies in which cerebral and domineering women become reeducated, to enjoy traditional women's roles (*Nebesnyi tikhokhod* [*Celestial Sloth* 1945, Timoshenko], *Vesna* [*Spring* 1947, Alexandrov]). *Celestial Sloth* is perhaps the most remarkable picture in the last category. This romantic comedy depicts Soviet women-pilots who in the course of the film strive to remain good housewives and to find good

---

[22] 23.7 million viewers watched Donskoi's *Rainbow* in the USSR. There are no data on ticket sales for Ermler's *She Defends her Motherland* (Kudriavtsev 1998, 435).

[23] Both films were released in England, France, Greece, Italy, and the US (Fomin and Deriabin 2008, 793, 798, 809).

husbands. Youngblood notes that "*Celestial Sloth* contrasts sharply
[... with World War II representations of women AP]. However gently
and amusingly, the film mocks the contributions of fighting women to
the war and foreshadows their removal from war cinema as it evolved
in the last years of the Stalin era" (2007, 84). I would argue that the
film is both a successful romantic comedy and an exercise in blatant
misogyny. Soviet cinema and the state's propaganda machine had a
very short memory of women's roles in combat and on the home front
during the Great Patriotic War. Given the postwar cult of Stalin as the
sole victor of the war, *Celestial Sloth* and similar romantic comedies
ensured that no other cultural narrative, such as the myth of Mother
Russia as the struggling nation, interfered with the monologic discourse of the Stalinist heroic myth of the war.

Despite the repressive policies of the late Stalinist period, the myth
of Mother Russia as the spirit of the land did not entirely disappear
from Soviet cinema. In 1947, the incorrigible Donskoi made *The Village
Teacher* [*Sel'skaia uchitel'nitsa*], featuring the exploits of a Russian
noblewoman, Varen'ka, who graduates from an aristocratic school in
Imperial St. Petersburg and, despite everyone's objections, chooses
to go to the Russian provinces to teach peasant children. She marries
a Bolshevik, but the potential ideological male lead conveniently dies
at film's beginning, and Donskoi leaves his viewers with the female
teacher of dubious class origins in charge of the entire film's diegesis.
Varen'ka spends the years of the 1917 October Revolution and World
War II in the village, bringing up generations of Russian children,
whom she motivates to become, above all, emotionally mature people
(the subtitle of the picture was "Vospitanie chuvstv" ["Education of
Feelings"]) and professionals useful to their motherland. At film's
end her former students return to a now middle-aged Varen'ka and tell
her that her maternal care inspired them throughout their lives. The
film ends with the victory in the Great Patriotic War, which appears
also as the achievement of the maternal teacher and her faithful students. While the film hardly challenges the Soviet regime (which the
village teacher fully supports), the rural locale as opposed to Moscow
(the nation's center, to which Stalinist socialist realist heroes aspired)
and the protagonist's surrogate mother identity (versus the cult of
the Soviet leader) anticipate the chronotope of the Thaw-era cinema
of destalinization and its sincere melodramatic maternal protagonists.

Donskoi's late-Stalinist film not only provided a narrative model antithetical to the cultic and male-dominated films of the late Stalinist period, but also pioneered a lyrical camera style that foreshadowed the aesthetics of post-Stalinist melodrama. The cameraman Sergei Urusevskii, a disciple of Aleksandr Rodchenko, would prove a crucial figure in Thaw-era lyricism, and Donskoi invited him to collaborate in the creation of just such a lyrical visual world in *The Village Teacher*. Many of Urushevskii's discoveries in *The Village Teacher* became essential for the new visual style of post-Stalinist Soviet cinema, with its lavish use of the mobile camera and deep focus cinematography. Moreover, Donskoi's gender politics, which placed a strong, committed woman at the heart of his narrative, would resonate with Thaw-era priorities.

Reintroduced into official mythology as part of the World War II propaganda effort and suppressed once the war ended, the myth of Mother Russia returned to Soviet cinema after Stalin's death. As the family melodrama story, it provided a critical alternative to the socialist realist master plot. The story of the family's destruction and rebirth, as well as maternal perseverance during World War II, became an allegory of Russia's survival in the face of brutal Stalinist modernization. In Mikhail Kalatozov's *Cranes Are Flying* [*Letiat zhuravli* 1957], Grigorii Chukhrai's *Ballad of a Soldier* [*Ballada o soldate* 1959] and *Clear Sky* [*Chistoe nebo* 1961], the myth of Mother Russia would become a vital narrative strategy for the destalinization of Soviet cinema.

References

Attwood, Lynne. 1993. "Woman, Cinema, and Society." In *Red Women on the Silver Screen*, edited by Lynne Attwood, 17–132. London: Pandora.
Aleksandrov, Grigorii. 2005. "Dokladnaia zapiska nachal'nika upravleniia propagandy i agitatsii TsK VKP(b) G.F. Aleksandrova sekretariu TsK VKP(b) A.A.Andreevu o fil'me *Ona zashchishchaet rodinu*." In *Kino na voine. Dokumenty i svidetel'stva*, edited by V. Fomin and Aleksandr Deriabin, 352. Moscow: Materik.
Baraban, Elena. 2007. "The Return of Mother Russia: Representations of Motherhood in Soviet Wartime Cinema." Unpublished paper presented at the Conference on Women In War at the University of Pittsburgh, November.

Berdiaev, Nicolas. 1948. *The Russian Idea*. New York: The Macmillan Company.

Bogdanov, Konstantin. 2007. "Pravo Na Son i Uslovnye Refleksy: Kolybel'nye Pesni v Sovetskoi Kul'ture (1930–1950-e Gody)." *NLO* 86. http://magazines.russ.ru/nlo/2007/86/bo1.html (last accessed 4 April 2008).

Bonnell, Victoria. 1997. *Iconography of Power: Soviet Political Posters Under Lenin and Stalin*. Berkeley: University of California Press.

Brooks, Peter. 1991. "The Melodramatic Imagination." In *Imitations of Life: A Reader on Film and Television Melodrama*, edited by Marcia Landy, 50–67. Detroit: Wayne State University Press.

Clark, Katerina. 1981. *The Soviet Novel. History as Ritual*. Chicago: Chicago University Press.

Cottam, Kazimiera J. 1983. *Soviet Women in Combat in World War II*. Manhattan, Kansas: Military Affairs.

Deriabin, Aleksandr. 2001. "'Kolybel'naia' Dzigi Vertova: Zamysel, Voploshchenie, Ekrannaia Sud'ba." *Kinovedcheskie Zapiski* 51: 30–65.

Dobrenko, Evgenii. 2008. *Stalinist Cinema and the Production of History: Museum of Revolution*. New Haven: Yale University Press.

Fischer, Lucy. 1996. *Cinematernity: Film, Motherhood, Genre*. Princeton: Princeton University Press.

Fomin, V.I. and Alexander Deriabin, eds. 2007. *Letopis' rossiiskogo kino 1930–1945*. Moscow: Materik.

Frye, Northrop. 1967. *Anatomy of Criticism. Four Essays*. New York: Atheneum.

Giunter, Gans. 1997. "Poiushchaia rodina. Sovetskaia massovaia pesnia kak vyrazhenie arkhetipa materi." *Voprosy literatury* 4: 46–61.

Hubbs, Joanna. 1988. *Mother Russia: The Feminine Myth in Russian Culture*. Bloomington: Indiana University Press.

"Iz stenogrammy zasedaniia komiteta po delam kinematografii 'O povyshenii kachestva literaturnykh i rezhisserskikh stcenariev.'" 2005. *Kino na voine. Dokumenty i svidetel'stva*, edited by V.I. Fomin and Aleksandr Deriabin, 458–67. Moscow: Materik.

Kudriavtsev, Sergei. 1998. *Svoe kino*. Moscow: Dubl'-D.

MacKay, John. 2007. "The 'Subjective' Camera in Vertov's *Lullaby* (1937)." Paper presented at the Society for Cinema and Media Studies (SCMS).

Mayne, Judith. 1989. *Kino and the Woman Question: Feminism and Soviet Silent Film*. Columbus: Ohio State University Press.

Mulvey, Laura. 2005. "Repetition and Return: Textual Analysis and Douglas Sirk in the Twenty-First Century." In *Style and Meaning: Studies in the Detailed Analysis of Film*, edited by John Gibbs and Douglas Pye Gibbs, 228–43. Manchester: Manchester University Press.

Norris, Stephen. 2006. *A War of Images: Russian Popular Prints, Wartime Culture, and National Identity 1812–1945*. DeKalb: Northern Illinois University Press.

Nowell-Smith, Geoffrey. 1991. "Minnelli and Melodrama." In *Imitations of Life*, edited by Marcia Landy, 268–74. Detroit: Wayne State University Press.

"Ob uluchshenii organizatsii proizvodstva kinokartin" (23 March 1938). 2007. In *Letopis' rossiiskogo kino 1930–1945*, edited by V. I. Fomin and A. Deriabin, 548–9. Moscow: Materik.

Pennington, Reina. 2001. *Wings, Women, and War: Soviet Airwomen in World War II*. Lawrence: University Press of Kansas.

Prono, Luca. 2001. "Citta Aperta o Cultura Chiusa?: The Homosexualization of Fascism in the Perverted Cultural Memory of the Italian Left." *International Journal of Sexuality and Gender Studies* 6, no. 4 (October): 333–51.

Sazonov, A. N. 2005. "Tezisy A.N. Sazonova k zasedaniiu komiteta po delam kinematografii 'O povyshenii kachestva literaturnykh i rezhisserskikh stsenariev.'" In *Kino na voine. Dokumenty i svidetel'stva*, edited by V.I. Fomin and Aleksandr Deriabin, 454–58. Moscow: Materik.

Shumiatskii, Boris. 1935. *Kinematografiia millionov. Opyt analiza*. Moscow: Kinofotoizdat.

Taylor, Richard. 1999. "Singing on the Steppes for Stalin: Ivan Pyr'ev and the Kolkhoz Musical in Soviet Cinema." *Slavic Review* 58, no. 1: 143–60.

———. 1994. "Ideology as Mass Entertainment: Boris Shumiatskii and Soviet Cinema in the 1930s." In *Inside the Film Factory*, 193–216. London: Routledge.

Williams, Linda. 2004. "Film Bodies: Gender, Genre and Excess." In *Film Theory and Criticism: Introductory Readings (Sixth Edition)*, edited by Leo Braudy and Marshall Cohen, 747–41. New York: Oxford University Press, c1991.

———. 1998. "Melodrama Revised." In *Refiguring American Film Genres: History and Theory*, edited by Nick Browne, 42–88. Berkeley: University of California Press.

Youngblood, Denise. 2007. *Russian War Films: On the Cinema Front, 1914–2005*. Lawrence: University of Kansas Press.

Zorkaia, Neya. 2005. *Istoriia sovetskogo kino*. St. Petersburg: Aleteia.

CHAPTER 3

Flight without Wings:
The Subjectivity of a Female War
Veteran in Larisa Shepit'ko's *Wings*
(1966)

Tatiana Mikhailova and Mark Lipovetsky

Paradoxically and despite their best intentions, contemporary works
on Soviet subjectivity draw attention to the gap between symbolic
representation and personal everyday experience as the constitu-
tive feature of Soviet culture and society. Seminal works by Stephen
Kotkin, Sheila Fitzpatrick, Igal Halfin, Jochen Hellbeck, Eric Naiman
and others discovered practices of internalization of ideological discourses as a continuous process that shapes and re-shapes Soviet
subjectivity. As a rule, these studies focus on various two-way nego-
tiations among three main elements: an explicit ideological doctrine
(official rhetoric), its unconscious undercurrents (cultural myths and
scenarios), and individual (or, rarely, group) experience. "[...] [W]hile
ideologies change, ideology itself—as a category seen in T.J. Clark's
terms as epistemological code or as the 'genre' through which individuals legitimize their position in the world—can never be transcended,"
write Christina Kiaer and Eric Naiman in their introduction to the
volume *Everyday Life in Early Soviet Russia* (Kiaer and Naiman 2006,
6). However, the process of internalization has its limits: there are
cultural situations and historical moments when explicit ideological
models as well as implicit ideological myths come into profound con-

---

[1] For examples of this methodology see: Kotkin (1995), Fitzpatrick (1999
and 2000), Halfin (2002 and 2003), Hellbeck (2006), Kiaer and Naiman
(2006), Kharkhordin (1999), Boym (1994), and Yurchak (2006). For
a survey of different approaches to the problem of Soviet subjectivity see
Chatterjee and Petrone (2008).

tradition with individual experience, leading to a cessation of the dialogue among ideology, myth, and a subject. That stoppage signifies the collapse of Soviet subjectivity.

We maintain that such a collapse of Soviet subjectivity is depicted in Larisa Shepit'ko's film *Wings* [*Kryl'ia* 1966; script by Valentin Ezhov and Natalia Riazantseva; camera by Igor' Slabnevich]. As we try to show in the following analysis, that collapse is produced by a failed attempt to internalize two incompatible ideological scenarios: that of a "normal" Soviet woman (as shaped in the fifties and the sixties) and a woman soldier, "gvardii kapitan"—the initial title of Shepit'ko's film, which sounds notably masculine, not feminine. Another reason for this collapse is the contradiction between the explicit ideological rhetoric of gender equality and the implicit patriarchal mythology, which is paradoxically justified by the former.

Women on War: The Soviet Vocabulary

To the degree that war is a symbolic focus of Soviet culture, holding a sacred place in the Soviet mentality, it is also a particularly condensed form of the Soviet patriarchal myth (the unconscious ideology). An obvious contradiction between this ideological mythology and the explicit Soviet discourse of gender equality is resolved in the official, socialist realist art of the war and the postwar era through the employment of two traditional archetypes of femininity: that of the long-suffering mother (obvious examples aside, this archetype can also be represented by a beloved, a wife, a nurse, and others); and that of the innocent girl, sacrificed or sacrificing herself (from Zoia Kosmodem'ianskaia and the female characters of *Young Guard* [*Molodaia Gvadiia*] in Aleksandr Fadeev's novel (1945) and Sergei Gerasimov's film (1948), to the heroines of such films as *The Dawns Are Quiet Here* [*A zori zdes' tikhie*, dir. Stanislav Rostotskii, 1972] in the seventies). The first archetype became the key component in the renewed mythology of the Motherland as a god-like, immortal force, cruel to her enemies and caring to her "children." The second archetype resurrected Christian motifs of martyrdom, simultaenously merging them with a subverted, sado-masochistic eroticism, especially noticeable in the representation of Zoia Kosmodem'ianskaia in Lev Arnshtam's *Zoia* (1944) and of female characters in Fadeev's/ Gerasimov's *Young Guard*.

Moreover, in addition to the socialist realist canonical representation of women during the war, one may detect two more archetypes, one full-fledged, the other an absent signifier. The first is the traditional archetype of the harlot or the "camp follower," which within the war chronotope may be situated both behind the front line, in occupied territory, and at the front. This archetype is hardly new, and represents the mirror image of both the mother and the innocent girl. Neither a mother nor innocent, the character of a harlot/female sutler epitomized by Brecht's *Mother Courage and Her Children* (1939) manifested sexuality and profiteering—the features excluded from any heroic mythology, and especially from its Soviet versions. This is precisely why it was so widely adopted by mass culture ranging from numerous folkloric songs blaming an unfaithful wife for her husband's death at the frontline to obscene jokes about PPZhs (*pokhodno-polevaia zhena*/the "field campaign wife"—a derogatory term for front-line officers' mistresses).

Perhaps due to its openly anti-patriarchal character, the archetype of the Amazon warrior did not find its way into Soviet culture. Yet, the scenario that would correspond to this archetype certainly existed in the Soviet experience: it is represented by women who undertook active combat roles. As Barbara Engel notes, "By the end of 1943, when female participation [in the war] reached its height, more than 800,000 served in the armed forces and partisan units; by the war's end, more than a million had done military service [...]. Although Russia's women had served as armed combatants earlier in the nation's history, never before had they served in such numbers, nor had their service been as crucial to military success" (2004, 250). In the patriarchal paradigm, the archetype signifies a much larger problem for cultural consciousness, thus presenting a challenge for the formation of subjectivity. Symptomatically, in Soviet mass culture the scenario of the woman warrior was basically suppressed by either the archetype of the mother figure (*She Defends the Motherland* [*Ona zashchishchaet Rodinu*, dir. Fridrikh Ermler, 1943] *Rainbow* [*Raduga*, dir. Mark Donskoi, 1944] or the archetype of an innocent and coquettish female pilot. Thus in *Celestial Sloth* [*Nebesnyi tikhokhod*, dir. Semen Timoshenko, 1945] one can see a friendly competition between the genders, with a strong emphasis on "cute femininity" and the heroines' joyful subjugation to male authority.

At the same time, Svetlana Aleksievich's *War's Unwomanly Face* [*U voiny ne zhenskoe litso*, 1988], based on interviews with real-life female veterans, demonstrates how the active participation of women in military actions was frequently seen as an unacceptable gender transgression, taking a woman beyond the bounds of "normal" social relations. In Soviet social practice, despite an increasing sacralization of the war, female veterans' war experience was frequently something to be ashamed of. Several of Svetlana Aleksievich's real-life heroines speak about becoming outcasts after the war:

> I returned to my village with two Glory medals and other decorations. I stayed [at home] for three days and on the fourth, my mother wakes me up with the words: "Honey, I prepared some stuff for you. Take it and go. You've got two younger sisters growing up. Who'll marry them? Everybody knows that you were at the front for four years [...]. (2004, 22)[2]

> How did the motherland meet us? I can't speak about this without tears [...] Forty years have passed, and still my cheeks are burning. Men kept mum, and women [...] They yelled at us: "We know what you were busy with at the front! You were sleeping with our husbands. Frontline whores [...] Army bitches." They insulted us in many ways. (2004, 243–4).[3]

> After the war. I lived in a communal apartment. All my neighbors were with their husbands. They insulted me: "Ha-ha [...] Tell us how you whored around with men [at the front]." They used

---

[2] "Вернулась в свою деревню с двумя орденами Славы и медалями. Пожила три дня, а на четвертый мама меня поднимает с постели словами: "Доченька, я тебе собрала узелок. Уходи, у тебя еще две младшие сестры растут. Кто их замуж возьмет [...] Все знают, что ты четыре года на фронте [...]."

[3] "Как нас встретила Родина? Без слез не могу [...] Сорок лет прошло, а до сих пор щеки горят. Нужчины молчали, а жещины [...] Он кричали нам: 'Знаем, чем вы там занимались! Вы спали там с нашими мужьями. Фронтовые б [...] Сучки военные.' Оскорбляли по-всякому."

to pour vinegar into my potato stew. Or put spoonfuls of salt into my cooking [...] And laughed with pleasure. Then my commander demobilized. He came to me. We got married. But in a year he left me for another woman, the director of our factory canteen. "She smells of perfume, and you reek of [soldiers'] boots and dirty socks" [he said]. (2004, 234–5)[4]

Engel comments on these and similar passages as testimony to the social marginalization of women with combat experience in postwar society:

In the postwar period, wives and mothers almost completely effaced the woman warrior. [...] Women received proportionally fewer medals than did men and most of those were rewarded posthumously. Women's most praiseworthy wartime activity became bearing and rearing the nation's soldiers. [...] The postwar experience of the women who had served at the front thus differed from that of the men who served beside them and whose exploits continued to be celebrated in the postwar period. In the words of one female veteran, the men "as victors, heroes, and marriageable men could wear their medals; they had a war, while people looked at us [women] as if we were completely different." (Engel 2004, 223–4)

It is also telling that the majority of women with combat experience were forced into retirement as soon as the war was over:

Most women performing military service were demobilized immediately after the war and *discouraged from pursuing a military career*: "Do not give yourself airs in your future practical work.

---

[4] "После войны. Я жила в коммунальной квартире. Соседки все были с мужьями, обижали меня. Ругались: 'Ха-ха-а [...] Расскажи, как ты там б [...] с мужиками.' В мою кастрюлю с картошкой уксуса нальют. Всыпят ложку соли [...] И довольные смеются [...] Демобилизовался из армии мой командир. Приехал ко мне. Поженились мы. А через год он ушел к другой женщине, заведующей нашей фабричной столовой. От нее духами пахнет, а от тебя тянет сапогами и портянками."

Do not speak of the services you rendered, let others do it for you," president Mikhail Kalinin advised recently demobilized women soldiers in July 1945. (Engel 2004, 224)

Possibly, the reasons behind this sociocultural perception of women-soldiers were not that women's military activities undermined male superiority and disrupted patriarchal gender opposition. In our view, the source of the problem (in addition to the prevailing archetype of the war harlot and the danger posed by the strong woman-warrior) was related to professional murder, which in traditional patriarchal culture— including Russian—is unacceptable for women as the givers of life.

In many traditional patriarchal cultures murder performed by a woman for a sacred cause received symbolic approval only if accompanied by self-sacrifice, as in the case of Judith and Holophernes, when the murder of the enemy was accompanied by the woman's death.[5] Death was the natural requirement for acceptance of the woman-killer in patriarchal culture. Exceptions were possible, but in Soviet culture they typically pertained to mothers who were avenging their children (biological or symbolic), i.e., the women who had already fulfilled their "life-giving duty" (*She Defends the Motherland, Rainbow*). Another group of exceptions comprise female warriors who were "protected" by *distance*—the epic distance of legendary time (for example, Ol'ga Danilovna [Valentina Ivashova] in Sergei Eisenstein's *Alexander Nevsky* [1939]) or by physical distance, such as between female pilots or female snipers and their targets—although even this requirement did not always protect the female veteran from social alienation, as documented in Aleksievich's book.

Tellingly, one of Aleksievich's heroines internalizes this cultural taboo, suggesting that she was punished for killing people during the war with an unhappy family life: "I'm punished [...] What for? Maybe, for killing? Sometimes I think like that [...] [My husband] left us, heaping reproaches on me: 'How can a normal woman go off to war?

---

[5] Characteristically, in American and British armies women were not allowed to participate in frontline combat—their military duties were limited to anti-aircraft units, various services and medicine. Although German women served in the military, they were also forbidden to fire guns until the last days of the war in 1945. See Campbell (1993).

Learn to shoot?' That's why you can't give birth to a normal child' [...] What if he's right?" (2004, 245).[6] One of Aleksievich's interviewees, however, directly challenges the notion that killing a military enemy is a specifically masculine duty: "We kept hearing that going off to fight was a masculine urge. That we were abnormal [...] Not quite like other women [...] That we were deranged [...] No! No, it was a [normal] human urge" (2004, 194–95).[7]

If the woman who killed professionally survived the war, her existence created an insoluble problem, whose poignancy increased in the atmosphere of Soviet culture's declarative feminism. On the one hand, officially proclaimed gender equality demanded that a female veteran receive the same symbolic rewards as her male compatriots. On the other, such a woman lost her "gender license" and was pushed outside stable gender scenarios—both legitimate (mother, innocent girl) and transgressive (harlot). From this point of view, the film *Wings*, created by one of the most prominent female Soviet directors, Larisa Shepit'ko (1938–1979), is particularly paradoxical, since it thoroughly problematizes all existing archetypes as well as other gender scenarios of the female veteran's self-realization in the postwar period, specifically during the Thaw.

A Paradigmatic Soviet Heroine?

This problematization is reflected even in the history of the film's creation. Originally a famous scriptwriter, Valentin Ezhov (already celebrated for his script of *Ballada o soldate* [*Ballad of a Soldier* 1959] by Grigorii Chukhrai), was slated to write a script for a comedy about a female pilots' unit during the war, which obviously recalled *Nebesnyi tikhokhod*. However, when he began working with Natal'ia Riazantseva,

---

[6] "Я наказана [...] За что? Может, за то, что убивала? Иногда я так думаю [...] [Муж] бросил нас с упреками: 'Разве нормальная женщина пойдет на войну? Научится стрелять? Поэтому ты и ребенка нормальног родить не способна' [...] А если он прав."

[7] "Мол, это было мужское желание—пойти воевать. Вы какие-то ннормальные. Не совсем женщины [...] Неполноценные [...] Нет! Нет, это было человеческое желание."

she changed the genre to a drama about a former female pilot's postwar life. According to an interview with Riazantseva, Shepit'ko's inattentiveness to Ezhov's opinions once she turned to the script led to his near-departure from the project, leaving Raizantseva to collaborate with the director alone: "Larisa [...], despite her youth, did not treat Ezhov as an authority, and he distanced himself from the work. Essentially, from that point on, we worked without him" (Gorovoi 2009).[8]

The protagonist of *Wings*, Nadezhda Petrukhina (brilliantly played by Maia Bulgakova), does not appear to be the victim of social repression. A former wartime pilot and a highly placed provincial official, she is not only the principal of a vocational school (*professional'no-tekhnichskoe uchilishche*) but also a deputy in the City Soviet. The film makes no mention of her forced expulsion from the profession of pilot, though it plays a very powerful role as the cause of her unrest. Characteristically, during a discussion of Shepit'ko's film in *Iskusstvo kino* [*The Art of Film*] in 1966, a former wartime pilot, A. Poliantseva, who called *Wings* a harmful film that depicts an atypical heroine, for some reason justified Petrukhina's retirement by referring to her serious injury—an injury never mentioned in the film.[9] Poliantseva's very comments nonetheless testified to a different category of injury: the *traumatic* effects of alienation from one's wartime self, experienced not only by Petrukhina, but also by her real-life critic, with a similar biography.

In the film, however, Petrukhina is seemingly respected by men and women alike, as evident in the scenes at the local beer pavilion: Petrukhina is gladly invited along with the men and receives special treatment from the female bartender, Shura. At the local air club that she had attended before the war she is also greeted with respect. Her portrait hangs in the city museum along with photographs of those who perished heroically fighting in the war—including Petrukhina's love, Mitia Grachev (Leonid D'iachkov). She has a grown-up daughter, though adopted. Moreover, her male suitor, Pavel ("Pasha") (Panteleimon Krylov), director of the local museum, is so devoted to Petrukhina that in one sequence she has only to whisper his name after

---

[8] "В результате мы стали работать с Ларисой, которая, несмотря на молодость, совершенно не считалась с Ежовым как с маститым, и тот надолго отошёл от этого дела. По сути дальше мы работали вдвоём."

[9] See "*Kryl'ia*" 15–18.

he leaves her apartment to have him return. (That "miraculous power," tellingly, fails to work with her daughter, Tania, whose departure from her mother's "domain" is irrevocable.) The only sign of gender repression—and an important one—surfaces in an episode where the heroine, tired of peeling potatoes (a task she performs in a rough, "masculine" rather than in a skillful, "feminine" manner) decides to go to a restaurant: "Why does a person have to peel potatoes on Sunday?" ["Почему человек в воскресенье должен чистить картошку?"], only to find herself refused entrance without a male escort after 6 pm. Perceived as an indecent oddity in the culture of the Thaw, an independent woman is excluded, both symbolically and literally here, from its readymade social structures.

Scholars describe the transformations of gender culture in the sixties as a paradoxical amalgam of contradictory tendencies: while some state and societal practices stimulated gender equality in terms of women's professional and social growth, others augmented the double burden, stipulating responsibility for housework and childcare as women's major patriarchal role. As Reid notes, "The relation between the Khrushchev state and society was not totalitarian; it was, nevertheless, paternal and patriarchal. And, as in other forms of modern welfare paternalism, the main objects of control and definition were women and children" (Reid 2004, 156). *Wings* fully reflects the ambivalence of gender changes in the Thaw period. On the one hand, Petrukhina belongs to a small stratum of women in positions of political authority. According to Engel, "At the end of Khrushchev's rule, in 1964, the proportion of women in positions of genuine political authority still barely exceeded 4 percent" (2004, 235). On the other hand, Petrukhina's social suffocation directly reflects the tightening of social conventions that make her more and more irrelevant to her social environment.[10] Her inability to find "a place of her own" par-

---

[10] A drama very similar to that undergone by wartime female pilots, and specifically by Petrukhina, unfolded a few years after the release of *Wings*, in relation to female cosmonauts. According to Nikolai Kamanin's diaries, "Summoned to the Central Committee in 1968, Tereshkova was appalled to discover the future they had in mind for her. Five years after her flight she was still working for the space programme, was studying at the Zhukovsky Military Aviation Academy, and fully intending to qualify as an engineer. Though Kamanin had attempted

tially explains the film's finale, which we read as implying Petrukhina's suicide. Though such a reading impresses us as the most justified in the context of the entire film, it would be a stretch to explain the finale entirely as a consequence of the cultural atmosphere of the sixties—marked by a shift from the societal modus of permanent mobilization, which also implied relative gender equality, to more relaxed, more "normal" conditions, which stimulated the restoration of many patriarchal models and conventions.

Quite possibly, Shepit'ko obfuscated almost all signs of social repression of female veterans because she wanted to reveal the problematic and even explosive nature of this poster case of public respect and veneration of the paradigmatic Soviet heroine. Such a reading of the film was convincingly presented by Dodona Kiziria in her article "Death of the Heroine," which contextualizes *Wings* among classic Soviet films about women: *Mother* [*Mat'*, 1926] by Vsevolod Pudovkin, *Member of the Government* [*Chlen pravitel'stva*, 1939] by Aleksandr Zarkhi and Iosif Kheifits, *Zoia* (1944) by Arnshtam, *Wait for Me* [*Zhdi menia*, 1943] by Aleksandr Stolper and Boris Ivanov, and *The Village Teacher* [*Sel'skaia uchitel'nitsa*, 1947] by Mark Donskoi. Finding numerous parallels between Petrukhina and the heroines of these films, Kiziria argues that Shepit'ko's heroine demonstrates the dead-end of molding the model Soviet woman from the twenties to the fifties. Petrukhina is indeed the "typical positive heroine of Soviet cinema" (Kiziria 1990, 133), yet her life is deprived of any tangible meaning—hence her suicide in the film's finale:

> The film narrative [...] leaves little doubt concerning the end of Petruxina's cinematic "road to life." It destroyed the woman in her and led her to a sterile existence. She failed as a mother, as an educator of Soviet youth and even as a beloved woman since she was

---

to steer her towards a life of public service, she continued to be entranced by space. Above all, the worldwide struggles of the women's movement simply did not interest her. When the Politburo duly rubber-stamped the decision without her consent she was devastated. Sitting in floods of tears in Kamanin's flat, there was nothing even he could do but lend a sympathetic ear: 'She kept coming back again and again to the same theme, "I've lost everything"—space, the academy, flying, and her family, her daughter'" (Bridger 2004, 235–6).

not capable of loving a living man. In this view her name Nadežda, "hope" in Russian, sounds bitterly ironic. There is no hope for her any more and the best she can do is to end her life. This would be her first independent decision, the one that does not follow the path paved by her predecessors. By killing herself Petruxina cuts her ties with them, deconstructs their image and transforms herself from a cinematic parody into a tragic figure. (1990, 143)

While agreeing in general with Kiziria's reading of *Wings*, one cannot help noticing that dramatic overtones dominate in the film, and that the deconstruction of the Soviet heroine fuses with a deep compassion for Petrukhina, whose cultural and social irrelevance testifies not only to the failure of Soviet ideological models, but mainly—as we would like to argue—to the irretrievable loss of specific gender subjectivity that appears to be inseparable from the war experience and the impossibility of creating an alternative gender identity. We would like to emphasize the gender aspect of this trauma, which, we argue, lies in the failure of new female identities offered by the "normal" life of the Thaw period, to secure for Petrukhina a degree of freedom and dignity that she apparently enjoyed during wartime. The novelty of *Wings* stems from the complete internalization of its focal conflict, which Shepit'ko situates within Petrukhina's subjectivity. The clash between the self shaped by wartime experience and postwar "mobilization," on the one hand, and her attempts to become a "normal" (i.e., socially acceptable) woman, on the other, resides at the film's conceptual center.

Petrukhina's "military" or, rather, "mobilized" personality manifests itself in many details and scenes. Of particular importance are her commanding, gruff manner of speech, her unbendingly straight back, and her official appearance—conveyed by her unchanging black suit and white blouse, which function as a uniform. Petrukhina's representative status is established in the film's opening sequence, which shows her being outfitted at a tailor's, the back of her head, with its almost masculine haircut, turned toward the viewers, so that her face is invisible. After a theatrical entrance, the tailor takes her measurements, then announces: "A standard size 12" ["Стандартный сорок восьмой"], thereby immediately inscribing her case as ordinary, and not unique. However, the camera's movements produce an effect that appears somewhat contradictory to the statement of the heroine's typicality:

Figure 3.1. Petrukhina tries to climb into the airplane

the film opens with a shot of an urban crowd moving along the street, then the camera moves back and we see the same crowd through a large window. As the camera moves further back, we see Petrukhina completely separated from the crowd, not seen by it or seeing it, as she is standing behind the wall of a dressing room with her face turned away from the viewer. We see her face only at the end of the scene. Thus, though average, one of many, she is at the same time isolated, cut off from "the masses"; her typicality paradoxically combines with her loneliness. No wonder that in the film's finale, the *standard* outfit, tailored for her in the first scene, transforms into a torturous restraint when, with an awkward smile, Petrukhina tries to climb into the cockpit of an airplane [Fig.3.1]—tangibly and painfully revealing the conflict between Petrukhina's social identity and her constricted self.

In the film's beginning, after a series of the heroine's "official" appearances (as a deputy of the local Soviet, as a school principal), we also see another Petrukhina, relaxing at the beach. The official outfit is removed, and the camera slowly slides along her body, surprisingly young and beautiful in an open swimsuit, thus contrasting with her image at the tailor's. Yet, as in the scene with the tailor, her face is hidden, covered

Figure 3.2. Petrukhina on the beach

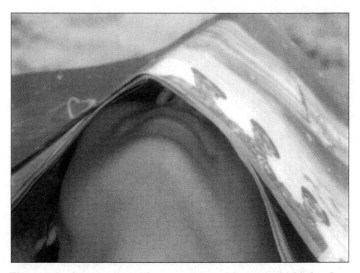

Figure 3.3. A magazine with cosmonauts on its cover shields her face

by a magazine with photographs of cosmonauts—the sixties' replacement for the earlier Soviet cult of pilots [Figs. 3.2, 3.3, 3.4]. This loaded
visual image unmistakably communicates the obliteration of Petrukhina's
embraced identity. From the outset we see her subjectivity split between
the sexless "suit" (the official or public self) and the feminine "body"

Figure 3.4. Petrukhina as the matriarch among matryoshkas

(her private self, supposedly encouraged in the cultural atmosphere of
the Thaw). The paradox lies in the fact that both selves deprive her of
herself, of her face, superseded by the impersonal signs of the power
discourse that corresponds to her venerated yet awkward position of a
former war heroine whose photograph hangs in a museum.

Both Petrukhina's rigidity and her irrelevance are painfully revealed
during her visit to her daughter, Tania (Zhanna Bolotova), who left her
mother's home for her 37-year-old university professor. Although this
motif remains unelaborated in the film, an attentive viewer might detect
a deeper conflict behind the awkward mother/daughter relationship. The
fact that Tania lives with her university professor suggests the young
woman's yearning for a strong paternal presence, for an authority figure,
which Petrukhina cannot be. The irrelevance of Petrukhina's authority
for Tania—i.e. for the generation of the Thaw—becomes obvious in the
following scene, when, unable to communicate with Tania's unofficial
husband and his intellectual friends, Petrukhina loudly proposes having
a drink, praises the apartment in impersonal, newspaper-style phrases,
cuts the cake she has brought with graceless, "masculine" gestures, and
finally bombards Tania's husband with tactless questions delivered as
though at an interrogation. Although this scene is usually viewed as

testimony to Petrukhina's "military" self, it is evident that Petrukhina "overplays" her part, like a bad actress: her self-parodic performance actually reflects and exaggerates the stereotypical perception of her as a rough, sexless veteran—a perception apparently shared by Tania and her circle. The awkward effect produced by Petrukhina, however, proves the opposite: that this stereotypical "identity" is as narrow and artificial for her as the suggested identities of a "party bureaucrat" or a "domestic woman." In short, here, as elsewhere, she cannot assimilate, cannot fit into a social group comprising mutually supportive members. She remains outside any recognized system of self-identification.

In a later conversation with Tania, when the daughter comes to visit her at home, Petrukhina acknowledges her own irrelevance. She characteristically explains her roughness by her wartime past: "Rough and unsophisticated [...] Army grunt. Unfit for cultured circles" ["Серая, необученная [...] Солдатня. Неприлично привести в интеллигентную компанию"]. Yet, immediately afterwards, in reaction to her daughter's suggestion that she leave her job and start a new life, Petrukhina delivers an angry monologue about her sense of duty, rooted in wartime experience and extended to the postwar period: "Let others do that—I never knew these words [...] [I always went] where I was ordered to, without thinking. I worked for myself and for others." ["Пусть другие—я этих слов никогда и не знала [...] Где прикажут, не разбираясь. И за себя, и за других"]. Subsequently, she adds: "Feel pity for me, do you? Well, don't. You'd do better envying me" ("Пожалела? А ты меня не жалей. Ты лучше мне позавидуй"). This riposte evokes a thematic intertext: the poem "My generation" ["Мое pokolenie," 1945] by the famous war poet Semen Gudzenko: "No need to pity us, since we wouldn't have pitied anyone either" ["Нас не нужно жалеть, ведь и мы б никого не жалели [...]"]. Though several Soviet critics, such as V. Kardin, have characterized Petrukhina as a blindly obedient Stalinist,[11] in this episode Shepit'ko clearly empha-

---

[11] See V. Kardin in "*Kryl'ia*" 12–15. A similar interpretation of the film's pro-tagonist as a Stalinist in the Thaw environment was indirectly promoted by Shepit'ko herself in one of her last interviews—during the ban on direct dis-cussion of Stalinism, which was in effect in the 1970s and early 1980s. See Rybak 1987, 181–2. This view also surfaces in an article (1987) by Arsen Medvedev published in the memorial collection Larisa.

sizes the wartime roots of the heroine's sense of duty, suggesting a fusion of independence, brutality, and responsibility rather than a simple subjugation to orders.

Although Petrukhina's soldier-like lifestyle is responsible for her emphatically "unwomanly" manners, Shepit'ko blurs rather than justifies the opposition between "warrior" identity and femininity. First, Petrukhina's memories of the war revolve above all around her beloved and her girlfriends. Second, her professional service to society in her present life entails the duties of a school principal. It is Tania's suggestion that she leave this job ("Leave your hoodlums" ["брось своих оболтусов"]) that causes Petrukhina's genuine indignation. Official decree alone assigns the meaning of a social service to what is basically and traditionally the patriarchal function of an adult woman as mother. This paradoxical blend of social duty with patriarchal femininity is ironically underscored by the episode in which circumstances force Petrukhina to play a giant matryoshka—a symbol of fecund maternity—in a school dance performance. Once again, much as in the sequence of Petrukhina's conversation with Tania and her friends, this episode strikes the viewer by its ironic artificiality: Petrukhina has to be carried on stage and supported by her students throughout the number. Moreover, that fact she, the school principal, substitutes for a student originally slated to play the part results from her failure as a pedagogue, as a "mother figure." Consequently, such a performance of maternity only reinforces Petrukhina's unsuitability for this venerated—albeit patriarchal—form of gender identification.

Petrukhina's failure as a mother figure on both the private and the social front constitutes the key element in her crisis. Fulfillment of the maternal function is precisely what could safely establish her in the prevailing patriarchal disposition of gender. Simultaneously, that function serves as a test of her professional competence, and the scenario of professional self-realization is vital for the Soviet rhetoric of gender equality. However paradoxically, maternity offers the perfect channel for the internalization of the patriarchal gender model as a social (soldier-like) duty, and vice versa. Yet Petrukhina fails in both directions. Her daughter leaves permanently, her departure presumably caused by Petrukhina's insensitive attack when Tania falls in love with her professor. Though Petrukhina's acknowledged earlier fear that Tania would learn about being adopted proves groundless, all her efforts to

Figure 3.5. Petrukhina with cherries under the cleansing rain

establish close relations with her daughter end in their mutual alienation ("Alien, no matter what" ["все равно чужая"]).

Tania's departure in the personal sphere of the family is paralleled with the disappearance of one of Petrukhina's students (the professional arena), Vostriakov (played by the young Sergei Nikonenko), whom Petrukhina unhesitatingly expels from the college for his refusal to apologize to a female fellow student. When Vostriakov, having being beaten by his father and having wandered around for two days without food and shelter, returns to the college and delivers a formal apology, Petrukhina tries to "reach out" to him, only to hear him cry, "I hate you!" ["Я вас ненавижу!"]. Though on the surface both Tania's and Vostriakov's alienation and hatred for Petrukhina appear unprovoked by her, such is not the case, for her commanding style, on the one hand, and her independence and unbending confidence, on the other, make her a "bad mother," at least from a patriarchal standpoint.

In any case, after Vostriakov's words Petrukhina takes a nose dive: maternity, as the only valid bridge between her private and public selves, collapses, leaving her subjectivity in shambles. Hereafter

Petrukhina attempts, without success, to reinvent herself within the paradigm of traditional femininity. After leaving the college, she sees a man in a pilot's uniform and suddenly metamorphoses from a rigid bureaucrat into an attractive woman, taking off her jacket and unbuttoning her blouse, only to be ignored by him. This scene is followed by a beautiful, sentimental scene, in which she walks along the street with a handful of cherries, as if offering her sexuality to the entire world. When she tries to wash the cherries, however, there is no water in the faucet. The onset of a rainstorm not only washes the fruit, but also turns her eyes to the sky—triggering the memory of her wartime love, when she and her beloved were both pilots. Figure 3.5.

The symbolism of this scene is quite transparent: the water absent in the faucet and descending from the sky obviously serves as a metaphor for life (evoking the traditional Russian trope of revivifying water (*zhivaia voda*) so common in folklore). Real-life conditions, in short, cannot satisfy Nadezhda's sexual and emotional thirst, for the source of love and life for her is located elsewhere—in the transcendental dimension (heaven) that is equated by Petrukhina with the realm of death (war).

Soviet Femininity and Thanatos

As already noted, for Petrukhina, love is inseparable from war. She seems capable of happiness only at the front, not as a wife but as a "battle companion" equal to her beloved, killing and risking death by his side. The absence of these conditions and of equality in heterosexual relations makes "peacetime" love, let alone marriage, impossible for her, and the failure of her attempts at "seduction" corroborate this impossibility.

The dead-end is particularly evident in the scene at the museum, where Petrukhina sees herself as a dead exhibit amongst the living visitors to the museum. Petrukhina heightens the paradox of the situation when she tells Pasha, the museum's curator, who is in love with her, "Pasha! Marry me [...]" ["Паша! Возьми меня замуж [...]"]. Despite his feelings for her, the request unnerves him—as a sensitive person and truly in love with Petrukhina, Pavel realizes that her suggestion reflects her utter despair. After the awkward pause that follows, Petrukhina sarcastically adds, "Imagine, a director of the museum marries his exhibit" ["Представляешь, директор музея и женится на своем экспонате"].

This dialogue is framed by two ironic images clearly analogized with the female protagonist: before Petrukhina's proposal, Pasha speaks excitedly of steak made of mammoth meat preserved in permafrost; it is still edible, but a little tough. After her proposal, Petrukhina looks around and, noticing a stuffed hen, sardonically exclaims, "A stuffed hen. The only one of its kind in the whole world" ["Единственное в мире чучело курицы"]. The prospect of marriage and family happiness for Petrukhina parallels eating a permafrosted mammoth steak. Both the mammoth (extinct) and the hen (dead and stuffed) reflect Petrukhina's "identities"—her wartime self and the self she might acquire if she becomes a "normal woman." Her genuine femininity, associated with the war, is dead, for the war and her beloved are long gone. Characteristically, she concludes this conversation with the rhetorical question: "Today one girl [at the museum] asked about me: 'Did she die [in the war]?' By the way, what do you think: did she die?" ["Сегодня одна девочка про меня спросила: А она погибла? Кстати, как ты считаешь: она погибла?"] Emotionally, she did, becoming an extinct species.

The alternate prospect, that of "domestication," which would entail giving up the ability to fly (wings!) for the possibility of laying eggs and protecting the nest, is equally dead and meaningless for Petrukhina, and she has no illusions about this option: a stuffed hen looks like a "normal" hen, yet is just an empty shell. The episode, in fact, evokes the colloquial patriarchal equation of a woman with a hen: "A hen's not a bird, a woman's not a human" ["Курица не птица, баба не человек"]. The heroine's desire to fly, to have wings, in this context reads as her resistance to the dehumanizing patriarchal reduction of a woman into a "domestic fowl."

It is also quite symptomatic that Petrukhina's first recollection of her wartime love is situated in an ancient, abandoned city of stone. Her beloved, Mitia Grachev, explains that the town's inhabitants left it for "a better life" and as a result forgot their art of masonry. In other words, having abandoned the stones, they lost themselves. In the same episode, Grachev answers Petrukhina's question "Where should we go?" ["Как нам теперь идти?"] with an ironic quote from the fairy-tale formula: "Go left, you'll find your horse's death, go right, you'll find your death" ["Налево пойдешь, коня потеряешь. Направо пойдешь, сам пропадешь"]. Grachev's narrative and response symbolically foreshadow Petrukhina's fate after his demise. The loss of self experienced by the stone-town's inhabitants tropes Petrukhina's "military" self, which crumbles and dries up outside of war and wartime conditions. And Grachev's reference to death in his folkloric response predicts his own physical and Petrukhina's spiritual-emotional death. Not only this scene, but also the next episode of Petrukhina's recollections— depicting Grachev's death—testify to the fact that Petrukhina's love and femininity are rooted in *the land of the dead*: the abandoned city of stone provides a powerful visual metaphor for this concept. These scenes, as well as the film's finale, reveal the paradox at the root of the nostalgia Petrukhina (and Soviet society at large) felt for the war: the relative freedom of wartime is based on the presence of *death* as a major fact of existence.[12]

Another, alternative, scenario of "normal" femininity is represented in the sequence following the scandal with Vostriakov, in which Petrukhina converses with the female bartender at a beer café, Shura (Rimma Markova), who functions as Petrukhina's double. Of the same generation, she likewise is a figure of authority among men (at least those men whose concept of manhood is inseparable from beer). Shura's family life is also far from happy: she has two children and "somebody else's husband" ["есть муж, да чужой"]. During their revealing conversation, Petrukhina admits that when she tries to write a letter to her wartime girlfriends, she has nothing to write about. Nothing she does brings joy to her or anyone else ("It turns out—I have no joy for myself, nor for others" ["Ни себе радости, ни людям, оказывается"]). Shura's response, that she finds her life interesting despite all the odds, inspires Petrukhina's recollection of her reputation in school as an actress, which in turn prompts Shura to remember how she used to love waltzing. In a rare moment that represents woman-to-woman bonding, the two begin to waltz, humming the melody of Strauss's *Blue Danube* as they twirl, only to stop when they notice the amazed faces of men staring at them through the window. Shepit'ko

---

[12] Svetlana Aleksievich in her book *Enchanted by Death* [*Zacharovannye smert'iu,* 1993] posits a tradition of fascination with death as inhering in Soviet and post-Soviet culture.

orchestrates this unusual sequence to present via Shura a gendered version of the "simple life" (a popular conclusion in many films of the sixties and especially the seventies[13]), one that flows outside the uniformity of the symbolic order, yet can engage a subject. However, it is quite obvious that the scenario of "simplification" is not one Petrukhina can and will adopt: she is too well known and too independent to live a "simple life." Moreover, her present life derives its sole meaning from the past, which she cannot jettison.

The collapse of Soviet gender identity leaves an insatiable void that manifests itself in Petrukhina's striving for the sky—a spatial metaphor for her desire to return, if only symbolically, to the war, when she was free, loved, and in love. This striving finds its fullest manifestation in the film's finale, which provoked a curious controversy among critics. Soviet-era commentators typically interpreted Petrukhina's last flight as an optimistic act of victory over "prosaic" gravity—a view also prevailing in the sentimental/transcendental interpretation of the film's finale in the post-Soviet period. In 1999, one critic declared, "The film's finale (when Petrukhina gets in the training jet and takes off) is highly significant: it becomes a metaphor for the heroine's recovery of a lost harmony with herself and others" (Kudriavtsev 1999).[14] In a similar if more romantic vein, a female Russian commentator asserted, "The pilot Petrukhina turned the plane and soared into the sky, into the absolute, where Mitia awaits her" (Zakrzhevskaia).[15] Similarly, Denise Youngblood remarks that "Regardless of her intentions, she [Petrukhina] is beaming with happiness as she ascends into the clouds (heavens)" (Youngblood 2007, 180). Other critics are more prone to interpret the film's conclusion as implying the heroine's suicide. Kiziria notes, "Shepit'ko chose to leave it to the audience to decide whether she [Petrukhina] would kill

---

[13] See, for instance, the characteristic finales of such films as *Afonia* by Georgii Daneliia (1975) and *Moscow Does Not Believe in Tears* [*Moskva slezam ne verit* 1979] by Vladimir Men'shov, as well as the entire plotline of *Snowball Berry Red* [*Kalina Krasnaia* 1975] by Vasilii Shukshin.

[14] "[...] финал ленты (когда Петрухина садится в учебный самолет и взлетает вверх) в высшей степени знаменателен. Он становится метафорой обретения героиней утраченной гармонии с самой собой и с людьми."

[15] "[...] летчица Петрухина развернула машину и взмыла в небо. Туда, к Мите, в страну абсолюта."

herself. The possibility of Petruxina's suicide was considered and discussed by Soviet critics, but the conclusion was too unusual and too
difficult to accept without some modification. [...] The film narrative,
however, leaves little doubt concerning the end of Petrukhina's cinematic 'road to life'" (2007, 143). Josephine Woll argues that "In the
film's last scene Petrukhina settles into the cockpit of a plane as a nostalgic exercise, only to roar off down the runway. She points her plane
towards the sky, the element where she is genuinely at home, and
although we do not see anything more, she will probably dive down in
a suicidal crash" (Woll 2000, 218).

When interpreting the finale of *Wings,* it is important to remember
that Petrukhina's nostalgia for war is also inseparable from her lost
power to kill—her war record proudly lists twelve destroyed enemy aircrafts, her trophies. An achievement from the standpoint of official ideology, this record is a sign of monstrosity from the perspective of 1960s
gender mythologies, which equated womanhood with birthing and nurturing. From the latter viewpoint, Petrukhina's nostalgia for the war
may be read as a variation on the Freudian death drive. In this context,
the film's conclusion, in which the heroine soars skyward in a plane
similar to the one she flew during the war, acquires an unambiguous
meaning. Shepit'ko clearly implies the suicide of the former "warrior"
woman unable to find her place in "normal" Soviet culture, for her
identity has been formed by the discourses and practices of extraordinary mobilization. Unwilling to break herself to fulfill the constrictive
gender demands of peacetime, Petrukhina simply leaves for the only
freedom she knows—one secured by her wartime connection to death.

While exposing the contradictions in the gender discourses and
mythologies of Soviet culture, Shepit'ko's film proffers no alternatives
to this logic. *Kryl'ia* is important for its systematic rejection of illusions
(both official and popular), for overcoming gender contradictions incarnated in the figure of the woman-soldier. Petrukhina's death certainly
does not offer a resolution to these contradictions; it presents a desperate escape from them. Soberly and pessimistically, the film reveals
the soldier-woman's death as a mandatory requirement for her symbolic
acceptance into the "modernized partiarchality" of the sixties. Indeed,
death seems to be the only honorable exit for Petrukhina, and Shepit'ko
infuses her lack of options with a bitter, tragic irony that is maximally
removed from both paternalist sentimentality and official pathos.

Conclusion

From the standpoint of contemporary studies of Soviet subjectivity, Petrukhina's drama may be construed as the conflict between two types of subjectivity: on the one hand, the "normative self," and on the other, the "banal self," grounded in the practices of everyday life. The "normative self," in accordance with Michel Foucault's dictum, is a direct product of the coercive power (the "anatomo-politics of the human body") and correlative utopian/revolutionary discourses "centered on the body as a machine: its disciplining, the optimization of its capabilities, the extortion of its forces, the parallel increase of its usefulness and its docility, its integration into systems of efficient and economic controls." The "banal self" only seems to be excluded from power relations, but in fact is both created and disfigured by the disciplinary and biopolitical power mechanisms "whose highest function was perhaps no longer to kill, but to invest life through and through" (Foucault 1978, 139).

Although contemporary historical studies place the dominance of the two types of subjectivity in the Stalinist and post-Stalinist period respectively, we consider it more reasonable to situate the complex dialectic of these selves within a single individual. At the time Shepit'ko was shooting *Kryl'ia*, this dialectic was represented quite mechanistically as the opposition of "true" and "false" selves, as evidenced, for instance, in the "youth prose" of the sixties (Vasilii Aksenov, Anatolii Gladilin, Anatolii Kuznetsov) or the works of Alexander Solzhenitsyn (*The First Circle* [*V kruge pervom* 1964–68] and *The Cancer Ward* [*Rakovyi korpus* 1963–68]). Only the literature of the seventies and eighties—above all Iurii Trifonov, in all his mature works but especially in *House on the Embankment* [*Dom na naberezhnoi* 1976] and *Time and Place* [*Vremia i mesto* 1980]—aesthetically explored the complexity of the self torn between "the normative" and "the banal."

However, the representation of this conflict in Shepit'ko's film is completely different from both Solzhenitsyn's and Trifonov's scenarios. The film not only links the "normative" self with war memory, which still functioned (and not just officially) as the Soviet sacred, but, most importantly, situates the gender aspects of Petrukhina's personality in the nexus of this conflict. Each of these models, the "normative" and the "banal," affects gender construction, yet, as it turns out in the film, the erosion of the normative (Stalinist) self does not automatically lead to the emergence of a banal, prosaic, and decentered subjectivity. Tested through gender, the opposition between the normative and the banal subjectivity blurs, for the femininity shaped by the normative conditions of World War II cannot simply redress itself in the prosaic world of the Thaw. Thus, the "progressive" transition from the normative to the decentered banal subjectivity turns into a gender tragedy: Petrukhina's power and freedom as a woman cannot manifest themselves outside of war conditions, outside of the realm of death.

It is quite plausible that a reading of the film as a gender tragedy escaped the interpretational filters of the sixties and even of the eighties, when the film was perceived mainly as a statement against the crippling effects of Stalinism, mediated by the heroic mythology of the war. Any attacks on *Kryl'ia* concerned its perceived assault on the sacred cow of Soviet (Stalinist) culture—the Great Patriotic War and its veterans. As we have argued, a reading of Shepit'ko's film as a story of the gendered collapse of Soviet subjectivity has a more far-reaching effect. It suggests, among other things, that Soviet culture, with its emphasis on extreme situations of total mobilization such as the war, permitted a much greater degree of freedom and personal self-realization in such situations than during relatively "peaceful" historical periods. In relation to gender models, this means that the most radical, novel, and revolutionary paradigms of femininity emerged during these liminal and critical periods, but became irrelevant and even dangerous once the crisis ended. This explains why relatively liberal periods of Soviet history, such as the Thaw or the late eighties and early nineties, witness not only the weakening of authoritarian/patriarchal patterns of power, but also the paradoxical increase of patriarchal influence on the lives of women.[16] This paradox had been noticed before—for instance, in Aleksei Tolstoi's *The Viper* [*Gadiuka* 1928], which depicts the dramatic transition of a heroine shaped by the Civil War into the more "normalized" NEP (New Economic Policy) culture; it is a little wonder that this novella was frequently mentioned in discussions about

---

[16] For an analysis of this situation during the period of perestroika see Goscilo (1996), 5–18.

Kryl'ia. Shepit'ko, however, was the first to present this gender tragedy as the psychological motivation behind personal nostalgia for the war (and Stalinism) and as the dark flip side of political liberation. This perspective deconstructs a simplistic binary opposition between "times of terror" and "times of freedom," acknowledging the presence of freedom during "dark times" and exposing the repression of women during relatively "liberal" periods. This nuanced vision emerges as the summation of all the components of the film narrative, enables *Kryl'ia* to transcend the cultural borders of the sixties, and accounts for the resonance of Shepit'ko film with today's, rather than yesterday's, concerns and anxieties.

REFERENCES

Aleksievich, Svetlana. 2004. *U voiny ne zhenskoe litso. Pervoe polnoe izdanie.* Moscow: Pal'mira.

Boym, Svetlana. 1994. *Common Places: Mythologies of Everyday Life in Russia.* Cambridge, MA: Harvard University Press.

Bridger, Sue. 2004. "The Cold War and the Cosmos: Valentina Tereshkova and the First Woman's Space Flight." In *Women in the Khrushchev Era*, edited by Melanie Ilič, Susan Reid, and Lynne Attwood, 222–37. Houndmills, Basingstoke, Hampshire: Palgrave Macmillan.

Campbell, D'Ann. 1993. "Women in Combat: The World War II Experience in the United States, Britain, Germany, and the Soviet Union." *The Journal of Military History* 57, 2 (April): 310–23.

Chatterjee, Choi and Karen Petrone. 2008. "Models of Selfhood and Subjectivity: The Soviet Case in Historical Perspective." *Slavic Review* 67, no. 4 (Winter): 967–86.

Engel, Barbara. 2004. *Women in Russia, 1700–2000.* Oxford: Oxford University Press.

Fitzpatrick, Sheila. 1999. *Everyday Stalinism: Ordinary Life in Extraordinary Times. Soviet Russia in the 1930s.* New York: Oxford University Press.

———, ed. 2000. *Stalinism: New Directions.* London and New York: Routledge.

Foucault Michel. 1978. *The History of Sexuality: An Introduction.* Vol. 1. Translated by Rovert Hurley. New York: Vintage Books.

Gorovoi, L. 2009. "Bolshevskie kryl'ia." http://mosoblpress.ru/kalin/show.shtml?d_id=5088 (last accessed 12 June 2010).

Goscilo, Helena. 1996. *Dehexing Sex: Russian Womanhood During and After Glasnost.* Ann Arbor: University of Michigan Press.

Halfin, Igal, ed. 2002. *Language and Revolution: Making Modern Political Identity.* London, Portland: Frank Cass.

Halfin, Igal. 2003. *Terror in My Soul: Communist Autobiographies on Trial.* Cambridge, MA and London: Harvard University Press.

Hellbeck, Jochen. 2006. *Revolution on My Mind: Writing a Diary under Stalin.* Cambridge, MA and London: Harvard University Press.

Kharkhordin, Oleg. 1999. *The Collective and the Individual in Russia: A Study of Practices.* Berkeley: University of California Press.

Kiaer, Christina and Eric Naiman, eds. 2006. *Everyday Life in Early Soviet Russia: Taking the Revolution Inside.* Bloomington and Indianapolis: Indiana University Press.

Kiziria, Dodona. 1990. "Death of the Heroine." *Indiana Slavic Studies* 5: 131–44.

Kotkin, Steven. 1995. *Magnetic Mountain: Stalinism as a Civilization.* Berkeley: University of California Press.

"*Kryl'ia*: Podrobnyi razgovor." 1996. *Iskusstvo kino* 10: 11–29.

Kudriavtsev, S. 1999. "Kryl'ia." *KM.RU*, 7 June. http://kino.km.ru/ magazin/view_print.asp?id={EED92DFB-8AED-11D3-A90A-00C0F0494FCA}&data= (last accessed 26 February 2009).

Medvedev, Armen. 1987. "Drugie i Nadezhda Petrukhina." In *Larisa: Kniga o Larise Shepit'ko*, edited by Klimov Elem, 261–6. Moscow: Iskusstvo.

Reid, Susan A. 2004. "Women in the Home." In *Women in the Khrushchev Era*, edited by Melanie Ilič, Susan Reid, and Lynne Attwood, 149–76. Houndmills, Basingstoke, Hampshire: Palgrave Macmillan.

Rybak, L. 1987. "Poslednee interv'iu." In *Larisa: Kniga o Larise Shepit'ko*, edited by Klimov Elem, 179–94. Moscow: Iskusstvo.

Woll, Josephine. 2000. *Real Images: Soviet cinema and The Thaw.* London and New York: Tauris.

Youngblood, Denise. 2007. *Russian War Films: On the Cinema Front, 1914–2005.* Lawrence, KS: University Press of Kansas.

Yurchak, Alexey. 2006. *Everything Was Forever Until It Was No More: The Last Soviet Generation.* Princeton and London: Princeton University Press.

Zakrzhevskaia, L. No date. "Kryl'ia." http://www.russkoekino.ru/books/ ruskino/ruskino-0070.shtml (last accessed 26 February 2009).

Plate 2.1. Pusia puts on black stockings resembling Nazi boots

*Plate 2.2. Donskoi reinforces the point by cutting from Pusia's feet
in black stockings to German soldiers' high boots*

Plate 2.3. Pusia inserts the phallic object in Kurt's mouth

Plate 2.4. Poster by Iraklii Toidze, The Motherland Calls!
[*Rodina-mat' zovet! 1941*]

Plate 6.3. Iraklii Toidze. The Motherland Calls!
When vulnerable, the USSR was feminized (*1941*)

Plate 2.5. Poster by Iosif Serebriannyi, Beat Harder, Son!
[*Bei krepche, synok! 1941*]

ВОИН КРАСНОЙ АРМИИ,
СПАСИ!

Plate 2.6. Poster by Viktor Koretskii, Red Army Warrior, Save
[Us]! [*Voin Krasnoi armii, spasi! 1942*]

Plate 6.12. Viktor Koretskii. Red Army Solider, Save [Us]! (*1942*)

Plate 2.7 Poster by an unknown author, Russia—for Truth
[*Rossiia—za pravdu, 1914*]

Plate 4.1. 1960s poster for the Four Tankmen and a Dog
[*Czterej pancerni i pies 1966, 1969–70*] *marketing it to young audiences*

Plate 4.2. Janek's first romantic interest, a Polish girl Lidka

Plate 4.3. Janek and his Russian girlfriend Marusia,
a romance that is both titillating and safe

Plate 4.4. The crew poses with their newly christened (and petted) tank

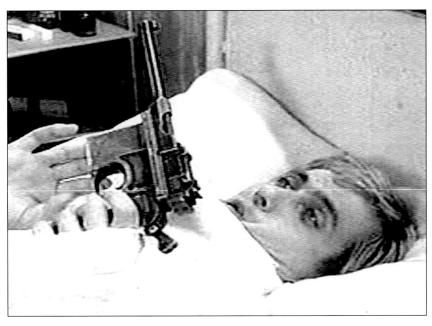

Plate 4.5. Wounded Janek in the hospital, admiring his phallic Mauser

Plate 4.6. Gustlik disguised as a German, with his sweetheart Honorata:
romance as slapstick

Plate 4.7. Everyone's love object: Janek and his dog Sharik

Adam Kiewicz Beata Kowalska

Pancerni

Materiały do zbiórek

www.muzeumczterechpancernych.pl
Młodzieżowa Agencja Wydawnicza

Plate 4.8. A Tankmen's Club [*Klub Pancernych*]
make-it-yourself kit for children; year unknown

Plate 4.9. Cover of the Polish television and film magazine Screen *[Ekran, 1969], featuring Małgorzata Niemirska (as Lidka) and the dog*

CHAPTER 4

Gender(ed) Games: Romance, Slapstick, and Ideology in the Polish Television Series *Four Tank Men and a Dog*[1]

Elena Prokhorova

Genre, Gender, and Generation

Within the long tradition of Soviet and Eastern European visual texts about World War II Konrad Nałęcki's *Four Tank Men and a Dog* [*Czterej pancerni i pies* 1966, 1969–70] presents something of an anomaly, comparable to the still lingering mystery of *Seventeen Moments of Spring* [*Semnadtsat' mgnovenii vesny* 1973, Tat'iana Lioznova]. When the first season of the Polish series aired in September 1966, it became an instant hit with national television audiences and constituted the first sign of television's serious competition with cinema.[2] Within the next few years, *Four Tank Men and a Dog* triumphantly marched through several Eastern European countries, including the USSR, where it was first broadcast in 1968 and acquired the informal nickname "Three Poles, a Georgian, and a Dog." In Poland, it enjoyed regular reruns until 1989, achieving cult status, evidenced by the dozens of fan sites on the Internet.[3]

---

[1] I am grateful to Helena Goscilo and Yana Hashamova for their helpful editorial suggestions, and to the participants of the conference "Women in World War II" (University of Pittsburgh 2007) for ideas and comments on the first version of this paper.

[2] The series created a challenge to Polish cinema by eating away a large chunk of its audience. See, for example, Haltof (2002), 112.

[3] See, for example, http://pancerni.twojeseriale.info and /http://www.muzeum-czterechpancernych.pl/index2.htm. The latter is a virtual museum of artifacts connected to the series: books, action figures, medallions, etc. (last accessed 10 January 2009).

Despite this lasting popularity, in 2006 *Four Tank Men and a Dog*, together with another popular Polish TV series, *More than Life at Stake* [Andrzej Konic, *Stawka wieksza niz zycie* 1968] was removed from the TV schedule by the Polish TV administration in response to a request by Army veterans claiming that the series glossed over the events of World War II.[4] The main objections were the depiction of Germans as a cartoonish, weak enemy (if they were bad soldiers, then Poles were not big heroes) and a distortion of the events of Polish national history.[5]

Meanwhile, for many viewers in post-communist Poland and Russia, the heroes of the series became a part of the nostalgic heritage of their own socialist childhood and adolescence, occupying an honorable place alongside Shtirlits, Cheburashka,[6] and other popular cultural icons.[7] In a 1993 issue of the film journal *Seans*, Aleksei Erokhin gives this nostalgia a romantic twist:

---

[4] Curiously, the dissociation from socialist Poland's ideological allegiance with the Soviet Union sixty years ago aligns these demands with the Russian nationalist agenda *now*, in particular with the use of World War II mythology as the cornerstone of the post-Soviet Russian identity. On 24 February 2009, Minister of Extraordinary Situations Sergei Shoigu suggested a new law stipulating criminal responsibility for any interpretations of the Great Patriotic War that "discredit" the role of the Soviet Union in the fight against Nazism. Available at http://www.rian.ru/politics/20090224/163016713.html (last accessed 10 July 2009). See also the website http://liewar.ru/, "The Great Falsified War," which "deconstructs" specific challenges to the official heroic version of the war.

[5] "We are outraged that the Germans were represented as a gang of morons, but it was a very strong army in the world at that time, and it was difficult to defeat it. Even children can defeat morons. The tragedy of war is not shown; the war in the film is like an adventure," said Tadeusz Filipkowski, deputy chairman of the organization *Armia Krajowa*. War veterans also resent what they see as a distorted picture of the events of the Polish national history in such films. Representatives of Polish television have already declared that they are planning to shoot a new series, based on a more "correct view of the national history." See http://www.lenta.ru/news/2006/08/07/zapret/ (last accessed 15 December 2008).

[6] Shtirlits is a Soviet super spy hero of the popular TV mini-series *Seventeen Moments of Spring*. Cheburashka is the hero of an animated film series (Roman Kachanov, 1969–83).

[7] Among post-Soviet tributes to the series is the film *Four Cabmen and a Dog* (Fedor Popov 2004), in which the cabmen fraternity includes a girl and a feisty Dachshund.

Four tank men, a dog—not counting love. Because your first erotic film was *Four Tank Men and a Dog*. It's not about the war at all... The Amazons' bare knees emit warm light. Male looks collide like tanks. War and love are male games. The street of our childhood played four tank men and their girlfriends. We played not war but love. The roles were set once and for all, only sometimes it was your turn to play Sharik [the dog] or a German sniper. But you learned to bark, to fall from a tree and—as the role demanded—not to be jealous of tenderness directed at others. [...] And no, a remake of our lives is impossible. But we learned that the most important thing about a tank is—to be in love or to be ready for it. Especially with such knees all around you. And, as if remembering that old role, you'd now yelp—hoping that a girl's light hand would pat you on your shaggy head... (1993). [Translation mine, EP]

This remarkably self-reflexive commentary suggests that, despite the official genre designation of the series as a war drama, viewers not only interpreted it through the prism of gender relations, but also used it for their own street games—a level of recognition afforded very few visual texts, e.g., *Chapaev* (Georgii and Sergei Vasil'ev 1934) and *The Elusive Avengers* [Edmond Keosaian, *Neulovimye mstiteli* 1966].

The titular heroes of the series are the crew of the T-34 tank, who participate in the liberation of Poland from the German occupation and, in the second and third season (1969–70), defeat the German army in Berlin as part of the joint Soviet-Polish allied forces. This serious war agenda was compounded by the political urgency to show Polish loyalty to the Soviet Big Brother, especially after the events in Czechoslovakia and the worker uprisings in Poland in 1968.[8] Any discussion of gender representation in an Eastern European or Soviet war film is inseparable from a consideration of political ideology. Both Polish and "shared" socialist war mythology, with the obliga-

---

[8] The authors of the 1974 Soviet book on Eastern European television, *Mnogolikii ekran*, praise the Polish series for its internationalism and "truthfulness of representation," but succinctly if cryptically note that this "television film is not lacking some flaws." See Nikolai Dostanko and Aza Plavnik (1974), 36.

tory motifs of heroism, sacrifice, and suffering, are present in the
series. Poland's traumatic past—the occupation, resistance, and the
brutal suppression of the Warsaw uprising—is evoked in the destroyed
towns liberated by the troops. The decision of the series' protagonist,
Janek Kos, to enlist is motivated by his search for his father, who participated in the fight against Germans at Westerplatte and has been
missing ever since.

As with *Seventeen Moments of Spring*, however, this narrative
outline can hardly explain the production's lasting popularity with
diverse television audiences, albeit the two TV dramas acquired cult
status for entirely different reasons. Made at the same time as the
first Soviet television series, the Polish series also uses the politically
safe theme of wartime heroism as the backdrop for an adventure plot.
Soviet mini-series set during the Civil War or World War II took as
their main subject the heroic agent who acts behind enemy lines to
subvert the enemy's efforts.[9] To accomplish this goal alone or in
a small group with any degree of verisimilitude and drama the hero
had to engage in role-playing. Wearing a mask of loyalty to the hostile
environment is a special kind of heroism that contemporary audiences
found congenial for a number of reasons that are beyond the scope of
this article.[10] What is important here is that the scenario of "our man

---

[9] The series *Drawing Fire* [Sergei Kolosov, *Vyzyvaem ogon' na sebia* 1963–64],
based on the novel by Janusz Przymanowski and Ovidii Gorchakov and considered the granddaddy of Soviet television series, set the tone by portraying
a group of Soviet partisans who, together with Polish pilots, wreck havoc
in the German rear. This production was followed by Evgenii Tashkov's
Major Whirlwind [*Maior Vikhr'* 1967] and *His Highness's Aide* [*Ad'iutant ego
prevoskhoditel'stva* 1969], and the Polish *More than Life at Stake* (Andrzej
Konic 1967–68), all of them spy thrillers—the genre that dominated Soviet
television programs in the late 1960s–early 1970s.

[10] Alexei Yurchak, for example, argues that after Stalin's death Soviet discourse lost its "master voice" and, as a result, the performative function—
faithful reproduction of pre-existing formulae—became the dominant
one. Yet underneath the ideological conventions of official discourse there
flourished multiple alternative views and modes of behavior that, while not
openly oppositional, created a gap between the ideological "norm" and the
meanings "sliding in unanticipated directions." Alexei Yurchak, *Everything
Was Forever Until It Was No More: The Last Soviet Generation*, Princeton:
Princeton University Press, 2005, 53.

among 'them'" by necessity structured the narrative around the fulfillment of the mission, precluding anything spontaneous or facetious,
such as romance or humor.

In contrast, the characters of *Four Tank Men and a Dog* are
enlisted in the regular armed forces (Polish and Soviet). As members
of a tank crew, the central characters are constantly on the move. In
pioneering the unstable setting of the "roads of war" the series pre-
dates *MASH* (1972–83), which introduced an environment of a
war hospital as a makeshift home for characters. *Four Tank Men*
took the premise of a movable frontline home even further, carving
out domestic space without compromising war mythology.[11] In fact,
the series has two quasi-domestic spheres: the tank, which is the site
of male bonding; and the crew's road through Poland and towards
Berlin, which becomes the site of romance, flirting, and occasional
body contact—a sort of war-time "dating service," which provides
fleeting titillation without heavy melodramatic consequences. The
series offers its viewers a war mythology packaged as the adventure
of four boys in a tank. In other words, war mythology articulated predominantly by male characters in a public setting—the fulfillment of
the patriotic mission—is mediated through the discourse of everyday
pleasures. The latter is constructed through the mixed genre of the
series—a hybrid of war drama and adventure, with elements of the
proto-sitcom—and formulaic characters whose appeal lies in spontaneity and transparent motivations, *not* psychological depth or patriotic
zeal.[12]

This revolutionary form—a light and humorous treatment of
the war theme in a production epic in scope (twenty-one episodes) if
not in style—challenged the conventions of representing both World

---

[11] The narrative of a journey, episodic plot, and focus on male brotherhood
invoke the conventions of a road and buddy movie.

[12] It is this fear of formula that at least in part explains the cancellation of the
series in Poland and that often produces self-apologetic gestures by filmmakers and critics alike. The contributors to the otherwise insightful 1986
collection *Dialogi o mnogoseriinom fil'me*, for example, note quite accurately
that heroes of adventure series originate in fairy tales, whose protagonists
are invulnerable, yet immediately claim that the serialized format allows one
to balance narrative twists and turns with a profound exploration of character psychology. See Mashchenko and Morozov (1986), 62.

War II and gender relations in war films. To be sure, there is nothing transgressive in the series' gender representation. Men fight and make important decisions; women appear in the supporting roles of nurses, radio operators, traffic controllers, and, of course, heroes' girlfriends. Women's purportedly "essential" qualities—domesticity, passivity, dependence on men—are inevitably mediated by the war agenda. As men's military comrades, women in the series are by necessity assigned more active roles than those of faithful fiancées. In fact, within the context of what Ann Kaplan calls "liberal" feminist criticism, which analyzes TV programs in terms of the kinds and frequency of female roles (1997, 254), *Four Tank Men and a Dog* would fare as less sexist than most Western TV shows of the 1960s. But while Kaplan notes that in terms of *sex roles* the USSR and other Eastern block counties were ahead of Western cultures, she admits that social changes represented in Eastern European visual texts often merely naturalized the essentialist treatment of women (1997, 253).

Conversely, the cultural context of the film, in particular the conventions of representing gender, largely determines the reading of a particular text. It is within the conventions of both Eastern European and Soviet war film and television series that *Four Tank Men and a Dog* stands out. Roads of war in the series are the perfect setting for a game—a game of adventure and romance, a game in which mechanisms of gender construction are not hidden and naturalized, but are instead *laid bare*. The series' officially designated primary consumers were children and "younger audiences"[13] [Plate 4.1]—a move on the part of the filmmakers that motivated a lighter treatment of the subject, while at the same time turning the series into a playground of gender relations.

The rest of this article will explore the construction of gender in the series as it supports and redefines the war narrative. In particular, I focus on Laura Mulvey's concept of the "gaze" as it manifests itself in *Four Tank Men* and the role of symbolic objects and slapstick humor in

---

[13] A generation of Polish youth grew up watching and enacting the series, including school performances based on the production and the organization of "Tankmen Clubs." Available at http://www.klubpancernych.pl/ (last accessed 24 November 2008).

the construction of gender(ed) communities.[14] I argue that while these structures of meaning mark the series as firmly grounded within patriarchal and Soviet ideological discourse, the show's reception was influenced by its deviation from the norms of Eastern European war film, in particular in the intertwining of official war mythology with popular culture entertainment.

Playing War, Performing Gender Rituals

Four Tank Men and a Dog is a television adaptation of a novel by Janusz Przymanowski, a colonel in the Polish Army who participated in the liberation of Poland from the Nazi occupation. Written between 1964 and 1970, Przymanowski's novel is an example of "trench war prose." Its heroes are the low echelon of the Polish Army, who are patriots, but for whom friendship and love are equally important. There are no epic scenes or extended meetings at the Commander's HQ, but plenty of details of everyday life at the front. The present--tense narration creates a sense of immediacy, which is underscored by the dialogue-driven action and a shifting perspective (including the dog's point of view), with multiple parallel sequences. The black-and--white series underscores this low-key, spontaneous atmosphere. After the first episode, which introduces all the major characters apart from Marusia, the narrative proceeds in a loosely motivated sequence of episodes that follow the logic of alternating "combat" and "rest."

The abnormal nature of the war motivates the temporary suspension of conventional narrative expectations in favor of situational, episodic structure. This deviation from the norm is signaled from the very beginning through displacement and the travelogue form of the narrative. The series begins with the Pole Janek Kos as a

---

[14] Following Ann Kaplan's distinction, I use the term "look" to mean a "relation and a process implying desire to know and curiosity about the other" and the "gaze" to designate the "extreme anxiety and fears that preclude knowledge." See Kaplan (1997), xvi–xxi. I am grateful to Yana Hashamova for her suggestion to differentiate the "look" of the male characters—and perhaps the audiences—from the controlling "gaze" of socialist censorship on inter-gender relationships in the series.

very young man in his mid-teens hunting in the Ussuri region of the Soviet Union's Far East. Both he and his dog, Sharik, are orphans: Janek's father has been missing since the Nazi occupation of Poland, Sharik's mother was killed by a wild boar. Here Janek meets Georgii Saakashvili, a Georgian who works as a tractor driver. When the news of the formation of the Polish People's Army reaches Janek, he and Sharik decide to enlist. The pairing of double orphanhood and the youth of the characters with the topos of "a boy and a dog" had clear emotional benefits. The "boy and the dog" gained special promi-nence after the airing of the TV series *Lassie*, which premiered in 1954 and became one of the *very* few Western TV shows to be broad-cast, albeit with some delay, in Eastern Europe, including the USSR. Significantly, Sharik is not a Collie but a German Shepherd, the breed used by both Germans and Soviets in the camps and the dog of choice in Stalin-era films about heroic border guards. While Sharik is a heroic dog, his dominant characteristic is being *Janek's* dog. Janek's qualities essential for the show—his youth, cheerful nature, loyalty to his friends and romantic entanglements—are mirrored and doubled in Sharik. Just like the characters' youth,[15] the dog's presence from the start is critical for disarming characters in the series as well as members of the audience.

The first episode—Janek's encounter with a Polish girl (with the Russian-sounding name Lidka) on the train [Plate 4.2], the medical exam, and the assignment of new recruits—introduces humor, fast-paced dialogue, some flirting, but above all comic situations that offer relief from the serious business of war.[16] At the recruiting office, Janek and Sharik are joined by Gustlik, who by his own admission was forced to serve the Germans but immediately escaped to join the Soviet army. With the addition of Olgierd, a serious and level-headed former mete-orologist (whose prototype, according to an unverified but popular

---

[15] Apart from Olgierd, who functions as a surrogate father for the crew, the main characters are known by the diminutives of their names.

[16] These features were also typical of 1960s Soviet war comedy. For example, see Youngblood (2007), 146–7. However, in these films all narrative com-plications and misunderstandings were resolved within 90 minutes. It was unthinkable to have an extended television film that would treat the war as a romantic setting.

"background" story, was a Soviet soldier[17]), the tank crew is complete: a displaced Pole, a displaced Georgian, a former "collaborator" (who throughout the series uses his acquired knowledge of German to trick the enemy), a Polish intellectual, and a "Soviet-Polish" dog, Sharik.

The hybrid and unconventional nature of the tank crew is mirrored in the two main female characters: the radio operator, Lidka, is Polish and the nurse, Marusia, is Russian. Whereas this international environment, complete with the "Babel tower" of languages, can be seen as the Polish filmmakers' concession to the political pressures of demonstrating loyalty to the Soviet Big Brother, the fast-paced narrative and multi-lingual dialogue introduce playfulness and a certain degree of transgression into what otherwise seems a "straight" war drama. The formation of the tank crew imitates the competition of epic warriors, which is represented as a spectacle for, among others, "beautiful maidens." Each of the crew members excels in something. Janek[18] is an excellent shot; Gustlik—a former village blacksmith—possesses incredible physical strength; Georgii is an expert driver; and Olgierd can predict the weather. These are fairy-tale heroes, who survive against all odds.[19] As the youngest member of the crew, Janek gets a free pass on "undisciplined" actions that, of course, are explained by his noble desire to get to the front as soon as possible. When a traffic jam delays the tank, Janek has Sharik perform tricks in front of a group of soldiers and thus distract the young Russian girl who controls the traffic, allowing the tank to squeeze into the car line. In this playful atmosphere, motivated by the episodic structure and vagaries of war, romance is not only guilt-free, but also separated from domesticity and the necessity to settle down and start a family until the victory and the return to normal living conditions, i.e., traditional patriarchal structure.

---

[17] See, for instance, Svetlana Bozhko, http://www.day.kiev.ua/167602/ (last accessed 12 October 2008).
[18] The name Janek in Polish is analogous to Ivanushka in Russian: the diminutive of Ivan, who is the staple "youngest brother" character of fairy tales.
[19] Though the tank is always on the frontlines, four out of five original heroes—including the dog—survive until the end of the series. The commander Olgierd is killed and buried at the end of season one, yet at the end of the series Gustlik claims to have seen him alive in Berlin.

Look but Don't Touch:
Teen Love between Voyeurism and Socialist Internationalism

The extended format of the series and its narrative premise of traversing Poland and Germany allow characters to meet various types of female characters typical of a more conventional war narrative. Age is the clear and unambiguous watershed in this gallery of "types": older women fulfill traditional roles, from symbolic figures of suffering to surrogate mothers who discipline the young crew members. Secondary characters primarily contextualize the series' war theme, teaching their target audiences about the heroic and tragic Polish past. For example, in Germany, the heroes liberate the inmates of a concentration camp. Emaciated, prematurely aged young women have no strength to greet their liberators, but simply stare at them like zombies. Another archetype of womanhood is the *mater dolorosa*, a half-crazed mother wandering the streets in search of her little son, who disappeared a year ago. Finally, there are middle-aged women who, while they do not participate in the war directly, are ready to put up a good fight if necessary, using anything from a houseplant to a submachine gun. Together with the inhabitants of liberated Polish towns, who line up along the streets and greet the tank crew with flowers and food, these female images are a *sine qua non* of a World War II drama. In *Four Tank Men and a Dog*, however, these archetypal female figures accentuating the themes of sacrifice, suffering, and resistance are marginal to the narrative.

At the center of the inter-gender communication in the series are Lidka and Marusia, both in their late teens. Their love interest, Janek, is no older, his youth underscored by his blond hair, baby face, and, not least, his constant playing with the "Soviet-Polish" dog, Sharik. All three are good-looking, innocent, and inexperienced, and the relationships within this love triangle offer perfect fare for "younger audiences." The teenage love in its romantic, sanitized version provides plenty of visual pleasure but wards off rough masculinity, "adult" desires, or any suspicion of sexual "impropriety." While within the rules of a socialist (realist) production this sanitized version of gender relations can be construed as "infantilizing" its audiences, within the teenage playground of the series it is simply pleasurably infantile.

The vagaries of war provide an ideal context not only for the fragmented serial form of the narrative, but also for reconfigured romantic relationships. Janek has a fleeting romance with Lidka before meeting Marusia. Because he is responsible for radio communication, his "business" exchanges with Lidka at the HQ are interspersed with laughter and flirtatious comments. The series works out an elaborate strategy of passing the baton from Lidka to Marusia as Janek's sweetheart [Plate 4.3]. As the Polish Army offensive reaches the suburbs of Warsaw, Lidka asks the crew to take her in their tank to look for her old house. Such a maneuver violates military regulations, which explains why in his radio transmissions Janek refers to her simply as a "soldier." Later, when street fighting begins, Lidka replaces a wounded local boy, running next to the advancing tank and showing it the way. Thus, while she is portrayed in a heroic fashion, she is also consistently infantilized and her gender identity blurred. For much of the series Lidka is portrayed as an imp, cute but "boyish."

At the same time, unlike the Russian nurse, Lidka is unattached. While she pines for Janek, she also flirts with various male characters. The shifting pairing is hardly promiscuous because nothing in the screen world of the series suggests that the relationships are ever consummated. The desire is only hinted at, and more often than not associated with the fiery gaze of the Georgian member of the crew, Georgii/ Grześ. But here too, the suggestion of the sexual nature of his longing is dissolved into humor, for the series pokes fun at his inadequate command of Polish, social awkwardness, and the comical disjuncture between his "hot" southern temperament and the more reserved Polish girls.

Despite these evasive strategies, the two central female characters are represented as alluring figures who provide an erotic spectacle both for the male characters and for the viewers. When not engaged in military missions, they sport tight tunics and short skirts. Their representation offers a textbook example of Mulvey's argument. Even though Marusia takes initiative in approaching Janek and showing him her interest *and* she is dressed in a soldier's blouse and pants, she is constructed as an object of the male gaze. As she sits next to Janek in a trench—an improvised quasi-domestic space—the other crew members observe her, and when she gets up and walks away past the smiling men, her oversized military pants emphasize her girlishness. Janek joins his friends and, even though he disapproves of their winking, his excited eyes also follow Marusia. The eyeline match to Marusia, her back to the camera, identifies her as the object of the male gaze on all three "fronts": the male characters, the camera, and the viewer.[20]

In the romantic plot of the series, Marusia represents the pure love that survives hardships and separation, and is rewarded in the end with marriage. While she participates in a scouting mission together with the Russian troops and occasionally appears on the battlefield as a nurse, early on in the series Marusia's place is anchored as the faithful fiancée. She never fights alongside Janek. The few rendezvous they manage to snatch are either watched by other members of the crew or are interrupted by Germans.

During the first attempt at a private meeting Marusia is wounded while trying to warn Janek of a German sniper. The couple's first kiss and Marusia's love dance in the hospital garden are watched by Grigorii, whose gaze is again identified with the camera's and the viewer's point of view. His presence, however, is non-threatening: indeed, he is not hiding and pleads with the lucky couple to continue their love game because it serves as an acceptable voyeuristic spectacle. Marusia's body is not only constantly on display for the male gaze, but is also portrayed as an exotic spectacle. Janusz Przymanowski repeatedly refers to her fiery red hair and her "black eyebrows, arched like a Mongolian bow" (Vol. 1, 138). While Pola Raksa's appearance can hardly be described as Asian, her "love dance" in front of Janek is a lyrical version of the Georgian *lezginka*, which she performs for both Janek and Grigorii.

The only truly private episode and a scene that hints at passion is the characters' walk in the destroyed German *Kirche*. Janek's embrace and his difficulty at controlling himself scare Marusia, who initially says "no," but is drawn to him. At this moment the lovers are captured by German soldiers hiding in the church. The sexual energy of the scene is diffused and transferred onto the more contained fear of violence from the aggressor. This shift channels the libidinal energy into normalized fear for Marusia's life, but *not* her virginity: nowhere in the series is there any hint of rapes perpetrated either by the Germans

---

[20] Mulvey (2009), 711–22.

or by the Allies. Janek and Marusia are promptly rescued by the tank crew, which had come over to the church hoping to sneak a peek at the lucky lovers. Voyeurism thus functions not only as a healthy impulse during the war, but as a positive alternative to the dangers of *complete* privacy, away from the cheering team members.

Accordingly, Lidka's position by the radio at the command post is frequently visited by the crew members. While the bunker offers an illusion of privacy, it is also a perfect setting for eavesdropping and voyeurism. Janek, Grigorii, and Gustlik all stop by to catch a glimpse of the girl looking into the distance with longing, combing her hair, and singing. Lidka's singing offers the first of three full-fledged musical numbers in the series. In each case, the performer is a woman, framed in medium close-up. These "numbers" are narratively unmotivated (Marusia, for example, sings a song in Russian while crossing a field at the beginning of an attack), a pure spectacle of female passive "looked-at-ness" (Mulvey 2009, 720).

Many of the crew's "missions" are spontaneous and accidental, not part of an organized offensive. Lidka joins the crew on several of these forays, which often consist of capturing German houses and castles—sites that provide an illusion of private space. On one occasion, Grigorii and Lidka are captured by a German couple and tied up in a cellar. Sharik as usual comes to the rescue, chews through the ropes, but, as the two are escaping, their captors return. In the ensuing struggle, the German woman comes at Lidka with an axe. Even though Grigorii is pummeling his male opponent a few feet away, it is the girls' fight that captures the camera's attention: a catfight, complete with pulling hair, twisting bodies, and screaming. Later in the episode, as the characters explore the castle, the men see Lidka trying on an elegant dress she has found in a closet. The low-cut, see-through gown transforms the impish girl, and the men crowd at the door, fascinated by the spectacle. Grigorii then joins Lidka in a mock dance and subsequently on the sofa, where the two enact a ritualistic courtship. But when Lidka attempts to position herself "languidly," the camera reveals the inappropriate lower part of her outfit: military pants and boots protruding from under the "ethereal" feminine silk. Scenes such as these form a recurring motif in the series: potential sexual meaning is deflated via slapstick humor or danger from the Nazis, with the characters playing, rather than behaving like, adults.

The playfulness and the "situational," fragmented narrative weaken the teleology of the series but do not cancel it. Susan Jeffords argues that in war films scenes of violence produce visual excess, a spectacle that simultaneously disrupts the narrative and provides motivation for its reproduction, the resolution of the conflicts externalized in the violence (1997, 990–91). Likewise it can be argued that voyeuristic moments and playful romantic spectacle suspend and break the narrative continuity of the conventional war plot, while at the same time reinforcing the correct ideological reading, from the "proper" gender roles to the current political priorities. It is no accident that the two most problematic issues in the series—representation of Poland's bourgeois past and its relationship with the Soviet Union—are encoded through gender relations. In one of the episodes, the characters meet a Polish officer who spent five years in a German concentration camp. He is left alone with Lidka and Marusia, who are anxiously waiting for news from Janek, fighting a landing force from a German submarine. The officer is psychotic and paranoid. He is shaken by his prison experience and troubled by the fact that Russians are in commanding positions all over Poland, and when Lidka introduces Marusia as Janek's Russian fiancée he looks at Marusia with open suspicion and hostility.

To take his mind off depressing thoughts, the girls ask him about the pre-war life in Poland. The officer ends his story with a telling comment: "Pani, a man has to leave his sabre in the coat room before entering the ballroom, just as he leaves women at home when he goes off to war." "So, you don't think of us as women?" Lidka chimes in coquettishly. "War is a dirty, bloody business [...] Women should preserve their tender hearts and loving eyes, so that they can greet those returning under the home roof" (Przymanowski 2006, 473). Unlike Lidka, Marusia is serious: "It probably was like this in the past. But now there are no roofs. They're destroyed. Maybe you're right, and there are women like that, but Lidka and I... Why didn't I go with the [tank] crew? [...]"

This scene is one of the most politically ambiguous in the series, and it places the officer's "paranoia" about Russians and his traditionalist views on women in a broader, historicized perspective through the juxtaposition of the "old," bourgeois Poland and the "new," emerging socialist Poland. The re-channeling of both patriarchal ideology and political tension through romance (the girls only fight because they are in love) finds perfect resolution in the combat scene. Eventually the officer and the two girls replace the killed crew of a machine gun. The barrage of fire they produce helps the Allied forces to win the battle, but in the process the officer is badly wounded and disappears from the narrative.

Marusia's romance with Janek also confirms the Polish-Soviet common cause (that is, "socialist internationalism"),[21] which is cemented by their engagement and blessed first by Janek's father, who appears in the last episode of the first season like a *deus ex machina*, and then by Marusia's commanding officer. Here language is essential to linking the private and the public, romantic comedy and the war myth, Polish patriotism and the Soviet imperial agenda. The Russian Sergeant Chernousov, who serves as Marusia's surrogate father, asks Janek's father, "Is he yours?" "Mine." In answer to his return question, "Is she yours?" Janek's father hears the word "Ours." While the Russian Marusia is being betrothed to the son of a Polish *hero*, Janek is betrothed to a daughter of the Soviet *people*. We know that they will get married, but not until the war is over. Romance and its culmination in engagement or marriage is a key element in the satisfying resolution of narrative and ideological conflicts. The series thus never questions traditional women's roles or stereotypes of gender behavior, but it does redefine the limits of the permissible in a war narrative.

Domesticating the War: Bonding, Pet(ting), and Slapstick

Despite the narrative, visual, and ideological importance of heterosexual romance in the series, at the center of it is the male community and all the pleasures that such bonding offers: from sharing food, drinks, and smokes to the culture of jokes and the joy of seeing your

---

[21] After the events in Czechoslovakia, the Soviet leadership identified a threat to Moscow-defined "socialist norms" anywhere in Eastern Europe as a threat to the bloc's stability. Socialist integration, based on "common interests," was deepened and translated into common (i.e., Soviet-inspired) policies. National interests were explicitly subordinated to the welfare of the socialist community. The choice was "socialist internationalism" or military intervention. For more on this see Ouimet (2003).

buddies alive. Women in the series lack such a community. When
not engaged in war missions as men's comrades, they pine for men
or compete for their attention. Though friendly with Marusia, Lidka
secretly hopes that Marusia's romance with Janek will end together
with the war and Marusia will have to leave for Russia. When she
hears that the commander has given permission for Marusia to stay in
Poland she delays telling this news to Janek.

But the girls' role is made more prominent because it changes the
status quo, the *normal* life of the tank's crew. After all, the most stable
wartime home for the characters is their T-34 tank. The cult of the
war machine belongs, of course, to the modernist utopia. In the series,
however, the tank is both a fighting machine and a domesticated space,
a tool of war and an object of love. The family that resides in it consists
of the four male characters, complete with a pet—their dog, Sharik.
The potential of this scenario's homosocial associations—four men
squashed tightly into a narrow and hot space—is neutralized by the
filmmaker's ingenious decision. Even before Janek and Marusia declare
their love to each other, the crew decides to name their tank "Rudy"
("red-haired") in honor of the red-haired Marusia, nicknamed Ogonek
(the little light). The four male characters then ride through Poland
on their heroic mission under the protection of love and Soviet-made
steel. At the same time, the ritual of the naming of the tank is a peculiar display of male bonding via a symbolic female body (the tank) and
of repressed sexual desire.[22] After the tank is christened "Rudy" and
Gustlik writes the name on the side, members of the crew take turns
leaving their hand imprints on the armor [Plate 4.4]. This collective
"fondling" reestablishes male brotherhood while marking the tank as
the main "romantic" interest of the crew.[23]

Much of the series' emotion and humor come from the scenes
of quasi-domestic bliss and slapstick situations of the tank crew's
everyday life. Because the crew has moments of rest at unpredict-
able, random moments, usually after fierce fighting, neither Marusia
nor Lidka is there to serve in their traditional roles of caregivers. More

---

[22] See Sedgwick (1997), 478–86.
[23] Petr Buslov's criminal drama *Bummer* [*Bimmer* 2003] uses a similar narrative motivation for his story about 1990s Russia: a BMW is the transportation, the protection, the friend, and the symbol of male brotherhood.

often than not, a clearing in the wood, the tank's armor, and a captured house serve as an improvised "domestic space" where food provision is a communal, male business. When Olgierd is killed and the peasant son Tomasz joins the crew, he fulfills the role of a dutiful wife. He "requisitions" food from the Germans, salvages provisions even under extreme danger, and milks a cow virtually under fire. His peasant mentality is the butt of jokes by the other crew members, earning him an unfair reputation of a slow-witted country bumpkin. Yet in the absence of women for long stretches of the series, Tomasz's obstinate hoarding of provisions serves multiple functions: it satisfies socialist censors as a mild critique of petit-bourgeois mentality, provides comforting images of domesticity, and motivates slapstick humor.

The pattern of alternating combat and rest sequences provides a weak motivation for the narrative; hence entire episodes seem to "go nowhere" in terms of the war narrative. These are pure units of entertainment, driven by sitcom logic, visual jokes, and verbal puns. When the crew is stationed in a captured German castle, in the middle of the night Janek and Sharik discover a wine cellar where *both of them* get drunk. The viewer is treated to a subjective shot, where Janek sees three dogs happily prancing in front of him. Janek's comment, "Well, that's enough. A soldier shouldn't see triple dogs," treats war mythology as slapstick material. After Janek finally goes to bed, the other male characters in turn look longingly at what seems to be the door leading to the cellar, suggesting that they too would like to sneak away and taste the wine. Yet in the morning the viewers discover that behind the door is the bedroom occupied by Lidka who, moreover, has barricaded herself in. Bodily pleasures (sex and alcohol) are both invoked in this episode, but as a culturally acceptable one, alcohol consumption is treated explicitly, while sexual desire is reduced to a gag.

The series is explicit in showcasing masculinity via visual jokes. During one of the battles the tank's barrel is damaged. As a temporary solution, a mechanic saws off a large chunk of it. This castration procedure plunges the crew into a veritable depression, especially amidst the girls' ironic sympathy, until the colonel takes pity on the crew and moves them to a new tank with a regulation-size barrel. Combat sequences in particular make visible the crew's masculine qualities with an excess that metaphorizes both the heroic and the sexual: long shells are pushed into the tank's canon in extended sequences that suspend the narrative. Among other phallic jokes is a large pickle, which Janek solemnly hands over to a local girl at a party; a sabre Grigorii finds in an aristocratic German house and uses to impress girls; and a long-barreled Mauser that a Russian sergeant gives to the badly wounded Janek in the hospital [Plate 4.5].

By the end of the third season Gustlik finds his perfect woman, Honorata. She is a little older than the two other girls, and their romance, while often slapstick in nature (for example, in trying to follow the tank Honorata clings to the armor, and Gustlik has trouble "detaching" her from it), is also more sexually explicit. When Gustlik first meets Honorata in Germany she offers to show the crew the strategic road to the bridge. In response to Gustlik's playful comment, "Pani Honorata will *show* Gustlik?" Honorata chimes in, "She'll show him *the bridge*." Later on, when the two are alone, Honorata makes Gustlik jealous by speaking in puzzles about the soldiers who visited her earlier: "I told them I would give them what has been hidden and what will make them happy." While Gustlik first interprets this tirade as Honorata's "promiscuity," she is in fact referring to the German baron and his wife whom she locked in a cellar and delivered to the Polish soldiers. As they escape from the Germans who show up at the castle, Gustlik and Honorata drive away in the Baron's car, Gustlik dressed as a German general and Honorata holding on to the china she "confiscated" from the Germans [Plate 4.6]. The dowry in place, the only thing missing is an engagement ring, which magically appears in the form of a bolt from the tank.

But the most important and flexible symbolic object is the crew's dog, Sharik. At the beginning of the narrative, the bond between Janek and the dog marks the series as both a traditional 1960s narrative of orphanhood and renewal, and a socialist realist story of a man's maturation in the process of fulfilling a patriotic mission. Very quickly, however, the dog's functions are expanded. In the action sequences Sharik fulfills the role of a messenger. When unable to reach the commanding post or supporting artillery on time, the crew sends the dog with instructions. More often than not, this communication line links Marusia, Janek, and Lidka, and thus the war and the romance subplots. For example, when Marusia's unit captures a remote German bunker they run the risk of becoming victims of "friendly fire." Marusia puts a note in Sharik's collar and tells him to find Janek.

In the romantic subplot, the dog's faithfulness comments on the relationship between Marusia and Janek. In the hospital scene, as Janek lies in bed, bandaged from neck to toe and resembling a living statue, the camera alternates between Sharik under the bed and Marusia-the-nurse sitting on the floor next to him. Marusia pleads with the doctor to allow Sharik to stay in the room with his wounded master, thus partaking of the dog's aura of loyalty. The dog also rescues characters in trouble, often in a situation when danger from Germans is a punishment for the couples' attempts to be alone, as with Janek and Marusia in the *Kirche* and Lidka and Grigorii in the German castle. The "Sharik as Lassie" paradigm consistently underscores the adolescent nature of the series' characters [Plate 4.7].

The two other, more "adult" roles Sharik fulfills are central to the landscape of an erotic playground, which he makes visible. On the one hand, in the absence of rough masculinity in the series, the friendly German Shepherd externalizes all the suppressed sexual drives that the male characters themselves cannot show. On the other hand, the dog serves as a perfect substitute object for physical contact. The last shot of the first season, which ends with Janek and Marusia's engagement, shows the two of them playing with the dog on the seashore—an acceptable metaphor for lovemaking. Sharik is the ultimate symbolic go-between, a liaison between men and women, war and love, ideology and entertainment.

Growing Up, Settling Down

Games do eventually come to an end. In the Polish series, the closure is signaled by the end of the war narrative and the German surrender in Berlin. At the end of the series the crew is joined by a Russian officer, a sapper called Ivan Pavlov, whose job is to dispose of explosives threatening to destroy a German town. His death at the hands of a lonely Nazi youth after the German surrender marks a return to ideological rigidity. First, the ending underscores *Soviet* suffering and *Soviet* wartime heroism as the foundation of liberated Europe. Second, this death is the final rite of passage from adolescence to adulthood for Janek: in despair, he throws Ivan's gun to the ground, but picks it up again when Gustlik tells him, "You've got no right to do that until everybody in the world drop his weapons." Third, Pavlov's death also reestablishes a normalized patriarchal structure. Right before he dies he shows the admiring crew members a picture of his wife in Siberia (who, of course, is faithfully waiting for him) and his two sons. Even though Pavlov is no older than the protagonists he has the dual authority of fatherhood and Russianness. All these meanings find their expression in the legendary "Blue Kerchief"[24] melody that plays in the background of the scene.

The end of *Four Tank Men and a Dog* collapses socialist and patriarchal ideology in a closure that bears more resemblance to Ivan Pyr'ev's kolkhoz musicals than to the preceding narrative. The viewer is abruptly transported into the near future of the socialist realist idyllic countryside, with troika rides, choir folk songs, and characters dressed in folk costumes. The former petit bourgeois suspect Pan Czereśniak ("Mr. Cherry," Tomasz's father) is discussing the new life at the collective farm, while the brides—Marusia and Honorata—are permanently attached to their men's sides. Lidka, who follows the happy couples with envious eyes, gets her wish fulfilled too. Grigorii asks her to marry him and she promises to follow him to Georgia—a radical departure from her previous repeated rejection of the Georgian's advances. The scriptwriter Przymanowski appears in the last scene as the photographer who takes a collective picture of the heroes and their faithful playmates.

Despite this socialist realist conclusion, which strives to resolve all conflicts in a vision of the bright future, *Four Tank Men and a Dog* is an unconventional war series. Its transitional nature manifests itself in the compromise and tension between the official war mythology, with its traditional gender roles, and an entertainment text, with a mixed genre and humorous, playful characters. Within the fragmented, episodic narrative structure of the series, even the traditional romance fulfills

---

[24] "The Blue Kerchief" is a Soviet World War II song made famous by Klavdiia Shul'zhenko's performance. In the series, the melody is played without the lyrics. This gesture would have a different meaning for different audiences. On the one hand, the song's tremendous popularity immediately evokes the theme of a faithful girl waiting for her hero, who is "firing his machine gun," defending "the blue kerchief." On the other hand, less well known is the fact that the song used the original melody by a popular Polish composer, Jerzy Petersburski.

the function of destalinization, giving its audiences a story of war that is both human and inspiring.

It is no accident that the heroes of the series became part of both children's and adult popular culture [Plates 4.8, 4.9]. Aleksei Erokhin's commentary in *Seans* not only identifies the entertainment potential of the "war-cum-love" plot, but also accurately points out the adolescent scenario into which *Four Tank Men and a Dog* encodes this male rite of passage. Since the collapse of communism, Russia and other Eastern European countries have gone through several waves of nostalgia—or *Ostalgie*—for things socialist. Material culture, as well as shared ideas, words, and images serve as signifiers of the imaginary "paradise lost" of the "common past." As the writer of this article herself can attest, no amount of historical knowledge and critical analysis can completely erase the comforting memories from one's late-Soviet childhood—the time of literal and ideological infantilism. And it matters little that Erokhin's comment constructs the audience for the memories—and the series—as exclusively male. For the rest of us, there is always Sharik, a Soviet-Polish mediator between men's war and women's romance.

REFERENCES

Bozhko, Svetlana. No date. "*Chetyre tankista i sobaka:* vzgliad cherez chetyre desiatiletiia." http://www.day.kiev.ua/167602/ (last accessed 9 March 2009).

Czterei pancerni i pies. 1996. Directed by Konrad Nałęncki and Andrzej Czekalsi. 21 episodes, 3 seasons, 1966, 1969–70.

Dostanko, Nikolai and Aza Plavnik. 1974. *Mnogolikii ekran: televidenie sotsialisticheskikh stran*. Minsk: Isdatel'stvo BGU im. Lenina.

Erokhin, Aleksei. 1993. "Chetyre tankista i sobaka." *Seans* 7 (October). http://seance.ru/n/7/chetyire-tankista-isobaka/ (last accessed 18 August 2008).

Haltof, Marek. 2002. *Polish National Cinema*. New York: Berghahn Books.

Jeffords, Susan. 1997. "Masculinity as Excess in Vietnam Films: the Father/Son Dynamic of American Culture." In *Feminisms: An Anthology of Literary Theory and Criticism*, edited by Robyn R. Warhol and Diane Price Herndl, 988–1010. New Brunswick, NJ: Rutgers University Press.

Kaplan, Ann E. 1997. *Looking for the Other: Feminism, Film and the Imperial Gaze*. New York: Routledge.

———. 1992. "Feminist Criticism and Television." In *Channels of Discourse, Reassembled: Television and Contemporary Criticism*, edited by Robert C. Allen, 2nd edition, 247–83. Chapel Hill: University of North Carolina Press.

Mashchenko, N.P., and Iu. Z. Morozov. 1986. *Dialogi o mnogoseriinom tele-fil'me.* Kiev: Mistetstvo.

Mulvey, Laura. 2009. "Visual Pleasure and Narrative Cinema." In *Film Theory and Criticism*, edited by Leo Braudy and Marshall Cohen, 7th edition, 711–22. New York: Oxford University Press.

Ouimet, Matthew J. 2003. *The Rise and Fall of the Brezhnev Doctrine in Soviet Foreign Police.* Chapel Hill: University of North Carolina Press.

"Poliakam bol'she ne pokazhut chetyrekh tankistov i sobaku." No date. http://www.lenta.ru/news/2006/08/07/zapret/ (last accessed November 2007).

Przymanowski, Janusz. 2006. *Chetyre tankista i sobaka.* Vols. 1 and 2. Moscow: Veche.

Sedgwick, Eve Kosofsky. 1997. "Gender Assymetry and Erotic Triangles." In *Feminisms: An Anthology of Literary Theory and Criticism*, edited by Robyn R. Warhol and Diane Price Herndl, 478–86. New Brunswick, NJ: Rutgers University Press.

Youngblood, Denise J. 2007. *Russian War Films: On the Cinema Front, 1914–2005.* Lawrence, KS: University Press of Kansas.

Literature, Graphics, Song

CHAPTER 5

Rage in the City of Hunger: Body, Talk, and the Politics of Womanliness in Lidia Ginzburg's *Notes from the Siege of Leningrad*

Irina Sandomirskaja

Narratives of the Leningrad siege rarely afford the city's civilian women the right to be enraged. In official histories, largely preoccupied as they are with the military and macro-political aspects of the siege, the lives of civilians serve as statistical material; their deaths are justified by the deplorable but unavoidable realities of war; and their individual destinies are deemed insignificant in comparison with the epic dimensions of war's tragic circumstances.[1] These narrative strategies abuse memories of the siege and disempower the civilian by divesting her of her ability (albeit minimal) to act as a responsible political and historical subject. Only recently have the voices of women in besiegement started to be acknowledged not only as a testament of insufferable privation but also as a valuable historical source (Simmons and Perlina 2005).

Evidence of rage rarely seeps into the controlled and (self-)censured narrative of what John Barber once referred to as "the betrayal of Leningrad" (Barber). This restraint may be attributed partly to the attitude of the memoirists themselves, their usually reserved emotional stance, their respect for the defence of Leningrad, the city's "unparalleled common cause"[2] of suffering, resistance, and restoration, and

---

[1] Demographic statistics of the siege, as well as the pre-war rates of population movement, were classified in the USSR. However, the opening of the archives after the fall of the Soviet regime has not made the picture clearer owing to lack of consequence in statistic records (Cherepenina 2001).

[2] "Besprimernoe obshchee delo," Ginzburg 2002, 185.

their unwillingness to bear witness to "the negative side." The survivors' own language is protective toward the history of the siege, and their speech often seems indistinguishable from the official discourse, since "it is only in the language of war that the language of the people for a moment merges with that of the newspaper" (Ginzburg 1995, 56).[3]

One can believe that rage also fuelled Lidia Ginzburg's project of writing in and about besiegement—a passion she never confesses to, preferring to discuss the more ethically transparent categories of guilt and remorse. Still, rage seems to transfuse the ice-cold, sharply penetrating and pitilessly analytical mode of her writing, which portrays the works and days of her fellow women under siege in philosophical fragments, Kafkaesque mini-novellas from Leningrad's everyday life, and Beckettian absurdist dialogues. Ginzburg's characters operate in an extraordinary situation: hundreds of thousands of civilians are exterminated, and decades-long (self-)censorship—during and after the siege—dominates the expression and working-through of the trauma.[4] Body and language in the City of Hunger find themselves under the triple pressure of (a) military law—the draconian biopolitical measures taken against the population for the sake of total mobilization; (b) unprecedented mass famine as a result of these measures; and (c) radical intensification of internal policing as a security precaution against the citizens, through total surveillance and police violence (Lomagin 2001; Lomagin 2005, 155–439).

---

[3] "Tol'ko v iazyke voiny narodnoe na mgnovenie sblizhaetsia c gazetnym," Ginzburg 2002, 645. Unless otherwise stated, quotations from Ginzburg refer to the English translation of part of her siege notebooks in Ginzburg 1995, but slightly modified.

[4] A possible effect of suppressing strong negative emotions, abnormally high blood pressure—the so-called "*leningradskaia gipertoniia*"—was a typical disease among siege survivors. It is explained by present-day medical research as caused by stress (Simonenko et al. 2003, 115–24; Magaeva 2001, 166–9). The lack of psychoanalytic data does not allow one to explain the stress itself. The latter might be hypothetically understood, among other factors, as the result of the suppression by self-censorship of internally devastating anger.

Body Desexed by Hunger and Regendered by Medical Research

With speech stifled and acts of self-rescue criminalized (Belozerov 2001), rage seems to have acted itself out in the body of the patient afflicted by alimentary dystrophy—Leningrad's own terminological invention to euphemize the protracted and almost complete starvation during the siege.[5] Life itself becomes a burden for an organism struggling to survive hunger, frost, air raids, and hard work. Sex, among other things, is a luxury that the body cannot afford and needs to get rid of in order to reduce the expenditure of energy needed for survival. The functions of the body become extinguished one by one, like burning candles in the wind, and the sex organs are the first to be sacrificed for the sake of survival. What remains is necessary for the preservation of life, not for its continuation. Physiologists compare the condition of the organism under prolonged and profound starvation to that of hibernation in animals: seeking to survive, life reduces itself to *vita minima* (M. V. Chernorutskii's term).[6] Yet hibernation is a mechanism of adaptation in animals, whereas in humans *vita minima* means dying: one cannot adapt to protracted hunger (Simonenko et al. 2003, 46).

---

[5] The term was invented by medical research in Leningrad and widely used as a diagnostic euphemism for death from starvation and hard labor in the Gulag. Military doctors who observed similar pathologies among the starved personnel of the Red Army suggested another term, alimentary cachexia (*alimentarnoe istoshcheniie*), which was more ambiguous as to the cause of the disease: absence of nourishment (Greek *trophe*, food). Chernorutskii (1947, 10) mentions that previously, starvation disease (*golodnaia bolezn'*) lacked nomenclature and had been denoted alternatively as nutritional edema, edemic disease (Ödemkrankheit, *otechnaia bolezn'*), hungry edema (*golodnyi otek*), epidemic edema (*epidemicheskii otek*), military edema (*voennyi otek*), and so on. Professor Mikhail Vasil'evich Chernorutskii (1884–1954) was responsible for the organization of medical service and medical research inside the besieged city. *Alimentarnaia distrofiia v blokirovannom Leningrade* (Chernorutskii), a compilation of his and other Leningrad doctors' contributions, was published in 1947 and contains observations and statistics obtained inside the siege.

[6] On the physiological understanding of the body in terms of consumption and waste of energy, see Magaeva 2001.

Figure 5.1. Three photographs of the Leningrad resident Sof'ia Nikolaevna Petrova, from the 1930s, May 1942, and October 1942. Jahn, Peter (Hrsg.). Blockade Leningrads 1941-1944. Dossiers / Blokada Leningrada 1941-1944. Dos'ie. Austellungskatalog, Deutsch-Russisches Museum Berlin-Karlhorst. Berlin: Christoph Links-Verlag, 2004.

With severe starvation understood as medical pathology, the diagnosis of alimentary dystrophy allowed medical doctors to consider the tragedy of Leningrad, its despair and rage in strictly biodeterministic terms, reducing the effects of starvation on sex and gender to pure endocrinology. According to Leningrad's doctors, starvation induced the dystrophy of sex organs in both men and women. First, they shrivelled, as did all other organs in the body, and with time, reproductive system dysfunction was further complicated as hunger attacked the production of male and female hormones. Officially, the first case of alimentary dystrophy was diagnosed and registered in November 1941 in a forty-year-old female patient.[7] Women, however, had begun to stop menstruating as early as August–September. Amenorrhea became a complaint on a massive scale in November, while by December it affected "almost all women" (Chernorutskii 1947, 196). Under the pressure of hunger, breastfeeding mothers stop lactating (Chernorutskii 1947, 238–9). In other words, the female body readied to endure the catastrophe by abandoning its traditional gendered biological function—that of a procreating female human being. [Figure 5.1]

---

[7] Chernorutskii 1947, 194. Incidentally, the first act of cannibalism registered in the classified reports of the NKVD was performed by a woman: a mother, the widow of a Red Army officer, killed her baby in order to feed her three older children. The case was reported in November 1941 (Lomagin 2001, 169).

Some women, though very few, did get pregnant, gestate, and give birth even during the worst winter, of 1941–42.[8] However, theirs seems to have been an unwilling motherhood, the female body expelling the being inside it so as not to expend more effort on anything other than its own preservation. Obstetricians registered a steep growth of premature births, up to 70 percent (Chernorutskii 1947, 357–8). Pregnant women developed an unusually high risk of eclampsia, a combination of hypertension and internal intoxication. The hungry body in gestation developed toxins and cramps, poisoning the child to evict it from the womb.

Leningrad's pediatricians also witnessed the collapse of sexuality and procreation in starved children, as the sexes became biologically undifferentiated, "a certain infantility" combined "with a somewhat senile, withered look in the patient," the growth of external sex organs considerably delayed, sometimes reversed (Chernorutskii 1947, 253).

Being a woman or man became meaningful exclusively in relation to matters of death: medical personnel recorded women dying a death different from that of men. The first victims of the siege were reported to have been "males, adults as well as adolescents, especially those with an asthenic constitution (Chernorutskii 1947, 196). The peak of male death from starvation was registered in the middle of December 1941. Women, it seems, developed critical stages of starvation much later, only by February 1942, after which they practically replaced men in the population of Leningrad's hospitals. During the first, fall/winter/spring period, marked by massive male death, the practice of releasing convalescents from hospitals was almost discontinued, indicating total lethality (Cherepenina 2001, 59). Leningrad medical research and statistics also identified three principal scenarios of death from starvation, and here some sexual differentiation also was observed—even though never made sense of. These were: (a) slow death, with bodily functions becoming extinguished one by one over the course of several days (with women dying more often than men); (b) accelerated death due to complications such as pneumonia (more men than women); and (c) a sudden death amidst "generally benign circumstances," i.e., without the onset of any lethal stage of starvation

---

[8] See a table of birth rates in Cherepenina 2001, 75.

at all (a category dominated by men) (Cherepenina 2001, 195). Why fewer women belonged to this last category—of "death from fear"—remained unexplained.[9] Medical statistics invariably seem to suggest that men were in greater danger and accordingly in greater need of emergency medical assistance.[10]

Male lethality was indeed considerably higher than female (Cherepenina 2001, 59–60), but there is another reason that men figure so heavily in the medical research of the time, whereas women appear only in statistics. As evident from Chernorutskii's survey of previous research, medical investigations of starvation had been conducted in connection with war and therefore concentrated on patients in homosocial male communities. As early as the eighteenth and nineteenth centuries, doctors were already describing starvation as "a peculiar disease with edemas" (Chernorutskii 1947, 9), for they noticed

---

[9] On "death from fear of death" (resulting from unidentified "emotional factors" and a "psychogenous" paralysis of regulation), see Magaeva 2001, 160, 162–3.

[10] For death rates by sexes, see Cherepenina 2001, 58; since males made up a third of the city's population, male lethality must be considered even higher than indicated in the table. As Cherepenina quotes from a private letter, "men and teenage boys have almost all died out; there are only women left" (Ibid., 57). Because of the disastrous figures of human loss, starting with the third quarter of 1941 until May 1943, Leningrad's demographic statistics were excluded from the all-Union Goskomstat records (Ibid., 66). According to the mini-census in summer 1942 (conducted for the sake of security rather than out of interest in the condition of the civilians), the population had shrunk to a quarter of its size in comparison with the 1939 census (which had included population movement resulting from evacuation and conscription). The number of men decreased sevenfold, women threefold, leading to a severe disturbance in the balance between the sexes (291 women per 100 men). For these and other vital population statistics, see Ibid., 73. It should be added that the central authorities discredited the possibility of such a catastrophic "natural movement" and blamed doctors for the horrifying figures of civilian fatalities. In May 1942, the city authorities demanded that hospitals work harder to reduce lethality "approximately eight times, if not more" (Ibid., 64). Chernorutskii mentions a visit by a representative of central medical authorities from Moscow who disbelieved that so many Leningraders were lethally ill until he saw what was happening in hospitals with his own eyes. His initial skepticism suggests that Moscow viewed Leningrad's civilians not only as potential traitors and hunger rioters, but also as malingerers.

how soldiers' bodies became swollen during long and trying campaigns. However, it was only when medical research went to internment and concentration camps for prisoners of war (first during the Anglo-Boer war in 1902) that the "peculiar disease" was diagnosed as a result of severe and prolonged starvation.[11] The Leningrad doctors' more pronounced interest in males accorded both with the tradition of medical knowledge and with the authorities' apparently greater investment in the survival of men, who were considered more valuable—whether as cannon fodder or as managers—for the purposes of resisting the siege. Men did indeed succumb first and in much higher percentages, but their rescue was also given priority, while women were apparently credited with greater ability to recover through their own "natural" resources. This form of sexual discrimination vis-à-vis survival was a biopolitically—scientifically, discursively, and administratively—engineered situation. Under the pressure of the military necessities of the siege, the sacrifice of women stemmed from the way the authorities coped with the situation. They relied heavily on bureaucratic routines to organize the population and on the use of expert knowledge—in the spheres of medical physiology and statistics discussed above—or of classified information about the population contained in NKVD reports (Lomagin 2001).

Administering *Vita Minima*

According to Ginzburg's notes, competition for survival took place almost exclusively among women, who also were responsible for the bureaucratic management of the dying city and occupied the lowest levels of the administrative pyramid. Women were in control of other women's lives, which they manipulated in their capacities as secretaries, saleswomen in food stores, and cooks in canteens. Women in petty administrative positions enjoyed both sanctioned and unsanctioned privileges, either by receiving a better ration or by stealing what they were

---

[11] See Chernorutskii's survey of predominantly German literature covering medical research on starvation between 1915 and 1935 (Chernorutskii 1947, 9–35).

appointed to distribute.[12] Female secretaries in the bureaucracy were representatives and agents on behalf of "hungry death" (*golodnaia smert'*):

> ... a sadistic type quite widespread among the administrative personnel [...] is the malicious secretary [...]. If she is placed where people who have lost their ration books need to go, she talks to them in a loud voice with the studied tone of rejection, gently restraining her administrative triumph. Then there is the languid secretary, with beautiful, heavily made-up eyes, not yet dressed siege-fashion. She is preoccupied with her own thoughts. She regards you without malice, her only desire to rid herself of distractions, and she rejects you lazily, even a little plaintively (complaining about distraction). There is, finally, the businesslike woman. [...] These savour their own efficiency, to the boundless irritation of those around them. [...] If the malicious secretary finds her work a source of power-loving enjoyment, if for the languid secretary work is a necessary concession to reality, the businesslike woman prizes the official process itself. She turns you down majestically, but circumstantially, with sermonizing and reasons. (Ginzburg 1995, 82)[13]

---

[12] On the popular "dissatisfaction with the work of canteens and food stores," on embezzlement, theft, and speculation as these are reflected in the NKVD files, see, e.g., Lomagin 2001, 246. A simple experiment was conducted privately during the winter 1941/42 to assess the actual amount of cereal in a portion of soup obtained in a canteen. Upon evaporation, the content of cereals proved 8.1 gram against the declared norm of 25 grams. The disappearance from the soup of over 60 percent of its nourishing matter gives one an approximate idea of the inefficiency of centralized control, on the one hand, and of the scale on which goods freely circulated in a city that was dying of starvation. See Cherepenina 2001, 56–7.

[13] "[...D]ovol'no rasprostranennyi sredi administrativnogo personala sadististichestkki tip. Eto zlaia sekretarsha. [...] Esli ee posadili tuday, kuda khodiat liudi, poteriavshie kartochki, ona govorit s nimi gromkin golosom s razrabotannymi intonatsiiami otkaza, slegka sderzhivaia administrativnoe torzhestvo. Est' tomnaia sekretarsha, eshche ne po-blokadnomu odetaia, s krasivymi, eshche zhirno podvenennymi glazami. Eta zaniata svoimi lichnymi voobrazheniiami. Ona smotrit na cheloveka bezzlobno, s edinstvennym zhelaniem poskoree otdelat'sia ot pomekhi, i otkazyvaet lenivo, dazhe neskol'ko zhalobno. [...] Est', nakonets, delovaia zhenshchina. [...] Oni perezhivaiut svoiu delovitost', vyzyvaia etim neuderzhimoe raz-

To escape the terror of the deadly secretaries, the besieged subjects worked hard to create difference. They "grab, hurriedly and greedily, at any marks, at anything that could distinguish and protect them" (Ginzburg 2002, 174).[14] Difference meant power, power meant status, status meant more food and in general a "normal life." It was therefore primarily food around which the games of power—competition for (often merely imagined but desperately sought for) marks of selectivity—were played between the more privileged and the less privileged women. Fully aware that no *essential* difference existed between them, they vigorously and viciously sought to construct a *symbolic* one:

> [I]n the writers' canteen there is a second room, for *ratsionshchiki* [convalescing dystrophic patients, non-writers assigned to receive food at the writers' canteen–I.S.], common women (*baby*) who are given a different ration. [...] While the lower room feels unconcealed envy and anger towards the one above [...], the latter treats the lower room with open spite. [...] "Short of rolls, again. I see. It's the usual story. *Ratsionshchiki* get everything first, we get things last. [...] [in response to an angry *ratsionshchitsa*]: If you don't like it here, who's keeping you from finding another canteen to be assigned to? We'll be only too happy, the fewer the better [...] This canteen is for writers." (Ginzburg 2002, 175)[15]

---

drazhenie okruzhaiushchikh. [...] Esli zlaia sekretarsha nakhodit v sluzhbe istochnik vlastoliubivykh udovol'stvii, esli dlia tomnoi sekretarshi sluzhba— neobkhodimaia ustupka deistvitel'nosti, to delovaia zhenshchina tsenit samyi sluzhebnyi protsess. Ona otkazyvaet velichestvenno, no obstoiatel'no, s poucheniiami i rezonami" (Ginzburg 2002, 726).

[14] "... toroplivo, zhadno khvataiutsia za vse znaki razlichiia, za vse, chto teper' dolzhno ikh vydelit', ogradit'..." (Ginzburg 2002, 174).

[15] "V pisatel'skoi stolovoi imeetsia vtoroi zal, dlia ratsionshchikov, dlia bab, kotorye poluchaiut *drugoe*. [..E]sli nizshii zal ispytyvaet k vysshemu neskryvaemye chuvstva zavisti i zloby [...], to vysshii otnositsia k nizshemu s neskryvaemym nedobrozhelatel'stvom [...] "Opiat' nekhvatilo bulochek. Poniatno, obychnaia istoriia, snachala vse ratsionshchikam, potom nam [...] Esli vam ne nravitsia, kto vam meshaet prikrepit'sia k drugoi stolovoi. Pozhaluista. My tol'ko rady budem, chem men'she, tem luchshe [...]." Eto stolovaia pisatel'skaia. (Emphasis by Ginzburg; translation mine–I.S.) (Ginzburg 2002, 175).

Gender in a Surrogate Social World: Conversations

As a by-product of such administration, transparent to the state and subject to manipulation in the most vital spheres of human existence, there emerges the subject of the siege, whom Ginzburg calls *blokadnyi chelovek*, the besieged human being. Her famished body becomes a mere envelope, a container for the bones and the residue of vital body organs—the remains of the brain, the heart, the kidneys—a bag of skin preserving an almost extinguished *vita minima* inside it. In addition, the self-identity of such a living envelope is reduced to an all-pervasive sense of internal emptiness. "Inside such a human, there is no longer anything left—neither love, nor pity, nor pride, nor even jealousy. By force of the habit of memory, he has a refined understanding of this and therefore is capable of feigning all these very well..." (Ginzburg 2002, 186).[16] Once an individual vested with multiple roles, identities, and responsibilities, a subject whose existence had been tightly interwoven with other lives (in the family, in a profession, and in citizenship) through a complex system of social relationships, the human in besiegement is totally and irreversibly alone, all connections having been severed under the blows of hunger, cold, and fear.

Whereas Leningrad doctors are overwhelmed by their inability to read sexual identities from the bodies of starved men, women, and children, and invent new criteria for differentiation (pathology development, type of death and lethality, body fat, hormones, and enigmatic "nervous-psychological factors"), the subject of the everyday life of the siege—with its unending hunt for food and the repeated hour-long queuing in the dark winter frost for a scanty ration doled out in food lines—knows the difference perfectly: those who stand in line and patiently wait for their turn to receive their 200–400 grams of bread are women. Those who sneak in, bypassing the long queue yet receiving their portion first, are men:

---

[16] "V cheloveke etom uzhe net nichego—ni liubvi, ni zhalosti, ni gordosti, ni dazhe revnosti. Po staroi pamiati on vse eto tonko ponimaet i potomu mozhet khorosho izobrazhat'..." (Translation mine–I.S.))Ginzburg 2002, 186).

Men cannot explain from where this feeling of inner rightness comes, despite the outward unfairness of their action. But one thing they do know: a queue is woman's business (*bab'e delo*). Perhaps they have a vague inkling that the justice of their claims rests on the fact that there are so few of them in the queue [...] [I]nwardly, he knows that even if she [the woman in the queue] works as much as he does, or even more, their relationship to time, its value, use, and allocation is different. And this relationship gives him the right to get bread without queuing for it. The shop girl, not being involved, understands this and normally encourages the men's claims. (Ginzburg 1995, 39)[17]

Such gender-marked behavior came as no surprise to Soviet working women such as Ginzburg, who had already learnt the politics of women's emancipation under Stalin. Soviet gender distinctions rested less on sexuality or work invested in production as opposed to reproduction than on a fundamental contrast with respect to the category of time and value:

Men cope particularly badly with queues, since they are used to the idea that their time is valuable. [...] Working women inherited from their grandmothers and mothers time which is not taken into account. [...] A man considers that after work he is entitled to rest or amuse himself; when a working woman comes home, she works at home. The siege queues were inscribed into an age-old background of things being issued or available, into the habitual irritation and the habitual female patience. (Ginzburg 1995, 39)

This "atavism" (Ginzburg 2002, 634), the age-old state of things, "normalized" by custom despite the official rhetoric of respect for woman and equality, results in the no less habitual definition of gender not as

---

[17] "Osobenno plokho perenosiat ochered' muzhchiny, privykshie k tomu, chto ikh vremia otsenivaetsia. [...] Rabotaiushchie zhenshchiny unasledovali ot svoikh babok i materei vremia, kotoroe ne uchityaetsia. [...] Muzhchina schitaet, chto posle raboty on dolzhen otdykhat' ili razvlekat'sia; vernuvshaiasia s raboty zhenshchina rabotaet doma. Blokadnye ocheredi vpisalis' v mnogoletnii fon vydavaemogo, dostavaemogo, v privychnuiu razdrazhitel'nost' i privychnoe zhenskoe terpenie" (Ginzburg 2002, 634).

an opposition of male versus female, but as an opposition of *muzhskoe* versus *bab'ie*. This opposition does not demarcate sexes but denotes differences of class, education, status, and values. To the working woman of the siege, these formulations were all too familiar from the comparatively well-fed existence of the pre-war era. Taking care of survival, procuring and cooking food, were treated with contempt as common women's occupations and games (*bab'i dela, bab'i igry*; Ginzburg 2002, 655 and 657). Yet the siege also disturbed this traditional balance between the two poles of virility and *bab'ie*, for the need to survive confused the roles. To survive, it was critical for men to be able to transgress the virile category of *muzhskoe* and to assume the habitus of *bab'ie*, to learn how to do woman's everyday work of nurture: "...during the period of the great hunger, the best in organizing the processes of satiety turned to be not the housewives [...], but the people furthest from household management, especially men [...]. Especially those same intellectuals who all their lives had feared to lay a finger on a besom or a pot, thinking it would cast doubt on their manhood" (Ginzburg 1995, 70–71).[18] Men who were not afraid for their virility, who were strong enough to trans-gender themselves into *domohoziaiki*, won in the war against hungry death and hungry insanity. Mother, wife, and nurturer, the *domohoziaika* is the performer of the "age-old" woman's role. It is important to remember, however, that in this instance these "age-old" statuses were produced as a modern phenomenon, by labor policy in the military economy rather than by "tradition."

Empty envelopes populating Ginzburg's besieged Leningrad acted out a theater of public performances that became a surrogate social reality, and Ginzburg emphasizes that the only medium of the social was conversation. Talk substituted for a social reality in the same way as *shroty*[19] substituted for butter, glue substituted for meat, and nettles substituted for vegetables: "The dystrophic winter queues were eerily

---

[18] "[...V] period bol'shogo goloda luchshimi organizatorami protsessov nasyshcheniia okazalis' vovse ne domokhoziaiki [...], a samye dalekie ot khoziaistva liudi, osobenno muzhchiny [...]. Osobenno te iz nikh, kotorye vsiu zhizn' boialis' pritronutsia k veniku ili kastriule, schitaia, chto eto postavit pod somnenie ikh muzhskie kachetsva" (Ginzburg 2002, 655).

[19] Remembered by all siege memoirists, *shroty* (from the German *Schrot*) is a by-product of vegetable oil extraction, the remaining waste of cut plant stalks, leaves, and seeds normally used as addition to cattle fodder.

silent. Gradually, with the increase in the bread ration, the spring
warmth, and the appearance of greens in the shops, [...] it [the queue]
began to converse. Man abhors a vacuum. The immediate filling in of
a vacuum is one of the basic functions of the word" (Ginzburg 1995,
40).[20] It is in this theater of conversation that womanliness was conceived, directed, staged, and acted out. It became a weapon in the
struggle against death, and later, when immediate survival was barely
achieved, for status and power.

Thus, standing in the queue, women talked about families and
children (many of them dead), hiding the pain of loss behind the
veneer of "eternal women's talk," "age-old" patriarchal womanliness
as nurture and motherhood. Here, the banality of the conversations'
topics stood in stark contrast to the "new and terrifying material" of
the siege: matters of life and death "within the unpretentious envelope
of a housewife's professional interests" (Ginzburg 1995, 43).[21] Talking
about food, the queue compensates for the "empty" reality of the
siege, which deprives humans of any representation, communicative,
emotional, cognitive, or narrative:

> It (conversation about food) had taken on a universal social
> meaning and importance paid for by the terrible experience of the
> winter. A conversation on how it's better not to salt millet when
> boiling, because than it gets to be just right, had become a con-
> versation about life and death (the millet expands, you see). [...]
> When this queue conducts a conversation about food, everything
> is included in it: emotional discharge in the reproaches and com-
> plaints, informative generalizations in discussions of the best ways
> of obtaining, cooking and sharing food, the narration of "interesting
> stories," and self-assertion of every kind. (Ginzburg 1995, 43)[22]

---

[20] "Zimnie distroficheskie ocheredi byli zhutko molchalivy. Postepenno, s
rostom khlebnogo paika, s vesennim teplom i poiavleniem zeleni [...] ochered'
stala razgovarivat'. Chelovek ne vynosit vakuuma. Nemedlennoe zapolnenine
vakuuma—odno iz osnovnykh naznachenii slova" (Ginzburg 2002, 635).
[21] "V nezateilivoi obolochke professional'nykh interesov domokhoziaek"
(Ginzburg 2002, 636).
[22] "On priobrel vseobshchuiu sotsial'nuiu znachimost' i znachitel'nost',
oplachennuiu strashnym opytom zimy. On, razgovor o tom, chto psheno
luchshe pri varke ne solit', potomu chto togda ono luchshe dohodit—stal

Conversational Homeovestism:
Perverse Strategies of Power

Being alive and being alive as a woman were not affordable to everyone and were best achieved with the support of an institution: the promotion from *domohoziaika* to an employee of a state organization and further up along its internal hierarchy qualitatively changed the fight for "normal life." Official standing was all because it gave entitlement to food. The second part of the *Blockade Diary* is dedicated almost entirely to conversation analysis and describes a group of educated women who were employed in propaganda by the Leningrad Radio Committee. They thus recovered from alimentary dystrophy in the privileged conditions of useful workers on the ideological front. In recording these women's conversations, Ginzburg explored the role of institutional power in the regeneration of the social and the reinstatement of a properly attributed, "normal," gendered subject. The women in the institution alternated strictly professional discourse with "feminine" small talk: flirting, discussing dressmakers and hairstyles, teasing rivals, and referring to lovers. Theirs, Ginzburg points out, was not a sexuality in recovery, but rather a sign of overcoming a severe social handicap, as power structures regenerated their socio-psychological sense of self. If in the bread queue nurturing femininity was mobilized towards survival, here it was deployed as a weapon in a struggle for power. Ginzburg understands sexuality along Foucauldian lines, as she also understands power—an all-pervading force that organizes people into a multi-dimensional field of dramatic, manifold, permanently reinstated and renegotiated inequalities:

> P. V. and Lipetskaia are engaged in a classic women's conversation: a seamstress and dressmaking. But this conversation takes place in an unusual, impossible situation (that of the siege).

razgovorom o zhizni i smerti (pshena ved' stanovitsia bol'she) [...]. Kogda eta ochered' vedet razgovor o ede, v nem soderzhitsia vse: emotsional'naia razriadka v poprekakh i setovaniiakh, i poznavatel'noe obobshchenie v rassuzhdeniiakh o nailuchshikh sposobakh dobyvaniia, prigotovleniia, raspredeleniia pishchi, i rasskazyvanie 'interesnykh istorii,' i vsiacheskoe samoutverzhdenie" (Ginzburg 2002, 637).

And the context gives the turns in the conversation quite special second meanings and underlying topics. To P.V.'s question about the price of the dress, Lipetskaia answers, delightedly, "expensive, expensive." The question opens up immense possibilities for her to assert her superiority as a professional, and not as a woman. All those feminine privileges—the dress, the stockings, the perfume— were acquired in exchange for bread, while bread, in its turn, is the price of her success as an actress. (Ginzburg 2002, 692–93)[23]

Here is a woman who performs a travesty of "femininity" in order to impress a less "feminine" (because less socially capable) conversation partner. This act of "conversational homeovestism"[24] illustrates how femininity is created as an instance of a perverse strategy by a subject who has barely escaped imminent death from hunger and is seeking to create an illusion of a "normal human life." The perverse strategy makes up part of the microphysics of power.[25] The "classic women's conversation," with its interest in dresses and perfume, is produced with the sole purpose of emphasizing how much bread had to be exchanged for these vain attributes of frail femininity. Feminine vanity and frailty, however, are here acted out by a hard-working, self-sup-

---

[23] "Mezhdu P. V. i Lipetskoi idet klassicheskii zhenskii razgovor: portnikha, nariady. No osushchestvliaetsia on v neobychainoi, neveroiatnoi (blokadnoi) situatsii. I situatsiia soobshchaet replikam sovsem osobye vtorye smysly i podvodnye temy. Na vopros, vo skol'ko oboshlos' plat'e, Lipetskaia s vostorgom otvechaet 'dorogo, dorogo.' Vopros otkryvaet pered nei shirochaishie vozmozhnosti dlia samoutverzhdeniia. Osushchestvliaetsia ono ne stol'ko v zhenskom plane, skol'ko v professional'nom. Vse eti blaga—plat'e, chulki, dukhi—oplacheny khlebom, a khleb, v svoiu ochered', tsena ee akterskogo uspekha" (Translation mine–I.S.) (Ginzburg 2002, 692–93).

[24] Conversational homeovestism is "the feeling of speaking as the same sex" (McIlvenny 2002, 20–1). In psychoanalysis, a hom(e)ovestite is "any person dressing in clothes of his or her own sex [...] A woman [...] who acts or dresses like some stereotyped notion of a woman [...]" (Kaplan 1993, 250–1).

[25] "What makes a perversion a perversion is a mental strategy that uses one or another social stereotype of masculinity or femininity. [...] A perversion is a psychological strategy. It differs from other mental strategies in that it demands a performance. [...] The enactment, or performance, is designed to help the person to survive, moreover to survive with a sense of triumph over the traumas [...]" (Kaplan 1993, 9–10).

porting, and successful professional woman (in fact, an actress) who
is proud of her ability not only to ensure her own survival, but also
to create a certain excess—the image of an unnecessarily wasteful and
coquettish femininity—to convince her interlocutor that she possesses
resources in the competition for a "normal human life":

> Nor for P.V. [the conversation partner] is it merely a conversa-
> tion about petty clothes. At this time, having a dress made means
> being able to partake of a normal human life. [...] But this is all
> far beyond her means; she even had her husband's coat remade
> into a coat for herself. "Nothing, nothing will ever come of it" is
> a lamentation about that, and a complaint about the fact that her
> mother is hungry and she [P.V.] must support the mother from
> her own food ration. However, as the conversation goes on about
> Lipetskaia's bread prospects, about the five eggs she's received as
> a gift, and so on, P.V. gradually develops a need to resist: it turns
> out, she could have also been able to overcome circumstances, not
> as a professional, however, but in her capacity as a woman: [she
> mentions] an admirer who's at the front. (Ginzburg 2002, 693)[26]

The prize in this little verbal competition is "normalcy," the deployment of (perverse) heteronormative femininity being part of asserting
supremacy. Supremacy is achieved thanks to the subject's ability to
create tropes in speech and behavior. In such a game, the winner is
the one who is sufficiently nourished to be able to think and talk about
something that is *not* food, such as a dress or a lover. Those socially
entitled to a better canteen or a larger daily ration of butter find themselves empowered enough to afford a conversation that digresses from
the direct expression of hunger. In rebuilding their surrendered self-

---

[26] "Dlia P. V. eto tozhe ne prosto razgovor o triapkakh. Seichas sshit' sebe plat'e—
eto prikosnut'sia k normal'noi chelovecheskoi zhizni. [...] No vse eto ei ne po
silam, dazhe sshit' pal'to iz pal'to muzha. 'Nichego, nichego iz etogo ne vyidet'—
lamentatsiia po etomu povodu i po povodu togo, chto mat' golodnaia i nado ee
kormit' iz sobstvennogo paika. No po mere togo, kak prodolzhaetsia razgovor o
khlebnykh perspektivakh Lipetskoi, o piati iaitsakh, poluchennykh v podarok, i
proch., u P. V. voznikaet potrebnost' soprotivleniia—okazyvaetsia, ona tozhe
mogla by pobezhdat' obstoiatel'stva ne professional'nym sposobom, a zhenskim
(poklonnik na fronte)." (Translation mine–I.S.) (Ginzburg 2002, 693).

hood, they use such digressions to establish their discursive dominance over those who are weaker (hungrier). Thus, the game of power and the respective construction of identities begin when language, previously so impoverished by starvation as to retain only the primary meanings of food and hunger ("intellectual horizon narrowed down" to a fixation on "the alimentary theme," as the siege doctors put it), find themselves strong and recovered enough to afford a metaphor. The badge of victory in the fight for "normal life" goes to the woman who demonstrates her newly recovered ability to avoid talking exclusively about eating, who manages to produce tropeic speech (about dresses) and transposed social behaviours (ladylikeness). Womanliness thus shows its constructedness as a form of transposed (satisfied, sublimated, eliminated, compensated for, *Aufgehoben*) hunger.

However, the tropeic language is still too weak, and the memory of the overpowering meaning of food is still capable of breaking down the visible signs of self-certain, self-identical womanliness that the subject is trying to create. As much emerges in one conversation at the canteen, a discussion about *kasha* (which, Ginzburg notes, during the siege became the universal exchange equivalent of all value):

> ... now [i.e., in the process of recovery from dystrophy since she receives a much better ration–I.S.] the human mind has expanded to be able to hold many other things [other than *kasha*–I.S.], as, for instance, whether women look attractive in military uniforms or how to apply lipstick. For the people of the siege, holding a conversation about normal subjects is a way of confirming their selfhood. But here is one conversation partner who, as compared to the others, has been delayed at an inferior stage of emancipation from the fixations of the siege. She still preserves [its] obsession and frankness. She's made a discovery of extraordinary importance for herself and of interest for the others: one should eat *two* portions of *kasha* in a row [instead of one, to satisfy hunger–I.S.] [... In her speech, she demonstrates] the straightforwardness of a hungry phraseology [...] (Ginzburg 2002, 704–5).[27]

---

[27] "[...] Seichas soznanie vmeshchaet uzhe i mnogoe drugoe—dazhe idet li zhenshchinam voennaia forma ili kak luchshe mazat' guby. A dlia blokadnykh liudei razgovor na normal'nuiu temu—eto rod samoutverzhdeniia.

A superior "stage of emancipation from dystrophy" is achieved when the subject learns to speak creating some excess of meaning beyond the meaning of eating. Thus, recovery from hunger—and that means rehabilitation on route to a "normal life," the movement from sexlessness to womanliness, from nonentity as a statistical unit of population to a certain degree of social agency—is indicated by one's ability to use a metaphor in speech. This language game is played for the sake of power, not for poetic pleasure or for the necessities of survival. The loser is the one not entitled to *Aufhebung*: she remains in the grip of dystrophy; she is dominated by her own inability to digress from the subjects of hunger and death; her speech acts are overpowered and debilitated by an impoverished language of literal meanings; and in her new situation of recovery among the privileged she is discursively handicapped in her inability to stop thinking and talking about eating. Her language is as hungry as her own being. Tokens of security, the insignia of sex, gender, and a generally privileged status (i.e., the social tropes produced by the less hungry, luckier player of social power games) are beyond her control.

Identity in Recovery, Regime in Restoration

Ginzburg's storyteller in the *Blockade Diary* is an imagined male figure under the name of "N," a man without properties. Apart from the masculine pronoun and one mention that N wears a tie, he appears sexless and genderless rather than male and masculine. The uncertain sexuality of Ginzburg's *alter ego* is not only a sign of belonging to the tradition of lesbian writing,[28] nor merely an effect of Russian

---

No vot odna iz sobesednits, po sravneniiu s drugimi, zaderzhalas' na bolee nizkoi stupeni osvobozhdeniia ot blokadnykh navazhdenii. Ona sokhranila oderzhimost', otkrovennost'. Ona sdelala otkrytie prakticheskoe, imeiushchee chrezvychainoe znachenie dlia nee, interesnoe dlia okruzhaiushchikh—nado s'edat' *dve kashi* podriad [...] vsia priamota golodnoi frazeologii...." (Emphasis in original; translation mine–I.S.) (Ginzburg 2002, 705).

[28] On Ginzburg's writerly approaches to female homosexuality and on her concept of same-sex love, see Emily van Buskirk 2006.

grammar (Russ. *chelovek* is masculine), but also an allegory of a devastated identity.

In Ginzburg's book, siege subjects appear as a parade of habituses, a catalogue of nightmarish *tableaux vivants*, enactments of stereotypical womanliness signifying the terrifying content of mass extermination. The fixity of these images as portrayed by Ginzburg—the evil secretaries, good housekeepers, or ladylike coquettes—indicates a perverse strategy in re-socialization, on the one hand, and a perverse strategy in writing, on the other. Ginzburg presents her own and other women's personal experiences of *vita minima* in an objectifying, pseudo-scientific language as if to detach herself both from the sufferings of her fellow victims, and from her own rage.[29] However, apart from the acting out of suppressed self-censored passion, she also seeks to prevent future attempts to extract a positive lesson out of the "betrayal of Leningrad" (as in the official version of the history of the Great Patriotic War).[30] The "normal life" that her characters so desperately seek to capture includes the restoration of the social hierarchy and the reinstatement of the ideological norm parallel to the return of heteronormativity. This is how the Soviet regime begins to re-establish itself in the City of Hunger.[31]

The social reality of the siege as it appears in Ginzburg's notes is represented through a complex game of impersonations and transdressings, as "fabrications manufactured and sustained through corporeal signs and other discursive means" (Butler 1990, 136). As distinct from queer theory that sees the citation of gender stereotypes as subversive of the norm, in Ginzburg, the iteration of the heteronormative stereotype consolidates hegemony.

---

[29] Van Buskirk, however, analyzes Ginzburg's "detachment" as an aesthetic principle of self-estrangement in prose writing.

[30] On the ideological, political, academic, and intra-disciplinary circumstances involved in the production of the historiography of the siege of Leningrad, inside and outside, during and after the USSR, see Dzeniskevich 1998, Lomagin 2006.

[31] Compare this interpretation with Lisa Kirschenbaum's (2006, 52–6) emphasis on the merger between the everyday language of the siege and its official narrative (as suggested by Ginzburg) and a compromise between the official Stalinist patriotism and grass-roots city patriotism.

A return of the heterosexual norm occurs in the context of regen-
erating networks of multiple, carefully constructed and maintained
inequalities on the level of the micro-physics of power. Womanliness
reappears as a transposed performable meaning, to be acted out in the
narrow interstices between the discursive limits of "normal" life and
the inexpressible experiences of actual survival.

REFERENCES

Barber, John. No date. "Stalin and the Betrayal of Leningrad." http://www.
bbc.co.uk/history/worldwars/wwtwo/leningrad_betrayal_01.shtml (last
accessed 29 December 2008).

Barber, J. D., and A. R. Dzeniskevich, eds. 2001. *Zhizn' i zmert' v
bokirovannom Leningrade: Istoriko-meditsinkii aspekt.* St. Petersburg: Dmitrii
Bulanin.

Belozerov, B. P. 2001. "Protivopravnye deistviia i prestupnost' v usloviiakh
goloda." In *Zhizn' i smert' v blokirovannom Leningrade: istoriko-meditsinkii
aspekt,* edited by J. D. Barber and A. R. Dzeniskevich, 245–64. St.
Petersburg: Dmitrii Bulanin.

Buskirk, Emily van. 2006. "Samoostranenie kak eticheskii i esteticheskii prin-
tsip v proze L. Ia. Ginzburg." *NLO* 81: 261–81.

Butler, Judith. 1990. *Gender Trouble: Feminism and the Subversion of Identity.*
New York and London: Routledge.

Cherepenina, N. Iu. 2001. "Golod i smert' v blokirovannom gorode." In
Zhizn' i smert' v blokirovannom Leningrade: Istoriko-meditsinkii aspekt, edited
by J. D. Barber and A. R. Dzeniskevich, 35-80. St. Petersburg: Dmitrii
Bulanin.

Chernorutskii, M. V. 1947. *Alimentarnaia distrofiia v blokirovannom Leningrade.*
Leningrad: Medgiz.

Dzeniskevich, A. R. 1998. *Blokada i politika: Oborona Leningrada v politicheskoi
kon'iunkture.* St. Petersburg: Nestor.

Ginzburg, Lidia. 2002. *Zapisnye knizhki, vospominaniia, esse.* St. Petersburg:
Iskusstvo.

———. 1995. *Blockade Diary,* translated by Alan Myers. London: Harvill
Press.

[Ginzburg, Lidiia]. 2007. "'Nikto ne plachet nad tem, chto ego ne kasaetsia':
Chetvertyi "Razgovor o liubvi" Lidii Ginzburg" (edited and with introductory article by Emily van Buskirk). *NLO* 88: 154–68.

Kaplan, Louise J. 1993. *Female Perversions: the Temptations of Madame Bovary.*
London: Penguin, c1991.

Kirschenbaum, Lisa. 2006. *The Legacy of the Siege of Leningrad, 1941–1995:
Myth, Memories, and Monuments.* New York: Cambridge University Press.

Lomagin, N. A. 2005. *Leningrad v blokade*. St. Petersburg: Eksmo Iauza.

_____. 2001. *V tiskakh goloda: Blokada Leningrada v dokumentakh germanskikh spetsluzhb i NKVD*. St. Petersburg: Evropeiskii Dom.

Lomagin, Nikolai. 2006. "Diskussiia o stalinizme i nastroeniiakh naseleniia v period blokady Leningrada." In *Pamiat' o blokade: svidetel'stva ochevidtsev i istoricheskoe soznanie obshchestva*, edited by M. V. Loskutkova, 296–334. Moscow: Novoe izdatel'stvo.

Magaeva, S. V. 2001. "Fiziologicheskie i psikhosomaticheskie predposylki." In *Zhizn' i smert' v blokirovannom Leningrade: Istoriko-meditsinkii aspekt*, edited by J. D. Barber and A. R. Dzeniskevich, 141–86. St. Petersburg: Dmitrii Bulanin.

McIlvenny, Paul, ed. 2002. *Talking Gender and Sexuality*. Amsterdam: John Benjamins.

Simmons, Cynthia and Nina Perlina. 2002. *Writing the Siege of Leningrad: Women's Diaries, Memoirs, and Documentary Prose*. Pittsburgh: University of Pittsburgh Press.

Simonenko,V. B. et al. 2003. *Leningradskaia blokada: Meditsinkie problemy—retrospektiva i sovremennost'*. Moscow: Meditsina.

CHAPTER 6

Graphic Womanhood under Fire

Helena Goscilo

"War is not women's history."
Virginia Woolf

"War's unwomanly face."[1]
Svetlana Aleksievich

"A really successful war, a psychologically Good
War, requires not merely the extirpation of a
cruel enemy abroad. It requires as a corollary the
apotheosis of the pure of heart at home."
Paul Fussell[2]

---

[1] *U voiny ne zhenskoe litso*, usually translated as *The Unwomanly Face of War*, is
the title of the Belarusian writer Svetlana Aleksievich's most famous book. A
hybrid that perhaps most closely resembles the genres of documentary prose
or oral history, it chiefly comprises interviews with women who saw action in
World War II, interspersed with authorial commentary. Originally published
in 1985, it was reissued in amplified form by Pal'mira in 2004. Aleksievich,
clearly, took lessons from her older countryman Ales' Adamovich, who co-
authored with Daniil Granin *Blokadnaia kniga* [*The Blockade Book* 1977–
81], an unsparing account of the prolonged siege of Leningrad during World
War II.

[2] Paul Fussell, "Writing in Wartime: the Uses of Innocence." In *Thank God for
the Atom Bomb and Other Essays* (New York, London, etc.: Summit Books,
1988), 53.

Mapping through Images

A frequently iterated truism about World War II holds that during that period of devastation, which cost approximately thirty million Soviet lives, culture served as a rallying point for Russians (von Geldern 1995, 52). Indeed, the imperative of uniting the population against the enemy prompted the government to mobilize all available modes of cultural production—radio, music, song, film, theater, journalism, literature, and graphics.[3] On 23 June 1941, just a day after Germany invaded the USSR, the first Soviet anti-Nazi poster launched a concerted propaganda campaign that exhorted, reassured, and inspired the Soviet people throughout its harrowing four-year struggle. Were all other records of the war eradicated, one could still map its general course through these visuals, which, together with documentary films[4] and radio broadcasts,[5] responded with lightning speed to developments at the front and, as a corollary, to the nation's immediate ideological priorities.[6]

---

[3] Of the voluminous scholarship on World War II, of particular relevance to my analysis are the following sources, in addition to those contained in my bibliography: Catherine Merridale, *Ivan's War: Life and Death in the Red Army, 1939–1945* (New York: Metropolitan Books, 2006); Denise J. Youngblood, *Russian War Films: On the Cinema Front, 1914–2005* (Lawrence KS: University Press of Kansas, 2007), especially 55–81. For a list of recent publications on women's contributions on the battlefield, see *Gender War in Twentieth-Century Eastern Europe*, edited by Nancy M. Wingfield and Maria Bucur (Bloomington and Indianapolis: Indiana University Press, 2006), 19, footnote 10.

[4] Peter Kenez reports that "[t]he first wartime newsreel, amazingly, appeared in movie theaters as early as three days after the outbreak of the war, on 25 June. In the following months a new edition came out every three days" (1995, 160).

[5] About radio, see von Geldern (1995), 44–61.

[6] Various veterans of the war interviewed by Nina Tumarkin remember the first two years of the war as a period of "*spontaneous de-Stalinization*," inasmuch as Soviet unpreparedness and disorder forced people "to make their own decisions" as "independent human beings." A consolidation of the war machine and the revival of full-fledged Stalinism, however, followed the vicious battle over Stalingrad (Tumarkin 1994, 65). The representation of gender in World War II graphic art, however, does not mirror this shift, though one could argue that in the last two years of the war, women's physical appearance undergoes increased feminization.

This array of affective images, accompanied by verses or compressed texts teeming with apostrophes and exclamation marks, was disseminated among the military, factories, and farms, as well as posted in TASS windows and along city streets.[7] The panoply offers a composite picture of the nation's self-presentation, in which rhetorical emphases and omissions draw on Russia's centuries-old master narrative of martyred heroism—in bifurcated, gendered form. The very function of war propaganda determines, *mutatis mutandis*, certain ecumenical stereotypes within war rhetoric: "our" rectitude, bravery, and patriotism versus the enemy's craven, brutal aggressiveness; "our" noble defense of sacrosanct values versus "their" numerically stronger military equipment but morally weaker fighting spirit; "our" troops' defense of women and children, as opposed to "their" defilement and murder of the defenseless, and so forth. Within this arsenal of generic conventions, even specific symbols transcend national boundaries: the demonization of the enemy as a dragon, hydra, snake, and ape reticulates in war graphics not only in England and the Slavic countries, but also in Germany, with the readymade iconography adjusted according to the specifics of national identity. Paul Fussell has argued that the ineluctably sanitized image of war as a heroic enterprise springs from the perceived necessity not only of withholding from the public the gruesome physical reality of violent death by wholesale bodily dismemberment, but also of concealing fatal errors in generals' and decision makers' judgment that lead to decimation of entire platoons or civilians (Fussell 1989, 267–97). The politics of gender, which encompassed a propagandistic iconography of unflagging heroism, played out that sanitization in full force.

"War," the historian Linda Grant De Pauw contends, "is the most powerful cultural intervention which [sic] serves to define gender" (De Pauw 1998, 15). More precisely, not so much the chaos of war as its

---

[7] In their study of wartime posters, Peter Paret et al. absurdly fault the Soviet government for having issued inferior World War II posters: "The Russian people deserved far better posters than their government produced." Peter Paret, Beth Irwin Lewis, Paul Paret, *Persuasive Images: Posters of War and Revolution* (Princeton: Princeton University Press, 1992), 160. For a comprehensive examination of TASS's graphic works during the war, see Zegers and Druick (2011).

public representation in sundry cultural genres performs that function, and nowhere more forcefully than in the widely distributed form of posters. Of the approximately one million Soviet women who enlisted (Stites 1995, 2), 800,000 engaged in combat as pilots, machine gunners, tank drivers, snipers, scouts, and signalwomen (*sviazistki*).[8] Yet Soviet World War II posters contain scant evidence of their frontline deployment. A handful of exceptions aside, these graphics reinforce the gender asymmetry undergirding Soviet life under Stalin, which overturned the commitment to gender parity proclaimed by the Bolsheviks, to equate masculinity with sociopolitical agency, femininity with reproduction and domestic nurturing.[9] Consolidation structured the male paradigm (the "ontological," primary identity or A), while dispersal characterized its female counterpart (the complementary or non-A). Whatever the orientation of individual posters—hortatory, morale boosting, inflammatory, or celebratory—the majority assigned a single overriding function to young, virile specimens of manhood: annihilation of the enemy in a heroic display of patriotism, physical courage, and "holy vengeance."

The rhetoric of graphic propaganda relied heavily on synecdoche to capture wartime masculinity, whereby one or several Soviet Aryans in uniform imaged the nation's male population fighting for the sacred cause of the homeland. Since the overriding exigencies of lethal militarism exposed the genre to narrowness and mechanical repetition, artists diversified male iconography not only through incorporation of subgenres, such as caricature, photomontage, and *lubok*, but also through two devices that strategically appealed to national memory.

---

[8] Tank drivers included Aleksandra Boiko (posthumously recognized as a Hero of the Soviet Union), Mariia Oktiabr'skaia, and Aleksandra Rashchupkina, a former tractor driver from Uzbekistan, who for three years passed herself off as a man in order to "fulfill her patriotic duty." See Zheltova and http://news.e63.ru/2366.html. For memoirs by female machine-gunners, see Zoya Matveyevna Smirnova-Medvedeva, *On the Road to Stalingrad: Memoirs of a Soviet Woman Machine Gunner*, edited and translated by Kazimiera Janina Cottam (New York/Ottawa/Toronto: LEGAS, 1996).

[9] Such changes in the Constitution of 1936 as restrictions on divorce and the repeal of abortion, plus the campaign of *kul'turnost'*, encouraged women to bear children, focus on domesticity, and forget about significant political activity.

The first invoked historical precedent—the visual resuscitation of instantly recognizable heroes from Russia's illustrious past, such as epic *bogatyri*, Aleksandr Nevskii, Dmitrii Donskoi, Kuz'ma Minin and Dmitrii Pozharskii, Marshal Suvorov, Mikhail Kutuzov, and so forth [Plate 6.1].[10] As Paul Parker, writing about American advertising art in the 1930s, notes, "new" methods of advertising usually involve "the investigation of past glories" (Parker 1937, 23). Soviet pledges of victory in the imminent future therefore leaned heavily on psychologically freighted reminders of a distinguished past, to convince the populace that "We've done it before, and we'll do it again." By labeling World War II the Great Patriotic War (*Velikaia Otechestvennaia voina*), Soviets directly linked it to the first "Patriotic War" of 1812, fought against Napoleon's *Grande Armée*, and posters elaborated on the connection through satirical treatment of the defeated French commander and his armies.[11] The second strategy entailed eloquent incorporation of earlier posters into new ones, notably when the Germans started their withdrawal, to highlight the Red Army's fulfillment of repeated vows that it would vanquish the invaders [Plate 6.2].

By contrast, multiplicity of roles marked images of women, which likewise mined age-old traditions, since the pragmatic benefits of suspending official Soviet anathematization of tsarist values were self-evident.[12] As Laurie Stoff in her monograph on Russian female soldiers

---

[10]   The roster of names duplicates the list of "great ancestors" cited by Stalin in his speech on 7 November 1941, during which he asserted, "The whole world is looking upon you as the power capable of destroying the German robber hordes! The enslaved peoples of Europe are looking upon you as their liberators" (quoted in Tumarkin, 63). For an analysis of masculinity, history, and metahistory in World War II graphics, see Helena Goscilo, "History and Metahistory in Soviet World War II Posters," in *Recalling the Past—(Re)constructing the Past: Collective and Individual Memory of World War II in Russia and Germany*, edited by Withold Bonner and Arja Rosenholm (Tampere: Aleksanteri Series 2, 2008), 221–41.

[11] As Tumarkin notes, the name originated in an article in *Pravda*, the Communist Party newspaper, published on 23 June 1941 (Tumarkin 1994, 61) and has remained Russians' name for the war, relegating the Allies' participation to insignificance.

[12] By the 1930s, the internationalist orientation of Leninism had yielded to Stalin's national-patriotic ideology, more tolerant toward the old regime than the earlier revolutionaries.

in World War I asserts, "Women's wartime roles, although traditionally prescribed as passive, are in reality more fluid and varied [than men's]..." (Stoff 2006, 6). Commenting on the impermanence of wartime transformations, Margaret and Patrice Higgonet similarly propose that women "assimilate new roles with astounding swiftness, possibly because of a sense that their identity is not bound up in the social roles they play" (Higgonet 1987, 33, 38). Joan Scott, however, justifiably wonders whether "the gender system" was genuinely transformed or reproduced in the course of wartime's drastic circumstances (Scott 1987, 26). In the case of Soviet graphics, there seems little doubt that, to the extent possible, posters assimilated women's new roles into stale paradigms. Despite their surface diversity, female images largely reinforced the code of gender differentiation prevailing during peacetime, which by definition included no historical precedents of female military glory. Instead, women retained their timeless allegorical significance as the nation or homeland, a trope partially naturalized by the feminine gender of the Russian word "*rodina*" and one that effectively short-circuited female subjectivity/agency in the sociopolitical sphere.[13]

Maternity as Allegory, Masculinity as Glory

Cast in their eternal role of mother, middle-aged women personified the threatened motherland (*rodina-mat'*). In that capacity they dominated some of the most famous wartime graphics, including Iraklii Toidze's early recruitment poster, *Rodina-mat' zovet!* [*The Motherland Calls!* 1941], probably the single most reproduced visual from these years [Plate 6.3/2.4]. In contrast to the youthful, prettified embodiment of America in World War II posters circulated in the United States, the Soviet woman's substantial body incarnated the unshakable steadfastness of the nation; bulk connoted bulwark. As the prospect of victory dawned, and later, when the Germans conceded defeat, the modality of this image altered, from exhortation to condign reward

[13] See Goscilo and Lanoux, "Introduction: Lost in the Myths" (2006), 3–29; Riabov, 183–202.

for valiant exploits and glorification of the forces that had routed the adversary. Thus women as nation conferred insignias of the Roman Empire upon allied Soviet troops [Plate 6.4] and restored to them the bounties of the Russian land, contravening the reality of domestic agriculture's plight and cities razed to the ground [Plate 6.5]. As in the majority of posters, the color red predominated, symbolizing the Red Army and passionate love of motherland, while also calling to mind blood spilled in a noble cause.[14]

A kindred allegorical iconography, in which old women implore young recruits, addressed as sons, to protect them, likewise troped the defense of endemic historical values. Images of aged frailty or urgency implied the peril looming over enshrined immemorial values [Plates 6.6, 6.7, 6.8]. These symbolic, often grandmotherly figures were the anonymous, abstracted female equivalent of the individualized male heroes from the past, for poster-propaganda followed Stalin's example in abandoning the standard Soviet policy of proselytizing the progressive new order vis-à-vis the shortcomings of the retrograde tsarist era to underscore hallowed national traditions to be safeguarded at all costs.[15]

Those costs defied the imagination. Yet, ignoring the staggering death toll, desertion at the front, and, at Stalin's command (the notorious order no. 227), Soviet officers' summary execution of their own troops if the latter retreated or seemed in imminent danger of capture,[16] graphic artists intent on raising the morale of both soldiers and civilians studiously avoided the faintest hint of male vulnerability, rarely depicting

---

[14] With the rise of the Red Army, red became the favorite color of Soviet visual genres. Its multiple associations rendered it a convenient shorthand. Its ubiquity may be inferred from the publication of an illustrated art book in Russia titled *Krasnyi tsvet v russkom iskusstve* [*The Color Red in Russian Art*] (St. Petersburg: State Russian Museum, 1997).

[15] This pragmatic policy also entailed suspending the ban on religious worship.

[16] In July 1941, Stalin issued his notorious order of "Not a step back!" It demanded that any Soviet combatant captured by the enemy be branded a traitor and dealt with accordingly (Merridale 2006, 155–60). Special battalions (the *zagradotriady*) simply shot front-line deserters (see Kukulin 2005, 3). The first five months of the war, "until its costly success in the battle of Moscow in December 1941, was an unmitigated catastrophe" for the Soviet Union (Tumarkin 1994, 60).

Soviet troops disabled or killed.[17] One of the rare exceptions is Viktor Koretskii's poster of 1943 [Plate 6.9], where, significantly, the casualty, an Azerbaijani named Samed, is visibly Asian, Soviet but not "pure" Russian. After all, the touted myth of the friendship of nations, which the poster's verbal text promotes—"Samed goes to death so that Semen won't perish"—failed to camouflage the Soviet Union's de facto ethnic and gender hierarchies.[18] Posters regularly displaced vulnerability onto women in various configurations consonant with wartime propaganda by both the Allies and the Axis powers, which "underline[d] the idea that fascism directly threatened women" (Gubar 231) [Plate 6.10].

The Mission of "Saving Our Women"

As in the iconography of World War I, women frequently appeared as beleaguered young mothers [Plates 6.11, 6.12/2.6], holding in their arms children, who, as emblems of the future, were the obverse of the old women incarnating traditions: the two categories functioned as ideologized temporal bookends. Occasionally artists strove for emotional intensification by replacing mothers with desperate but resolute girls as maternal protectors of still younger children [Plates 6.13, 6.14], thereby fomenting hatred for the Nazis and eliciting compassion for a generation forced into premature responsibilities by the exigencies of war—perhaps most poignantly depicted in Andrei Tarkovsky's first feature film, *Ivanovo detstvo* [*My Name Is Ivan* 1962].[19]

---

[17] The practice of glossing over the phenomenon of invalids and survivors variously incapacitated by the war in order to emphasize Soviets' ability to overcome all odds likewise marked Soviet film. See Beate Fieseler, "The Wounds of War: Experiences of War-Related Disablement in Soviet Feature Films," in *Recalling the Past—(Re-)constructing the Past: Collective and Individual Memory of World War II in Russia and Germany*, edited by Withold Bonner and Arja Rosenholm (Tampere: Aleksanteri Series 2, 2008), 277–88.

[18] See Wolf (2012), 116. For thorough commentary on all posters by Koretskii included in this chapter, see Wolf's fine, copiously illustrated volume.

[19] Though inexplicably titled *My Name Is Ivan* when shown in Anglophone countries, the film emphasizes maimed childhood and the accurate translation of its original title is *Ivan's Childhood*.

An equally widespread mode of dramatizing feminine vulnerability cast women as victims of rape, death, or imprisonment [Plate 6.15]. This series typically reduced the Germans to bestial primitives [Plate 6.16], and the integrated verbal texts (frequently, verses composed by Samuil Marshak) explicitly gendered the victims of their brutality. Though Nazi concentration camps teemed with male and female prisoners, posters focused on the latter, either singly or projected against a background of grouped fellow-sufferers, smaller in scale and often ill-defined [Plates 6.17, 6.18]. Yet, unlike Anglophone graphic artists, Soviets circumspectly opted for intimation over explicitness in conveying sexual violence against women, shunning images of Neanderthal Axis aggressors carrying naked women tossed over their shoulders as war booty (Gubar 1987, 231, 234). In general, Soviet prudishness proscribed the customary eroticization of female bodies that marks some of the Allies' World War II posters, which feminist commentators decry as "reif[ying] gender arrangements as rigidly as they had been demarcated in the Victorian period" (Gubar 1987, 231).

While eschewing blatant eroticization, Soviet graphics nonetheless propagated pre-revolutionary and Stalinist gender configurations. The war emerged as the salvation of endangered Soviet women and offspring, with intrepid men as their saviors—a topos originating in some of the earliest Russian icons, in which St. George (*Sviatoi Georgii pobedonosets*) slays the dragon of heathenism in the name of Orthodox Russia, personified as a threatened maiden[20] [Plate 6.19]. The implied identification with an earlier saintly warrior evoked both historical mythology and the iconography of World War I, which also had adopted the discourse of the sacred war.[21] In fact, one of Russia's oldest war decorations (and its most prestigious) was the order of St. George, institutionalized by Catherine the Great via a statute of 1769. In effect until 1920, it was officially revived under Putin in 1994, awarded for exceptional military feats [Plates 6.20, 6.21]. St. George also figured prominently in Polish and English posters, the rhetorical power of his knightly aura

---

[20] Boris Pasternak's *Doktor Zhivago* transfigured the nature of St. George by analogizing the novel's poet protagonist, a demilitarized savior, with the medieval saint.

[21] On the iconography of World War I and the recycling of images throughout centuries, see the excellent study by Norris (2006).

deriving from the conceptual economy of an icon that neatly united the virtues of sanctity and self-sacrificing protection of imperiled innocence.

Retrograde Roles

Portrayed chiefly within the context of the home front, women appeared in their customary roles of nurturers and suppliers, working in both fields and factories to produce food and arms for compatriots at the battlefront [Plates 6.22, 6.23, 6.24]. Texts accompanying these visuals underscored the indivisibility of the two. Here, also, cobwebbed gender codes obtained, recalling Vera Mukhina's renowned sculpture of the female collective farm worker and the male industrial laborer (1937), welding together two disparate, value-freighted temporalities. The vaunted gender equality guaranteed by the Soviet Constitution notwithstanding, the 1930s equation of women with domesticity and nature inevitably spawned associations between womanhood and the conservative countryside, while urban industry and progressive tendencies remained male spheres. Thus Mukhina's monumental statue eloquently materialized not only the "*smychka*" urged during the decade, but also the period's gender politics. Vertical disposition of figures within agricultural images similarly affirmed a gendered, hierarchical division of labor, as in the 1942 poster by Viktor Ivanov and Ol'ga Burova, *Traktor v pole—chto tank v boiu!* [*A Tractor in the Field Is Like a Tank in Battle*] [Plate 6.25], where one of two women tractor-drivers gazes upward at a train, packed with waving male soldiers and tanks, speeding along elevated railroad tracks: here "looking up at" literalizes the notion of "looking up to." Posters of women in factories visually and verbally insisted on their temporary replacement of absent men—a substitution unambiguously articulated in Vladimir Serov's *Zamenim!* [*We'll Replace* [*Them*]*!* 1941] [Plate 6.26]. Such graphics confirmed that, once back home, men would resume these jobs, thereby returning their female counterparts to their "natural" pre-war occupations as part of normalcy's reinstatement.[22] This scenario, whereby women

---

[22] Many of such images were produced by Eremina and Vitolina, the two best known of the few female graphic artists.

merely fill "interim *man*-power shortages" (Higgonet 1987, 39), partially clarifies why so many women in England and America "experienced World War II as a resurgence of patriarchal politics" (Gubar
1987, 227).

Essentialist Soviet notions of biological reproduction as
women's "natural" function and destiny discouraged portraying their
termination of human lives as an officially sanctioned deed,[23] for, as
the chapter by Tatiana Mikhailova and Mark Lipovetsky demonstrates,
logical consistency demanded that such actions appear "unnatural,"
aberrant. Reluctance to violate the image of "nurturing femininity"
partly explains why posters bypassed Soviet women's unmediated participation in combat as pilots, tank drivers, and gunners,[24] though a
few images feature women in the auxiliary roles of armed partisans and
nurses [*druzhinnitsy*] aiding the wounded.[25] Female partisans tend to
be mature, solidly built, and unprepossessing as well as mannish in
appearance, for their readiness to exterminate the enemy implicitly
analogizes them with men, potentially destabilizing the bedrock binarism of Stalinist gender configurations [Plates 6.27, 6.28]. By contrast,
nurses usually look young and attractive, as befits "ministering angels,"
and the accompanying texts specifically define their role of compas-
sionate helpmates [Plates 6.29, 6.30]. Within war iconography, in
other words, the scarcity of women fighting at the front as full-fledged
members of the Red Army (also conspicuously underrepresented
in wartime songs, as Robert A. Rothstein notes) corresponds to the
virtual absence of severely or fatally wounded men, thereby affirming
expectations based on fabled gender distinctions.

---

[23] Tellingly, pronatalist policies under Stalin included the decree of 27 June
1936 banning abortions on demand.
[24] Reina Pennington (2001) and Kazimiera Cottam (1998) have thoroughly
detailed these activities. Films containing scenes of Soviet women executing
Germans "justified" their actions by framing their violence as righteous
revenge for the foe's murder of their children, as in Fridrikh Ermler's *Ona
zashchishchaet rodinu* [*She Defends the Motherland* 1943].
[25] Of course, nursing traditionally was the quintessential female profession,
the logical extension of women's allegedly inborn nurturing/maternal
impulses.

From Exhortation to Celebration

As the Allies forced the Germans westward and offensive displaced defensive strategies, posters increasingly conveyed the message of liberation [Plate 6.31]. Unsurprisingly, women dominated this series—a positive inversion of the gendered iconography of incarceration—typically expressing heartfelt gratitude by gesture or word to their stalwart male rescuers. Predictably, children alternated with women as the other category of helpless sufferers who, having passively awaited rescue, saw their faith vindicated. Posters enveloped these beneficiaries of masculine agency in smiles, which also irradiated the faces of the triumphant military liberators, in sharp contrast to the grim solemnity of previous images. Such scenes evoked the conclusions of numerous fairy tales, where the hero kills the dragon, weds the princess released from its clutches, and inherits a kingdom—here, the beloved Motherland.

Cheerfulness and determination permeated graphics as the war neared its end. With entire cities reduced to rubble, rebuilding became an imperative for the entire nation, and posters faithfully recorded this priority, in an unfailingly optimistic key. Whereas graphics designated destruction of the enemy as a predominantly male enterprise, countless posters assigned reconstruction to women—in a sense a responsibility paralleling their frontline roles as nurses aiding recovery.[26] Iosif Serebriannyi's 1944 poster, *A nu-ka, vziali!* [*So, Let's*

---

[26] A notable exception is Arkadii Plastov's 1944 poster *Vosstanovim!*, which features a balding, bearded peasant pulling back the sleeves of his *kaftan*, readying to pick up the foregrounded ax buried in a felled tree trunk by his side, while two young men in uniform, disproportionately small, mend a telegraph wire a few paces behind him. In the distance a roughly sketched-in peasant woman behind a horse is presumably sowing. Projected against the horizon is a blasted landscape of bare trees and remnants of buildings. Though the visual image reinforces the verbal text, which vows to restore what the Nazis have destroyed—a formula in graphics of reconstruction— the fierce, joyless expression on the old peasant's face and the absence of the customary ebullient red underscore hardship and the enormity of the task facing those who have survived. Empirical circumstances also account for women's predominance in images of reconstruction, for the war dramatically reduced the Soviet Union's male population.

Get to It!], Serov's *My otstoiali Leningrad. My vosstanovim ego* [*We've Defended Leningrad. We'll Restore It*], and Viktor Ivanov's and Olga Burova's *Otstroim na slavu!* [*We'll Do a Grand Job of Rebuilding!* 1945] anticipated the reality of laborious restoration throughout the post-war Soviet Union, but emphasized women's enthusiasm for the task [Plates 6.32, 6.33]. The verbal messages echo the encouraging avowals of victory (now fulfilled) that overran early war posters, and the extraordinarily upbeat mood in *Otstroim na slavu!* is visually buttressed by the buxom, beaming, rosy-cheeked young woman with a red headscarf wielding a shovel, as well as the smaller figures in the background vigorously engaged in rebuilding under a symbolically cloudless blue sky [Plate. 6.34]. Though images of reconstruction included men, presumably recovered from the trials of combat and prepared to resume their civilian lives, a disproportionate number of women populated the graphic narrative of Soviet citizens' eagerness to reclaim their past and construct their future through colossal physical effort.

Victory (8 May 1945)[27] likewise validated the strategic optimism of previous years, generating an iconography of jubilation. Curiously, whereas the pressing challenge of ceaselessly designing inflammatory posters that would incite the citizenry to resistance and abhorrence of the enemy occasioned a sizable body of highly original satirical works, notably by Viktor Deni, Dmitrii Moor, and the Kukryniksy, graphics inscribing happiness at victory were aesthetically inferior. Bland and unimaginative, they bordered on the crudely amateurish. In the proliferating sanitized images of soldiers' repatriation, women as safekeepers of domestic values welcomed them home [Plates 6.35, 6.36]. Mothers, wives, and offspring exultantly hailed the conquering heroes, with no allusion to the catastrophic cost in military and civilian lives or to the war's traumatic effects on survivors, many of them maimed or incapable of reintegration into society—a theme explored in such 1950s war films as Sergei Bondarchuk's *Sud'ba cheloveka* [*Fate of a Man* 1959] and Marlen Khutsiev's *Dva Fedora* [*Two Fedors* 1958].[28] Numerous soldiers had established second families and either failed to return or did, but with the intention of enjoying two wives and homes.

---

[27] In Russia, 9 May, owing to the time difference between Berlin and Moscow.
[28] Larisa Shepit'ko's *Kryl'ia* [*Wings* 1966] is unique in its portrayal of a *female* fighter pilot who cannot adjust to peacetime conditions.

The writer Lev Kopelev, a father and married man, frankly admitted to having taken a second "wife" at the front, following a pattern common among Russian officers (Merridale 317). Masculine self-indulgence during the war sprang partly from the ever-present likelihood of annihilation, and subsequently from the war's decimation of the USSR's male contingent, which not only rendered men a rare and therefore prized commodity in post-war Soviet society, but also exerted an incalculable impact on gender relations in succeeding decades.[29] Yet literature and film imputed the possibility of sexual infidelity under wartime conditions chiefly to women, and posters sidestepped the issue altogether in order to promote the inspiring mirage of conjugal and romantic solidarity amid slaughter and dread.[30]

Ladies in Waiting: Sexual Fidelity as Magic Charm

Needless to say, not all women "remained true" throughout the war. Yet the theme of female (in)constancy, widely explored in Soviet, British, and American wartime literature, film, and song, never penetrated graphics, though it appeared, albeit seldom, in unofficial songs (see the chapter by Robert A. Rothstein). Countless works in other genres inflated unwavering commitment to frontline soldiers by "the girls back home" into a prerequisite for fighting men's survival. "Dear John" letters or the deaths of sexually betrayed combatants were empirical markers of the consequence-laden distinction between "the ones [women] who waited and the ones who didn't," as the narrator of Leon Uris's *Battle Cry* (1953) categorically phrased it (Gubar 1987, 246).[31] Konstantin Simonov poem "Zhdi menia" ["Wait for

---

[29] For an astute analysis of these repercussions, see Elizabeth Brainerd, "Uncounted Costs of World War II: The Effects of Changing Sex Ratios on Marriage and Fertility of Russian Women." *NCEEER Papers* (15 February 2007), available at http://www.nceeer.org/Papers/papers.php (last accessed 6 July 2009).

[30] For a discussion of the toll the war took on domestic life, especially in rural areas, see Merridale (2006, 366–7).

[31] "A Woman's a Two-Face," the title of a poem by a corporal, expresses the sense of betrayal, whether real or merely suspected, by many a soldier. See Gubar (1987), 246.

me" 1941], summarizing in exalted tones soldiers' psychological dependence on their loved ones' forbearing faithfulness across the miles, became a mantra for Soviet men at the front, many of whom carried the poem in their pockets as a talisman. And Boris Ivanov and Aleksandr Stolper's identically titled film melodrama (1943), with the screenplay written by Simonov, credited female devotion with uncanny power in a scenario resembling religious narratives of faith's miraculous efficacy. Liza's unshakable fidelity and conviction that her pilot-husband, Kolia Ermolov, is alive, despite overwhelming odds to the contrary and the almost unanimous assumption of his death by the military, which reports him "missing in action," not only "infects" Ermolov's comrades with her faith, but also implicitly ensures his preservation. Her frivolous friend Sonia's contrasting behavior illustrates the maxim "female infidelity predestines male fatality": her husband perishes, as does the betrayed spouse in the song "In a Certain Town There Lived a Couple" ["V odnom gorode zhila parochka"] (see Rothstein).

More than a decade after the war, directors continued to invest female steadfastness with mystical salvific significance for men in battle, as may be deduced from Mikhail Kalatozov's Thaw-era *Letiat zhuravli* [*Cranes Are Flying* 1957],[32] where montage straightforwardly establishes a cause-and-effect relationship between Veronika's unfaithfulness and the death of her soldier-fiancé, Boris.[33] Songs such as "Katiusha," "Temnaia noch,'" "Zhdi menia" (Simonov's verses set to music, in multiple variants), "Zhdu tebia," "V zemlianke," "Ogonek," and many others likewise centered on the crucial assurance of women's loyalty.[34] An essential component of women's patriotic duty, fidelity at home mysteriously sustained men and their fighting spirit at the front. A fall from grace transformed women into irredeemable whores

---

[32] The screenplay by Viktor Rozov reworked his signally titled play *Vechno zhivye* [*Alive Forever*].

[33] For a perceptive analysis of the values and cultural conventions underlying these and similar scenarios, see Aleksandr Prokhorov, *Unasledovannyi diskurs: paradigmy stalinskoi kul'tury v literaturei kinomatografe "ottepeli"* (St. Petersburg: Akademicheskii proekt, DNK, 2007), especially 167–91.

[34] On gender disposition in World War II songs, see Suzanne Ament, "Reflecting Individual and Collective Identities—Songs of World War II," in Goscilo and Lanoux (2006), 115–30.

or worse, for their inconstancy robbed men not only of lives, but also of honor, as made explicit in *Letiat zhuravli*, in which a "Dear Ivan" letter elicits uncompromising condemnation: "Girls like that are worse than Nazis" and "Women like her—we men despise them. There can't be any forgiveness for her." Such negative female images, of course, ran counter to the *telos* of World War II posters—to rally, inspire, and comfort the population for the duration of the war—hence their omission in that genre. Moreover, after the German capitulation (8 May 1945), other initiatives occupied graphic artists, who had given unstintingly of their time and talent to the nation's war propaganda campaign. Whereas retrospective reassessment of women's flaws and frailties during the years of armed conflict may have attracted literati and film directors, in posters they would have been nothing short of grotesque.

Blocking out the Blockade

The perceived need for posters to "accentuate the positive" necessitated neglecting some of the war's most traumatic events, endured by multi-generational families and entire cities, such as the horrendous nightmare of Leningrad's protracted blockade (1941–1944)—the "900 days" of "an ordeal unprecedented in the history of warfare" (Tumarkin 1994, 69).[35] Encircled and trapped by the Nazis, lacking adequate food, fuel, and transportation, an estimated million inhabitants perished from starvation, disease, sub-freezing temperatures, and enemy fire. Lack of foresight and advance planning by the city's administration—"failure to stockpile food," delays in rationing and in evacuating children while still possible—contributed to the death toll, which reduced the city's population by more than a third. Leningrad trans-

---

[35] *The 900 Days: The Siege of Leningrad* (1969) is Harrison Salisbury's deservedly praised chronicle of the daily struggle for survival by civilians and soldiers in the city encircled and trapped by Hitler's forces, cut off from food and other supplies. For the substantial scholarship on this topic in more recent years, see Kirschenbaum and the sources listed in Cynthia Simmons, "Leningrad Culture under Siege," in *Preserving Petersburg: History, Memory, Nostalgia*, edited by Helena Goscilo and Stephen M. Norris (Bloomington and Indianapolis: Indiana University Press, 2008), 180, ft. 7.

formed into a carceral space combining the exhaustion, hunger, and anxiety of the home front with the "dismemberment and death" of military combat (Kirschenbaum 2006, 222, 220).[36] Unimaginable deprivation, daily confrontation with corpses lying on the streets, and steadily worsening conditions bred panic, callousness, insanity, and cases of cannibalism. Both official and unofficial accounts of the siege, however, focused not on starvation, but on German bombing and shelling, and hailed survivors in military terms as courageous "heroes" and "heroines" who voluntarily had sacrificed themselves for the nation's sake.

As bodies started to resemble skeletons, gender distinctions underwent erasure (see the chapter by Irina Sandomirskaja). Yet, as Lisa Kirschenbaum points out, writers such as Lidiia Ginzburg, who acknowledged the physical effects of starvation and "recognized that the starving body potentially subverted the comforting conclusion that even as they starved, Leningraders served a higher purpose," nonetheless adopted a "redemptive stance," despite feelings of shame at surviving starvation (229). A less sanguine viewpoint emerges from the memoirs of Ol'ga Berggol'ts, "the voice of Leningrad radio," who "made the disappearance of the gendered body a measure of the degradations caused by war" (Kirschenbaum 2006, 229). Both Ginzburg and Berggol'ts, like other female survivors, however, hardly mentioned their own desexed bodies. In a psychological retreat from eliciting pity as objects of defacement threatening a core identity, they focused on the skeletal, degraded bodies of other women or on the generalized body. Though alert to the myriad of suppressions during those dreadful years, Ginzburg in her sensitive memoirs seems strangely unaware of her own reluctance to place herself squarely in the midst of her own experience.[37] Deflection

---

[36] Kirschenbaum's (2006) fine article refers to Leningrad as the "city front"—comprising mainly women, children, and the old (*passim*).

[37] One can only speculate on the relationship between Ginzburg's desexualized body, her lesbianism, and her choice of a mediating male figure (the abstract N) for her perspective on the siege in *Chelovek za pis'mennym stolom*, of which *Blockade Diary* is a section. Symptomatic of her preference for distancing herself from what she narrates are the addenda to the *Blockade Diary*, above all "Paralysis (Confessions of a survivor of malnutrition")," which opens with the following statement: "This psychological episode has been reconstructed by me (in the first person) on the basis of siege experience, as reflected in the stories of the people who lived through it" (95).

and decorousness, in short, formed a bridge between official and unofficial descriptions of the inhumane existence instituted by the siege.

On the rare occasions that posters actually mentioned the blockade, it was to announce it breached, as for instance in Vladimir Serov's *Blokada Leningrada prorvana!* [*The Blockade of Leningrad Is Breached!* 1943]. Tellingly, city-specific posters such as Solomon Boim's *Krov' leningradtsev vyzyvaet k mesti!* [*The Blood of Leningraders Calls for Revenge!* 1944] depicted faceless corpses thinly scattered in the snow only after the blockade lifted, and they proclaimed the Germans' withdrawal from Leningrad (Serov's *My otstoiali Leningrad* [*We've Successfully Defended Leningrad*] 1944) only when there was reasonable cause for the expectation of Soviet victory. Neither these images nor the more general calls to avenge Nazi atrocities portrayed the ravages and desperate plight of the northern capital's inhabitants. The sturdy young female bricklayer gracing Serov's red-dominated reconstruction poster, in fact, glows with health and resoluteness. Moreover, her facial features, shape, and longish wind-blown hair are unmistakably coded as feminine [Plate 6.33]. To an incomparably greater degree than memoirs, fiction, and film, posters subsumed Leningraders' grisly tribulations amid inhumane conditions, as well as the enduring consequences of their traumas, under the heartening formula of "city under attack–city liberated" in a standardized exultant mode.

Kenotic Comrades

In the World War II graphic revision of Russia's lofty matrix narrative of martyred heroism, traceable to medieval times, gender dictated the distribution of roles: the male prerogative of invulnerable heroism prescribed martyrdom and passivity as women's lot. Yet, that overdetermined polarization notwithstanding, Soviet posters bypassed two entrenched derogatory stereotypes of femininity. Unlike their American and British counterparts, Soviet graphic artists adamantly refused to associate indiscretion exclusively with women either as gossips or seductresses.[38] As

---

[38] Recall Nathaniel Hawthorne's memorable dismissal of female logorrhea—a "mob of scribbling women."

Susan Gubar notes, in posters "enjoining silence as a protection against spies," Allied propaganda "spoke directly about and to servicemen's fear of their women's betrayal" through irresponsible garrulity (Gubar 1987, 240) and warned males to beware of seductive female spies. G. Lacoste's famous poster *Keep Mum, She's not so Dumb!* (c. 1940), for example, displays the physical charms of a lounging sophisticate in a tight-fighting dress using her feminine wiles so as to overhear or extract information from the three gullible males surrounding her. In this respect Soviet posters proved less misogynistic, for they not only presented careless chatter as independent of gender, but also entrusted women with the task of urging caution, as in the indefatigably reproduced *Ne boltai!* [*Don't Chatter!* 1941] [Plates 6.37, 6.38].

Secondly, in congruence with Soviet conventions, war graphics scrupulously avoided sexual exploitation of women as "desirable bodies," chiefly configuring them as mothers, comrades, and sisters. Unlike in cinema, no sexy spies or glamorous pin ups—mainstays of Anglophone wartime propaganda—appeared in posters, decorated barracks and bombers, or lent their names to artillery tanks (Gubar 1987, 238–9). Even in (the few) scenes of pillage and implied rape, Soviet graphic artists exercised discretion, merely sketching in prone women's bodies, leaving their faces indistinct, and emphasizing their maternal role by coupling them with small children. For instance, a 1942 poster by Leonid Golovanov depicts a brutish Nazi staring down at a dead, presumably raped woman [Plate 6.16]. A child lying across her supine body discreetly covers part of it, and the rhyming couplets below the image further desexualize the viewer's reading of the visual through domestication and the conceptual progression from family to homeland: "Za chest' zheny, za zhizn' detei, / Za schast'e rodiny svoei, / Za nashi nivy i luga— / Ubei zakhvatchika-vraga!" [For your wife's honor, for your children's lives, / For the happiness of your motherland, / For our fields of grain and dales— / Kill the enemy invader!]. Such posters are bifocal, in the sense that the pathos of the verses and of the violated woman represents a Soviet perspective, with her vestigial eroticization implicitly attributed to the Nazi barbarian, her understatedly disarrayed clothes serving as traces of *his* animalism.

A variation on the device of bifocalism operates vividly in the most dramatic image of female kenosis in World War II posters, which deviates from the canon in several respects. The prolific Viktor Deni's

1942 *Ubei fashista-izuvera!* [*Kill the Nazi-Monster!*] [Plate 6.39] derives
its emotional power not only from the repellently unambiguous juxtaposition of the necrophilic Nazi and the truncated corpse of the semi-
exposed, hanged young woman over whom he salivates, but also from
its relationship to a famous photograph of a historical icon shrouded
in national mythology. Deni's image graphically duplicates the widely
circulated snapshot of Zoia Kosmodem'ianskaia, the heroine of Lev
Arnshtam's 1944 film, *Zoia*, and a household name during and after
the war. According to the officially scripted account of her life, Zoia
was an eighteen-year-old Komsomol partisan who, when captured and
tortured by the Nazis, preferred death to betrayal of her comrades and
country.[39] Touted as the unparalleled martyr of World War II (Sartorti
1995, 182), this Soviet Joan of Arc volunteered for the partisan movement at the outbreak of war. Sent behind the front line on a military
assignment near Moscow, she was seized by the Germans when trying
to set fire to a stable in the village where they were camping overnight. Interrogated, tortured, and finally hanged, she preserved a stoic
silence, and reportedly died proclaiming, "To die for my people is happiness... Stalin is with us" (Sartorti 1995,185; English adjusted).[40]

Patently modeled on medieval hagiographies, this narrative of
secular canonization—consolidated through articles, drawings, a play,
and other cultural genres—acquired additional pathos with the publication of the photograph taken by the frontline photographer Sergei
Strunnikov (1907–1944)[41] [Plate 6.40]. It shows Zoia's frozen, mutilated body lying in the snow, her breast bared and the noose still pulled

---

[39] Kenez has argued that in 1943 and early 1944 watching a Russian woman's
violent death or seeing it unavenged would have demoralized Soviets audiences at screenings—for instance, of Fridrikh Ermler's *Ona zashchishchaet
rodinu* [*She Defends the Motherland*] (1943) and Mark Donskoi's *Raduga*
[*The Rainbow*]. By the summer of 1944, however, the realistic expectation
of victory over the Germans rendered consolatory omissions superfluous;
hence the ending of Arnshtam's film actually shows Zoia's execution
(Kenez 1995, 168).

[40] Tarkovskii's boy protagonist Ivan presumably suffers an analogous fate (see
Ivanovo detstvo).

[41] The photograph also inspired the poster *Zoia* (1942/43) by the Kukryniksy.
For additional details of Kosmodem'ianskaia's transfiguration, see
Tumarkin (1994), 76–8.

tight around her neck (Sartorti 1995, 184).[42] The homology between the photograph snapped in 1941 and Deni's poster just a year later was indisputably intended to incense Russians at the Nazis' merciless savagery.[43]

The inestimable hold that national mythologies possess over the collective imagination may be inferred from the failure of recent voices raised in the demythologization of Kosmodem'ianskaia to tarnish her halo. Despite copious evidence of the myth's fictitious nature, she remains a gendered icon of the sacred war that for the majority of contemporary Russians constitutes the single uncontaminated event in their troubled history. To assume that official views of the war were imposed upon a citizenry with strikingly divergent recollections and interpretations of its unendurable hardships, however, requires dismissing uncensored retrospective accounts of individual war experiences. To highlight the united population's courage, stoicism, and "heroic self-sacrifice," many of these reminiscences downplay such factors as fear, vacillation, and the instinct of self-preservation strong enough to prompt collaboration with the enemy. As Nina Tumarkin's detailed study documents, within the continuing reassessment of Soviet history ushered in by glasnost', some Russians deplore the cult of World War II orchestrated by the state, for in sweeping aside unwelcome facts it instances the self-serving unscrupulousness of a largely discredited political system.[44] Yet Kirschenbaum's nuanced scholarship on the siege of Leningrad reveals the degree to which recollections by survivors at a considerable temporal and geographical remove from

---

[42] Given the manufactured nature of the myth at every stage, whether the body is actually Kosmodem'ianskaia's remains questionable.

[43] For the Kukryniksy poster inspired by the photograph, see the large, superbly illustrated volume that accompanied the exhibition in the Art Institute of Chicago in 2011 (Zegers and Druick 2011).

[44] Some of the credit for demythologizing the war belongs to publications by Ales' Adamovich, Daniil Granin, Vasilii Grossman, and other writers and war correspondents. See *Blokadnaia kniga* by Adamovich and Granin; *Khatynskaia povest'* [*The Khatyn Story* 1972] and *Ia iz ognennoi derevni* [*Out of the Fire* 1977] by Adamovich; *Chernaia kniga* [*The Black Book*, pd. 1993] by Grossman and Il'ia Erenburg; Grossman's *Zhizn' i sud'ba* [*Life and Fate*, pd. 1980) and *Vse techet* [*Forever Flowing*, pd. 1970].

the events overlap or coincide with the official Soviet master narrative of incorruptible heroism.

Few challenges tax the cultural historian more than the distinction between "Truth" and myths, for the latter have their own psychological truth. Tumarkin recounts a telling moment during her interaction with a circle of Russian friends in 1985, when one of the members' joking remark about "Pavlik"[45] Matrosov—a canonized World War II hero—was unanimously greeted with stern reproaches. Tumarkin sympathized with the group's rebuke for cogent reasons:

> It was [and is, HG] impossible to make fun of the lavish cult of the Great Patriotic War without in some way deriding the actual war experience. The horrific and in some ways majestic stories that came together as a collective memory were solid pieces of the mosaic of lies and truth that for decades had made up the sustaining myth of the Great Patriotic War, a mosaic that served both to evoke the past and to cover up selected portions of it. (Tumarkin 1994, 45)

The humorous remark evidently violated the majority's sense of the war's sacredness, while also expressing a minority attitude. Like other cultural genres recruited for war propaganda, posters targeted the populace's loyalties, fears, prejudices, and desires so as to rally the people, inducing them, at a horrific cost, to translate unlikely avowals of victory into reality—or Truth. Though posters hardly reflect either the price of this victory or women's contribution to it, they provide insight into the mass psychology deemed effective for the ultimate achievement of that hard-won triumph.

In today's Russia, the publishing house Kontakt-Kul'tura ensures the availability of World War II posters, reproduced in an anniversary volume published in 2005 (Snopkov), for example, and in postcards sold in major bookstores. The huge 2011 exhibition of TASS World War II posters at The Art Institute of Chicago and the large volume of visuals cum commentary based on it (Zegers and Druick) represent

---

[45] The hero's real name was Aleksandr Matrosov, and the joke resides in the speaker's ironic yoking of two cultural icons: Matrosov and Pavlik Morozov.

the largest compendium in the West. From the special popularity of postcards replicating such posters as *Rodina-mat' zovet!, Ne boltai!,* and *A nu-ka, vziali!,* one tentatively deduces that the woman-centered graphics possess an appeal lacking in the iconography of male soldiers. Whether these images are artistically superior or whether their market value merely instances the seemingly universal proclivity to construct women as more gaze-riveting than men remains an open question.

REFERENCES

Bonner, Withold, and Arja Rosenholm, eds. 2008. *Recalling the Past—(Re)constructing the Past: Collective and Individual Memory of World War II in Russia and Germany.* Helsinki: Aleksanteri Series 2.

Cottam, Kazimiera J. 1998a. *Women in War and Resistance.* Nepean, Ontario: New Military Publishing.

———, ed. and trans. 1998b. *Defending Leningrad: Women behind Enemy Lines.* Revised edition. Nepean, Ontario: New Military Publishing.

———. 1983. *Soviet Women in Combat in World War II.* Manhattan, Kansas: Military Affairs.

De Pauw, Linda Grant. 1998. *Battle Cries and Lullabies: Women in War from Prehistory to the Present.* Norman: University of Oklahoma Press.

Fussell, Paul. 1989. *Wartime: Understanding and Behavior in the Second World War.* New York and Oxford: Oxford University Press.

Geldern, James von. 1995. "Radio Moscow: The Voice from the Center." In *Culture and Entertainment in Wartime Russia,* edited by Richard Stites, 44–61. Bloomington and Indianapolis: Indiana University Press.

Ginzburg, Lidiya. 1995. *Blockade Diary.* Translated by Alan Myers. London: Harvill Press.

Goscilo, Helena and Andrea Lanoux, eds. 2006. *Gender and National Identity in Twentieth-Century Russian Culture.* DeKalb, IL: Northern Illinois University Press.

Gubar, Susan. 1987. "'This Is My Rifle, This Is My Gun': World War II and the Blitz on Women." In *Behind the Lines: Gender and the Two World Wars,* edited by Margaret Randolph Higonnet et al., 227–59. New Haven: Yale University Press.

Higgonet, Margaret Randolph et al., eds. 1987. *Behind the Lines: Gender and the Two World Wars.* New Haven: Yale University Press.

Higgonet, Margaret R. and Patrice R. Higgonet. 1987. "The Double Helix." In *Behind the Lines: Gender and the Two World Wars,* edited by Margaret Randolph Higgonet et al., 31–47. New Haven: Yale University Press.

Kenez, Peter. 1995. "Black and White: The War on Film." In *Culture and Entertainment in Wartime Russia,* edited by Richard Stites, 157–75. Bloomington and Indianapolis: Indiana University Press.

Kirschenbaum, Lisa A. 2006. "'The Alienated Body': Gender Identity and the Memory of the Siege of Leningrad." In *Gender & War in Twentieth-Century Easter Europe*, edited by Nancy M. Wingfield and Maria Bucur, 220–34. Bloomington and Indianapolis: Indiana University Press.

Kukulin, Il'ya. 2005. "The regulation of pain: The Great Patriotic War in Russian literature from the 1940s to the 1970s." *Eurozine* (5 June), translated by Mischa Gabowitsch. Original published in *Nepriskosnovennyi Zapas* 40 and *Osteuropa* (4 June 2005). www.eurozine.com (last accessed 4 February 2007).

Merridale, Catherine. 2006. *Ivan's War: Life and Death in the Red Army, 1939–1945*. New York: Metropolitan Books.

Norris, Stephen. 2006. *War of Images: Russian Popular Prints, Wartime Culture, and National Identity 1812–1945*. DeKalb: Northern Illinois University Press.

Parker, Paul. 1937. "The Modern Style in American Advertising Art." *Parnassus* 9, no. 4 (April): 20–3.

Pennington, Reina. 2001. *Wings, Women, and War: Soviet Airwomen in World War II*. Lawrence: University Press of Kansas.

Pisiotis, Argyrios K. 1995. "Images of Hate in the Art of War." In *Culture and Entertainment in Wartime Russia*, edited by Richard Stites, 141–56. Bloomington and Indianapolis: Indiana University Press.

Riabov, Oleg. 2007. *"Rossiia-Matushka": Natsionalizm, gender i voina v Rossii XX veka*. Stuttgart: Ibidem-Verlag.

Sartorti, Rosalinde. 1996. "On the Making of Heroes, Heroines, and Saints." In *Culture and Entertainment in Wartime Russia*, edited by Richard Stites, 176–93. Bloomington and Indianapolis: Indiana University Press.

Scott, Joan W. 1987. "Rewriting History." In *Behind the Lines: Gender and the Two World Wars*, edited by Margaret Randolph Higgonet et al., 21–30. New Haven: Yale University Press.

Snopkov, P.A. et al. 2005. *Plakaty voiny i pobedy: 1941–1945*. Moscow: Kontakt-Kul'tura.

Stites, Richard, ed. 1995. *Culture and Entertainment in Wartime Russia*. Bloomington and Indianapolis: Indiana University Press.

Stoff, Laurie S. 2006. *They Fought for the Motherland: Russia's Women Soldiers in World War I and the Revolution*. Lawrence, KS: University Press of Kansas.

"Tri goda tankist skryval, chto on—zhenshchina." No date. http://news.e63.ru/22366.html (last accessed 2 October 2007).

Tumarkin, Nina. 1994. *The Living and the Dead: The Rise and Fall of the Cult of World War II in Russia*. New York: Basic Books.

Vilinbakhov. G., and T. Vilinbakhova. 1995. *Sviatoi Georgeii Pobedonosets*. St. Petersburg: "Iskusstvo—SPB."

Wingfield, Nancy M., and Maria Bucur. 2006. *Gender & War in Twentieth-Century Eastern Europe*. Bloomington and Indianapolis: Indiana University Press.

Wolf, Erika. 2012. *Koretsky: The Soviet Photo Poster: 1930–1984.* New York: The New Press.

Zegers, Peter Kort, and Douglas Druick, eds. 2011. *Windows on the War: Soviet Tass Posters at Home and Abroad 1941–1945.* Chicago: The Art Institute of Chicago.

Zheltova, Ekaterina. "Zhenshchiny—tankisty." No date. http://www.volkey. ru/admin/print.php?subaction=showfull&id=1140824280&archiv (last accessed 22 September 2007).

Plate 6.1. Petr Aliakrinskii. The rhetorical device of using past victories as a guarantor of current military success (1942)

КРАСНОЙ АРМИИ ·СЛАВА!

Plate 6.2. Leonid Golovanov. Glory to the Red Army!
Fulfillment of the promise in a 1944 poster by Golovanov (1944) that the Soviet
Army would reach Berlin and rout the Germans (1945)

Plate 6.3. See at Plate 2.4.

Plate 6.4. Iraklii Toidze. For the Motherland! (*1943*)

Plate 6.5. *Viktor Ivanov*. Liberated Soviet People! You Are Delivered from the Enslavement of Nazi Oppression—Return as Soon as Possible to Your Homeland! (*1945*)

Сынок родимый мой! Словами не сказать, Освободитель мой! Дай мне тебя обнять,
Как настрадались мы от гадины немецкой... Расцеловать тебя—по-русски, по-советски!

в. ЛЕБЕДЕВ-КУМАЧ

Plate 6.6. Fedor Antonov. An iconic representative of the older generation effusively thanks the young soldier ("son" and "savior") for liberating the population from the German "louse." Text by V. Lebedev-Kumach (1943)

Сын мой! Ты видишь долю мою...
Громи фашистов в святом бою!

Plate 6.7. Fedor Antonov. My Son! You See My Fate! Crush
the Nazis in [Our] Sacred Battle! (*1942*)

Plate 6.8. Dementii Shmarinov. Soldier, Answer [the Needs of] the Homeland with Victory! *(1942)*

Самед на смерть идет, чтоб не погиб Семен,
Собою жертвует Семен за жизнь Самеда...
Пароль их „Родина" и лозунг их „Победа"!

*Plate 6.9. Viktor Koretskii. The "friendship of nations," which dictates
that all Soviet citizens willingly risk death for their compatriots.
Verses by Dem'ian Bednyi (1943)*

Plate 6.10. Nina Vatolina. Nazism Is Women's Worst Enemy! (*1941*)

Plate 6.11. Dementii Shmarinov. Revenge [Us]! *(1942)*

Plate 6.13. See at Plate 2.6.

Plate 6.13. Viktor Ivanov & Ol'ga Burova. Red Army Soldier,
Fight Boldly and Stoically for Children's Lives, for Wives' Honor,
for Home, and for Homeland! (*1942*)

Plate 6.14. Dementii Shmarinov. Death to the Germans-Murderers! (*1944*)

БОЕЦ КРАСНОЙ АРМИИ!
Ты не дашь любимую на позор
и бесчестье гитлеровским солдатам.

*Plate 6.15. Fedor Antonov. Appeal to the Red Army for protection from "shame
and dishonor"—presumably rape as "a fate worse than death"—perpetrated by
Hitler's army (1942)*

За честь жены, за жизнь детей,   За наши нивы и луга—
За счастье родины своей,   Убей захватчика-врага!

Plate 6.16. Leonid Golovanov. A list of what is at stake—children, women's honor, and the Soviet land (1942)

Plate 6.17 Leonid Golovanov. A female prisoner, identified by her number tag, urges "valiant soldiers" to press west and free all of the "Soviet land" (1943)

Plate 6.18 Viktor Ivanov. An affectively tearful young prisoner of war as one of countless Soviets awaiting liberation by the Red Army (1945)

Plate 6.19. Icon of St. George visually documenting his biography, the stages of his life arranged clockwise around his central saintly achievement (fourteenth century)

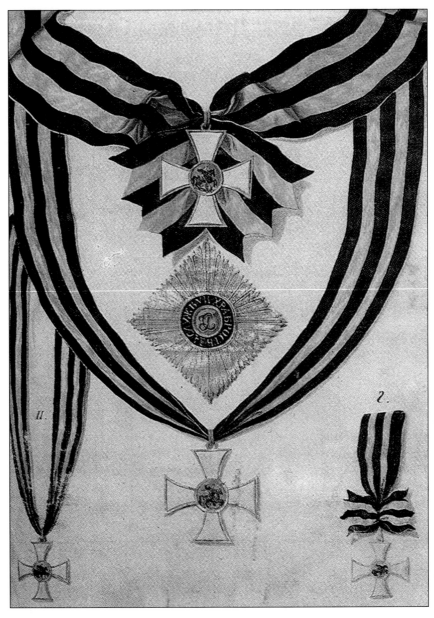

Plate 6.20. Order of St. George (1769)

Plate 6.21. Order of St. George (contemporary)

Plate 6.22. Tat'iana Eremina. Homefront dedication to harvesting the entire crop "to the last seed" (1941)

БОЛЬШЕ ХЛЕБА
ДЛЯ ФРОНТА И ТЫЛА

УБРАТЬ УРОЖАЙ ПОЛНОСТЬЮ

*Plate 6.23. Nikolai Denisov & Nina Vatolina. The same message,
with the explicit addition that the fruit of women's labor will provide bread
for those "at the front and the rear" (1941)*

Plate 6.24. Viktor Koretskii. We Have but One Target—Berlin.
*Four years after the Nazi invasion, smiles had replaced imploring
expressions and cries for help (1945)*

ТРАКТОР В ПОЛЕ –
ЧТО ТАНК В БОЮ!

*Plate 6.25. Viktor Ivanov & Ol'ga Burova. Women in the fields, helping
men bound for the front (1942)*

Plate 6.26. Vladimir Serov. We'll Replace [Them]! (*1941*)

Plate 6.27. Tat'iana Eremina. Partisans, Wreak Vengeance without Mercy!
(*1942*)

ОТ НАРОДНОЙ МЕСТИ
НЕ УЙТИ ВРАГУ!

Plate 6.28. Isaak Rabichev. The Enemy Won't Escape the People's Vengeance!
Only the kerchief (plus absence of beard) indicates the
otherwise desexed woman's gender (1941)

*Plate 6.29. Viktor Koretskii & Vera Gitsevich. The young field nurse
as the soldier's "aide" and "friend" (1941)*

Plate 6.30. Viktor Koretskii. A Red Cross nurse helping a soldier from the battlefield and simultaneously rescuing his weapon (1942)

Plate 6.31. Dementii Shmarinov. Ukraine as woman embracing the Red Army "liberators" (1943)

Plate 6.32. Iosif Serebriannyi. A 'feminine' enthusiast eager to rebuild (1944)

Plate 6.33. Vladimir Serov. Encouraging reassurance by another young female
optimist that post-blockade Leningrad will be rebuilt (1944)

ВИКТОР ИВАНОВ-4

ОТСТРОИМ НА СЛАВУ!

Plate 6.34. Viktor Ivanov and Ol'ga Burova. Reconstruction,
yet again imaged as a cheerful young woman (1945)

Plate 6.35. *Nikolai Kochergin.* Glory to the Victors! Long Live Our Free Soviet Fatherland! *No longer under German threat, the USSR has metamorphosed from vulnerable Motherland to triumphant Fatherland (1945)*

**ТЫ ХРАБРО ВОЕВАЛ С ВРАГОМ—
ВОЙДИ, ХОЗЯИН, В НОВЫЙ ДОМ!**

Plate 6.36. Nina Vatolina. Woman as keeper of hearth and home welcoming her returned husband as "master" of their new domicile (1945)

Plate 6.37. Konstantin Ivanov & Veniamin Briskin. Chatter and Gossip Suit the Enemy Nicely—*and are not solely women's preserve (1954)*

БУДЬ НА ЧЕКУ,
В ТАКИЕ ДНИ
ПОДСЛУШИВАЮТ СТЕНЫ.
НЕДАЛЕКО ОТ БОЛТОВНИ
И СПЛЕТНИ
ДО ИЗМЕНЫ.

НЕ БОЛТАЙ!

Plate 6.38. Nina Vatolina & Nikolai Denisov. Don't Chatter!—*a warning featured in the wartime graphics of most participants in WWII (1941)*

УБЕЙ ФАШИСТА-ИЗУВЕРА!

Plate 6.39. Viktor Deni. The Nazi as repellent necrophile drooling over the lifeless body of the idealized 'heroine' Zoia (1942)

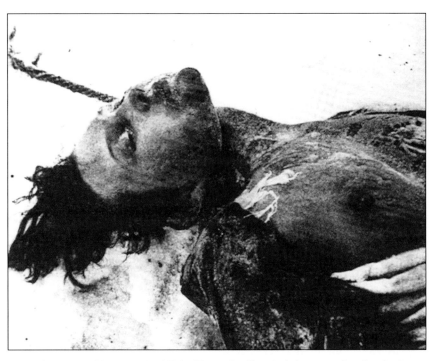

Plate 6.40. Photograph of Zoia Kosmodem'ianskaia's corpse that inspired both Deni and the Kukryniksy

Plate 9.1. Scene from Jasmila Žbanić Grbavica *(2006).*
Sara (Luna Mijovic) reciting a poem

Plate 9.2. Sara demands to know the truth about her father (Grbavica 2006)

Plate 9.3. Esma (Mirjana Karanović) shares details of her violation
(Grbavica *2006*)

Plate 9.4. Sara joins her classmates signing "Sarajevo, my love"
(Grbavica 2006)

CHAPTER 7

Songs of Women Warriors and Women Who Waited

Robert A. Rothstein

For fish [the natural element is] the river,	[Рыбам – речка,
For women, the stove,	Бабам печка
For us, the campaign.	Нам поход.]

These three lines from the refrain of a 1943 Russian song, "Where the Eagle Spread Its Wings" [Где Орел раскинул крылья], reflect the general image of women in World War II songs—waiting on the home front for their sons, husbands, or boyfriends to come home from the war.[1] But alongside songs presenting this dominant image there are also (often lesser-known) Russian songs that portray women as front-line nurses and soldiers, pilots and guerilla fighters. Songs of both

---

[1] The song, with words by Sergei Alymov and music by Anatolii Novikov, was written in August 1943 as a march for the 129th Infantry Division of the Red Army after the Division liberated the city of Orel. The first line of the text, which became the song's title, plays on the homonymity of the Russian word for eagle and the name of the city. The lines quoted here are from Alymov's original text as published in 1944 and reproduced in Lebedev (1986), 314–15. Lebedev points out that the text was constantly being amended by frontline soldiers. He cites a totally different refrain recalled by a veteran of the Division in 1973 (317). In the version of the song published in some other collections of wartime songs (Lukovnikov 1975, 150–2; Lobarev and Panfilova 1994, 26) the stove is associated with houses (Хатам – печка) rather than with women. Perhaps already by the 1970s the original line, with its less than respectful term for "women," seemed politically incorrect.

kinds are valuable not only as documents of official and unofficial attitudes of the time, but also as elements of the cultural heritage of present-day Russians. A front-page picture in *The New York Times* on 15 February 2009, for example, showed a placard carried by demonstrators in Vladivostok. The text of the placard echoed the 1945 song "The Enemies Have Burned [His] Home Down" (discussed below).[2]

In what follows, I propose to begin with the songs that depict women waiting, which represent the vast majority of songs about women during World War II. One small sample: the Lobarev and Panfilova anthology includes one hundred songs about women waiting, seven about nurses, and six about female fighters.

First, however, a bit of context may be useful. A line from *Gone with the Wind*—"War is men's business, not ladies'"—is echoed in the title of Svetlana Aleksievich's "documentary novel" [документальная повесть] *War Doesn't Have a Woman's Face* [*У войны – не женское лицо*]. The title of the Belarusian writer's book is somewhat ironic, since it is based on interviews with hundreds of Soviet women who participated in World War II, or what the Soviets called the Great Patriotic War, in roles ranging from cooks and laundresses to nurses and surgeons to tank commanders and fighter pilots. Yet the book begins with the following passage, remarkable in its essentialist view of gender:

---

[2] The original text by Mikhail Isakovskii begins:

Враги сожгли родную хату,	The enemies have burned his home down,
Сгубили всю его семью.	Killed his entire family.
Куда ж теперь идти солдату,	Where can the soldier go now,
Кому нести печаль свою?	To whom can he take his grief?

The placard reads:

Враги сожгли себе в угоду	The enemies have for their own convenience
большую славную страну,	burned down a glorious, big country,
куда ж теперь идти народу:	where can the people go now:
в бомжи, в рабы иль на войну?	[to become] homeless or slaves or go to war?

Everything that we know about woman fits best into the word "loving-kindness" [милосердие].[3] There are other words as well: sister, wife, friend, and the most lofty—mother. But isn't loving-kindness present in their content as their essence, as their purpose, as their ultimate meaning? A woman gives life, a woman protects life; woman and life are synonyms.[4]

This attribution of inherent traits to women, which ignores social and political forces in identity formation, is precisely what feminists such as Hélène Cixous and Luce Irigaray assailed in their milestone publications. The contrast between the reality of women's participation in the war and the romanticized image of women presented in Aleksievich's opening paragraph reflects a dichotomy in Soviet approaches to the "women's question" described by Lynne Attwood in her account of representations of women in the Stalinist press (Attwood 2001). Attwood adopted terminology from Barbara Ehrenreich and Deirdre English to describe how the Soviet Union initially followed a "rationalist" approach that saw women as "a vital economic resource," since "women were innately no less suited than men to work outside the home" and "differences in male and female personality and behavior were largely cultural constructs." This approach was in contrast to the older, "romantic" one, which viewed differences between men and women as rooted in nature and saw women as "naturally more tender, loving and nurturing" (Attwood 2001, 159, citing Ehrenreich and

---

[3] "Loving-kindness," introduced into English by William Coverdale in his 1535 translation of the Bible, seems a more appropriate translation of Russian *miloserdie* than the usual dictionary equivalent of "mercy" or "kindness." *Miloserdie* is a calque of Latin *misericordia* (the Vulgate's translation of Hebrew *chesed*, as in Psalm 25:6), for which Coverdale chose "loving-kindness." I am grateful to Halina Rothstein for this translation suggestion.

[4] "Все, что мы знаем о женщине, лучше всего вмещается в слово 'милосердие.' Есть и другие слова—сестра, жена, друг и самое высокое—мать. Но разве не присутствует в их содержании и милосердие как суть, как назначение, как конечный смысл? Женщина дает жизнь, женщина оберегает жизнь, женщина и жизнь—синонимы" (Aleksievich 1989, 12).

English 1978). Except for the alliterative contrast with "rationalist," perhaps "idealized" would be a better term than "romantic."[5]

The late 1920s, Attwood argues, brought a realization of the need for stability after the turmoil of the Revolution, Civil War, and the first Five-Year Plan. The family began to be seen as a potential source of such stability. If women had a natural propensity for domestic work, moreover, there was less need for the authorities to finance institutions and services (such as cafeterias and daycare centers) to take over the functions that women performed in the family. There was also opposition to the proposed elimination of the individual kitchen on the part of women themselves.[6] But the program of rapid industrialization meant that women could not be allowed "to devote themselves entirely to domesticity." Women were a vital economic resource, so "the Soviet state tried to have it both ways" by promoting rationalism and romanticism simultaneously, periodically adjusting the balance between them according to "the changing economic and demographic needs of the state" (Attwood 2001,159–60).[7]

When the war began, rationalism required that women replace men in the workforce, but romanticism dominated the imagery employed to encourage men to defend Mother Russia and their vulnerable wives, mothers, sisters, and girlfriends. As the defense of the homeland began to push women onto the front lines, this shift, too, was explained in terms of the romantic model. Women were effective as fighters precisely because of their "natural femininity, maternal care and tenderness." On the pages of the magazine *Peasant Woman* [Крестьянка] the writer Vera Ketlinskaia explained that these wives and mothers "passionately love their children, their families, their hearths. But they do not want to rear children for captivity, they do not want to see their loved ones turned into slaves... Love and motherhood [...] do not deaden their urge to

---

[5] Helena Goscilo proposes the term "restrictive" since "idealization or romanticization of women by definition removes them from both social and political spheres, confining the area of their activity to 'home'" (author's private correspondence).

[6] Women's attitudes on this subject are discussed in Rothstein and Rothstein (1997), 178–84.

[7] The balance, or rather lack of balance, led to women's bearing a "double burden"—working full-time outside of the home and then returning home to a "second shift" (to use the term popularized by Hochschild 1989).

fight to the end for the independence of the motherland, but fan it into a terrible flame" (Attwood 2001, 169).

The song texts considered here, especially those by professional poets and lyricists, mostly embody the romantic view of women, whether portraying them as waiting on the home front that Soviet fighting men were defending, or as providing tender care to wounded soldiers as nurses—"sisters of mercy" [сестры милосердия], to use the archaic Russian expression that echoes Aleksievich's definition of the essence of a woman cited above. It is primarily in the texts written by non-professional or folk poets, however, that we see women who equal or outdo men as soldiers.[8] The official image promoted by professional poets and lyricists, however, was also widespread in the many unofficial songs that were collected during the war and later by folklorists.

The theme of waiting is explicit in some songs, even providing the title for one of the most popular wartime songs, "Wait for Me" [Жди меня]. The first twelve-line stanza repeats the imperative of the title eight times:

Wait for me, and I'll return,	Жди меня, и я вернусь.
But wait very hard.	Только очень жди,
Wait when yellow rains	Жди, когда наводят грусть
Bring melancholy;	Желтые дожди,
Wait when the snows swirl;	Жди, когда снега метут,
Wait when it's boiling hot.	Жди, когда жара,
Wait when others are not waiting,	Жди, когда других не ждут,
Having forgotten yesterday.	Позабыв вчера.
Wait when no letters come	Жди, когда из дальних мест
From distant places.	Писем не придет,
Wait when everyone who's waiting	Жди, когда уж надоест
Together is sick and tired of waiting.	Всем, кто вместе ждет.[9]

---

[8] Ament's article contains many pertinent observations about the reflection of gender roles in wartime songs, including the comment that "an accommodation between ideal and real was what rendered a song effective and powerful" (2006, 127).

[9] The text by Konstantin Simonov, first published as a poem in *Pravda* in January 1942, was set to various melodies; Matvei Blanter's became the most popular. See Shilov (1967), 3:101–3, 262.

The motif of melancholy or sadness [грусть] sounded in "Wait for Me" and the injunction to resist it also appears in such songs as "Good-bye, Cities and Village Houses" [До свидания, города и хаты],[10] written in 1941, which polarizes gender as it contrasts the brave young men who are about to leave at dawn for war with the young women whom they ask to see them off [На заре, девчата, выходите / Комсомольский провожать отряд]. The departing Komsomol members tell their girlfriends not to grieve in their absence, since they will come back victorious [Вы без нас, девчата, не грустите, – / Мы придем с победою назад].[11] A similarly optimistic view of the end of the war motivates the advice not to cry in the 1943 "Song of the Red Navy Men" [Песня краснофлотцев]:

Don't cry, wives, wipe away your tears,	Не плачьте жены, утрите слезы.
Let the storms howl behind the stern!	Пусть воют штормы за кормой!
An experienced sailor will pass through the thunderstorms	Моряк бывалый пройдет сквозь грозы
And will come home unharmed.	И, невредим, придет домой.[12]

The image of the wife at home wiping away a tear appears as well in one of the most beloved of wartime songs, "Dark Night" [Темная ночь, 1943], as the soldier at the front pictures his wife at home:

I know, darling, that this dark night you're not sleeping,	В темную ночь ты, любимая, знаю, не спишь,
And [standing] by the crib you secretly wipe away a tear.	И у детской кроватки тайком ты слезу утираешь.[13]

---

[10] While most dictionaries translate the word *khaty* of the title as "cottages," the reference is to peasant dwellings in Ukraine, Belarus, and southern Russia.

[11] The words are by Mikhail Isakovskii, music by Matvei Blanter. The text and music can be found in Shilov (1967), 3:11–12.

[12] The words are by N. Lobkovskii, music by A. Aleksandrov. The song is rarely included in Soviet or post-Soviet song anthologies; it is quoted in part by Gudoshnikov (1959), 16, and is available at http://www.sovmusic.ru/text.php?fname=morskay4 (last accessed 9 June 2008).

[13] The song was written for the film *Two Soldiers* [Два бойца]. The words by Vladimir Agatov and music by Nikita Bogoslovskii can be found in Shilov (1967), 3:165–7.

The soldier is calm in battle, comforted by his faith in his wife, who he knows will greet him lovingly no matter what happens to him [Знаю встретишь с любовью меня, что б со мной ни случилось].[14]

The formula of the tearful, devoted woman comforted by her stoic Red Army soldier survived long after the war. A song written in 1972 by professional songwriters adopts the folk style of a dialogue between a young couple that expresses the familiar active/passive gender roles:

Darling, where are you going?	Дорогой, куда ты едешь?
Darling, to war.	Дорогая, на войну.
Darling, take me with you.	Дорогой, возьми с собою.
Darling, I can't [or: I won't].	Дорогая, не возьму.

She asks him to write and to hurry home, to which he agrees (напишу, [...] поспешу), and the song ends with the traditional images of waiting and crying:

Darling, I'll dissolve in tears.	Дорогой, зальюсь слезами.
Darling, [they'll be too] salty.	Дорогая, солоны.
Darling, winter will set in.	Дорогой, зима настанет.
Darling, wait for spring.[15]	Дорогая, жди весны.

Not all the women who waited were nameless. A 1942 song that repeats the motifs of grieving and insomnia takes its name from its lyrical heroine:

You wait, Lizaveta,	Ты ждешь, Лизавета,
For word from your beloved.	От друга привета,

---

[14] The image of the steadfastness and loyalty of the women waiting is later questioned in unofficial songs.

[15] The song, with music by Valerii Gavrilin and words by Al'bina Shul'gina, can be found in Medvedeva (1985), 62. It was part of a vocal cycle called "War Letters" [Военные письма]. It is reminiscent of such songs as the Polish "Where Are You Going, Jaś?" [Gdzież to jedziesz, Jasiu?—see Kolberg 1986, 238–9] or the Yiddish "Tell Me, Pretty Maiden" [Her nor, du sheyn meydele—see Mlotek 1977, 32–3].

You don't sleep until dawn,	Ты не спишь до рассвета,
Worrying about me.	Все грустишь обо мне.

The most famous of the women waiting for their men to come home, however, was undoubtedly Katiusha, who made her appearance in the song of the same name in 1938. At that point Katiusha was sending her song not to a soldier at the front, but "to [her] fighting man at a distant border post" [бойцу на дальнем пограничье]. The division of labor was clear: he was to defend their native land, while she would keep love safe [Пусть он землю бережет родную, / А любовь Катюша сбережет].[17] Immensely popular during and after World War II, lending its name, for example, to the Red Army's BM-8 and BM-13 rocket launchers,[18] the song gave rise to numerous reworkings, in many of which—as we shall soon see—Katiusha played a more active role.

Songs about women patiently waiting probably were intended to reassure men that they need not worry about unfaithful wives and

---

[16] The music of *Lizaveta*, by Nikita Boguslovskii, was apparently written before the war (according to Sokhor 1959, 180), but it was first used with words by Evgenii Dolmatovskii in the 1942 film *Aleksandr Parkhomenko*. Although the film was about the Civil War, the song seemed to address the situation in 1942 and therefore became popular independently of the film. The text and music can be found in Shilov (1967), 3:91–3.

[17] The text by Mikhail Isakovskii and music by Matvei Blanter can be found in Shilov (1967), 1:136–8. 1938 had brought armed conflict with Japanese forces on Lake Khasan in the Soviet Far East, on the border of Japanese-occupied Manchuria. "Katiusha" became so associated with World War II that it was often assumed to have been written during that war.

[18] A 2008 internet article by an anonymous historian of Soviet automobiles (www.avto.ru/review/post_8871.html, last accessed 9 June 2009) suggests that the name originated in the marking KAT (for "Cumulative thermite artillery [shell]" [Кумулятивный артиллерийский термитный], but caught on because of the popularity of the song. In 1943 Vasilii Shishliakov, a soldier serving on the Karelia front, composed "A Song about 'Katiusha'" [Песенька о «Катюше»] in the form of a dialogue between a mother and her son. The mother asks about "the Katiusha that you've fallen in love with at the front" and hopes that when the war ends, he will bring her home. Her son answers that he has never had such a good friend, and that their friendship and love grows stronger every day as they strike the Germans together. But he adds, "when the storm ends and the last battle is over," he will return but he won't be able to bring "Katiusha" home. The text can be found in Lebedev (1986), 236–7.

girlfriends and therefore could concentrate on defeating the enemy. At the same time, they provided a model for female behavior on the home front. Yet there were also very popular songs that raised the possibility of unfaithfulness and made light of it. The hero of the 1942 song "Vasia-Vasilek" is in a bad mood because he has not received any mail from his beloved in five weeks. His comrades reassure him that if she loves him, she will write; if no letter arrives, it means that she has forgotten him and, moreover, never loved him. Yet that is no cause for gloom, since "if your heart is passionate, a girl will turn up. It's painful today, but don't be sad; tomorrow is your day." The general tone of the text and melody is upbeat.[19]

The same is true of a song about pilots written in 1945 right after the war. In the refrain to "Time to Hit the Road" [Пора в путь-дорогу] the singer tells his waiting girlfriend that she should not let anyone else into her heart, since he will be watching from on high, from where he can see everything.[20] One unusual song reverses the roles: a woman waiting at home raises the possibility of male infidelity. She tells her soldier that if he is unfaithful to her, she will recover from that wound, but if he is unfaithful to his military oath, her disdain for his cowardice will never fade.[21]

When *glasnost'* and eventually the breakup of the Soviet Union made it possible to publish and record previously unacceptable songs that until then had circulated only in *samizdat* or *magnitizdat,* it turned out that the women at home had not all shared Katiusha's attitude—as Russians, of course, had known for decades. If the soldier in "Dark Night" could rest assured that his wife would be waiting for him, no matter in what condition he returned, not so the officer in the newly available song "This Happened Not Long

---

[19] Если сердце горячо – / Девушка найдется. / Нынче больно - не тужи, / Завтра - твой денёчек. The words by Sergei Alymov and music by Anatolii Novikov can be found in Lukovnikov (1975), 46–9.

[20] Ты к сердцу только никого не допускай.
Следить буду строго,
Мне сверху видно все – ты так и знай! The words by Solomon Fogel'son and music by Vasilii Solov'ev-Sedoi can be found in Shilov (1967), 4:20–4.

[21] The text of the 1941 song, "If You Are Wounded, Darling, in the War" [Если будушь ранен, милый, на войне] by Iosif Utkin (music by Sigizmund Kats) can be found in Lobarev and Panfilova (1994), 339.

Ago" [Этот случай совсем был недавно]. Receiving his letter, which informs her that he has been wounded in battle and is now missing his left arm and both legs, his wife of ten years writes back that she has no use for a cripple:

I'm only 32,	Мне всего еще 32 года,
I can party and dance.	Я могу и гулять-танцевать.
You'll come home [and], like a log,	Ты приедешь домой, как колода,
All you'll do is lie in bed.	Только будешь в постели лежать.

But at the bottom of the letter his little daughter has scribbled her reply, telling him not to listen to what her mother wrote, but instead to hurry home, since she will be happy to see him:

I'll wheel you in your wheelchair	Я в коляске катать тебя буду
And pick flowers for you.	И цветы для тебя буду рвать.
If you get sweaty, papa, on a hot day,	В жаркий день, если, папа, вспотеешь,
I'll tenderly wipe [your brow] with a handkerchief.	Буду нежно платком вытирать.

It turns out that the officer was only testing his wife; when his train arrives, his daughter is amazed to see him uninjured:

It's OK, dear daughter.	"Ничего, ничего, дочь родная.
You see, your mother didn't come to meet me.	Видишь, мама встречать не пришла.
She's become a complete stranger to us;	Она стала совсем нам чужая,
We'll forget her forever.[22]	Мы забудем ее навсегда."

I have only anecdotal evidence that this song, and perhaps some similar ones, was in circulation during the war or shortly thereafter. Such songs would have been unacceptable during the war as poten-

---

[22] The full text is available at http://www.shansonprofi.ru/archiv/lyrics/narod/wX/p2/etot_sluchay_sovsem_byil_nedavno_.html (last accessed 9 June 2009).

tially undermining morale at the front; then and in later years they would have violated the official Soviet image of women on the home front. Yet we have the testimony of songwriter Konstantin Vanshenkin, who fought at the front during the war. Commenting on the lyrical songs of the period, he wrote:

> The appearance of these essentially officially recognized songs fully coincided with the needs of the fighting nation. But there were also unofficial songs […] that were also deeply moving. And the main thing is that all the official songs were about fidelity in love, while all the unofficial songs were about infidelity, about betrayal. And there was also a burning need for those songs, since they also contained life.   (Vanshenkin 2000)

The Rousseauian view of children as vessels of untainted purity likewise informs another song with a negative image of a woman who abrogates her "sacred duty" by not waiting, "In a Certain Town There Lived a Couple" [В одном городе жила парочка]. The twelve-year-old Allochka reports to her father at the front—apparently an ordinary soldier, not an officer—about her mother's behavior:

"Hello, papa dear," Allochka writes.	Здравствуй, папочка,- пишет Аллочка -
"Mama has begun to forget you.	Мама стала тебя забывать.
She's started going out late at night	С лейтенантами и с майорами
With lieutenants and majors…"	Поздно вечером стала гулять…

Allochka's information that the day before, her mother had told her to call Uncle Petia "father" leaves no doubts about the woman's infidelity. After reading the letter the soldier is so distraught that he stops being careful (не стал уж собой дорожить) and soon is killed in battle,[23] the sequence of events unambiguously laying the blame for his death at his unfaithful wife's door.

---

[23] The text of one version can be found in Uspenskii and Filina (2001), 399–400. Another version is at http://www.shansonprofi.ru/archiv/lyrics/narod/wV/p3/v_odnom_gorode_zhila_parochka_.html (last accessed 9 June 2009). The song is sung to the melody of "Little Bricks" [Кирпичики] (see Rothstein 1980).

Women "back home," whether faithful or not, also faced danger from the enemy, as portrayed in sundry films (for example, Sergei Bondarchuk's *Sud'ba cheloveka* [*Fate of a Man* 1959]) and attested by statistics for civilian deaths.[24] Indeed, the line between the home front and the war front constantly shifted, as the 1945 song "The Enemies Have Burned [His] Home Down" [Враги сожгли родную хату] reminds us. Instead of celebrating his safe return to his wife after four years at war, a soldier finds only an overgrown grave:

Don't blame me, Praskov'ia,	Не осуждай меня, Прасковья,
For coming to you like this:	Что я пришел к тебе такой:
I wanted to drink to your health,	Хотел я выпить за здоровье,
But I have to drink for the repose of your soul.[25]	А должен пить за упокой.

Not all women remained at home, however, and many sought involvement in the war rather than those who, like Praskov'ia, were overtaken by it. A traditional wartime role for women is that of the military nurse, and it is well represented both in songs by professional songwriters and in those written by anonymous soldiers.[26] One of the first such songs seems to have been "Aniuta the Nurse" [Медсестра Анюта, spring 1942], with the text by Mikhail Frantsuzov and music by Iurii Slonov, who had observed a lack of songs about nurses. In Frantsuzov's text the image of the female nurse is mediated by the male perspective of

---

[24] Discussions about the totals of Soviet wartime deaths (military and civilian) have not ceased in the historical and demographic literature. To cite only one respected source, Barber and Harrison state the following: "Premature deaths under occupation have been estimated at 13.7 million, including 7.4 million killed in hot or cold blood, another 2.2 million taken to Germany and worked to death, and the remaining 4.1 million died of overwork, hunger, or disease. Among the 7.4 million killed were more than two million Jews who vanished into the Holocaust; the rest died in partisan fighting, reprisals and so forth" (2006).

[25] The text by Mikhail Isakovskii can be found in Lobarev and Panfilova (1994), 162–3, together with an account of the resistance to the song on the part of various editors, producers etc. The music is by Matvei Blanter.

[26] Recall Aleksievich's definition above of loving-kindness as the essence of a woman's character.

a wounded soldier. Through his first-person narrative, we learn that he lies weak and bleeding on the winter snow until Aniuta crawls to him, whispers, "He's alive" [Живой], and carries him to safety. In the process, she tries to keep his spirits up by reminding him of heroism as the military imperative.

Turn around, look at Aniuta.	Оглянись, посмотри на Анюту,
Prove that you're a hero.	Докажи, что ты парень-герой.
Don't give in to cruel death;	Не сдавайся ты смертушке лютой —
You and I will laugh at it.[27]	Посмеемся над нею с тобой.

This early song contains three motifs later repeated (singly or in combination) in other songs about nurses: going under fire to reach a wounded soldier, encouraging him not to give up, and carrying him back to safety. We find them, for example, in another early song, written in a military hospital, probably in 1942, which encourages young women to serve as nurses:

Our own army has sent for you;	Родная армия послала за тобой
And called you a military nurse.	И назвала военною сестрой.
Hurry up, girls, get to the battlefield quickly;	Спешите, девушки, скорей на поле боя,
A young Red Army soldier is wounded.	Красноармеец ранен молодой.
Excited birds are flying over him;	Над ним летят взволнованные птицы;
He hears the roar of threatening batteries.	Он слышит грохот грозных батарей.
Crawl over to him and give him a drink.	Ты подползи и дай ему напиться,
Protect him, warm him with [your] words.[28]	Ты защити, словами обогрей.

---

[27] The text of the song and Slonov's comments about the lack of songs about nurses can be found in Lobarev and Panifilova (1994), 369.

[28] The full text is available at http://www.info.dolgopa.org/library/12_03.htm (last accessed 9 June 2009).

And in one of the many reworkings of "Katiusha," the young woman hears the call of a Soviet fighter, wounded in a "blizzard of lead" [метелица свинца]:

See her fly forward like a bird;	Вот летит вперед она, как птица;
See her crawl along the edge of the woods.	Вот ползет по краешку леска.
Our Katia is not afraid of bullets,	Наша Катя пули не боится,
She doesn't fear an enemy bayonet.	Не боится вражьего штыка.
She'll say something to the wounded soldier	Катя слово раненому скажет
That will immediately make his heart sing.	Так, что сердце сразу запоет.
She'll bind his wounds up tightly,	Катя раны крепко перевяжет,
She'll carry him off the battlefield on her back.[29]	На плечах из боя унесет.

In the anonymous "Where the Ancient Pines Murmured" [Где шумели сосны вековые] a reversal of roles unexpectedly follows this typical scene. A nurse saves a wounded young soldier:

A nurse ran to him under fire	Под огонь к нему сестра бежала
Over the steppe torn up by explosions,	По изрытой взрывами степи,
And, bending over him, she whispered:	И, над ним склонившись, прошептала:
"Be patient, comrade, be patient."	"Потерпи, товарищ, потерпи".

A month later, after his recovery and return to his unit, she is wounded, and he, in turn, carries her to safety:

Bloodstains were visible on the grass.	На траве виднелись пятна крови,
He crawled among explosions in the steppe.	Он пополз под взрывами в степи,

---

[29] The text can be found in Kirdan (1995), 64–5, reprinted from Gusev (1964), 317. It was collected in 1943.

And, bending over her, he said:	И, над ней склонившись, он промолвил:
"Be patient, comrade, be patient."[30]	"Потерпи, товарищ, потерпи."

Soviet military nurses took on other tasks as well, including those of repelling or attacking the enemy. "Our Girl" [Наша девушка], a song written by a sailor in 1943, describes the "girl's" courageous versatility:

If someone's wounded in battle, she'll bind his wounds	В бою кого ранят—она перевяжет
And carry him back from the battlefield.	И вынесет с поля к своим.
If a machine-gunner's killed, the girl will lie down	Погиб пулеметчик—и девушка ляжет
Behind the formidable and accurate "Maxim."[31]	За грозный и меткий "максим».

As in other cultural genres (for instance, film and graphics), women replaced men when and where the need arose, including on the battlefield, as another 1943 song about a nurse titled "A Song about a Front-Line Friend" [Песня о боевой подруге] makes clear:

If I fall, you'll replace [me]; You'll take up my rifle.[32]	Если я упаду,—ты заменишь, Ты поднимешь винтовку мою.

Songs about women who served not as nurses but as soldiers are relatively few. Such military activists—usually referred to as "girls" (*devushki*)—are routinely identified by their military greatcoat [шинель]. For instance, "A Song about Anka Graiterova" [Песня об

---

[30] The text, in Kirdan (1995), 66–7, is reprinted from Svitova (1985), 37–8. It was collected in 1949.

[31] The text, written by A. Shevchuk, can be found in Lebedev (1986), 301–2. The song was sung to the melody of "Kakhovka," a 1935 song about the civil war written by poet Mikhail Svetlov and composer Isaak Dunaevskii (see Shilov 1967, 2:23–6).

[32] The text, by M. Volkov, a veteran of the Stalingrad battle, can be found in Lebedev (1983), 172.

Анке Грайтеровой] pays tribute to a real-life female combatant at the front. It describes how the girl from Elets, in a standard issue great-coat, marches along with the soldiers [И рядом с бойцами в шинели походной / Елецкая девушка шла] and fights every bit as heroically as her male comrades. According to an item about Anka in a front-line newspaper from 1942, the young machine-gunner killed seventy Germans in one battle—an achievement that the text of the song references:

Remember, comrade, the whine of the mortar shells,	Ты вспомни, товарищ, как мины визжали,
How the machine gun hit the enemy,	Как бил пулемет по врагу.
How the Germans ran in fright from Anka	Как немцы в испуге от Анки бежали
And found their death in the snow.	И смерть находили в снегу.

Anka also found her death there, and the song invokes the common motif of vengeance against the enemy widespread in war graphics and film. Her comrades promise that:

For the untimely death of Anka the machine-gunner	За раннюю смерть пулеметчицы Анки
Her friends will wreak vengeance on the fascists.[33]	Фашистам друзья отомстят.

Much is made of the greatcoat in another song about a female soldier who leads a group of scouts in a grenade attack on a German pillbox.

---

[33] The text, originally published as anonymous, was written by the poet and later songwriter Iakov Khelemskii to the melody of "Kakhovka," written by Isaak Dunaevskii for the 1935 film *Three Comrades* [Три товарища]. The young soldier's name was actually Gaiterova (Lebedev 1986, 104–7). She was killed on 18 December 1941, one day before her seventeenth birthday. After graduating from the seven-year school in 1940, she started working as a bookkeeper to help support her family. In the fall of 1941, she joined the Komsomol and the local army reserve (народное ополчение), where she got military training. During the German occupation of Elets, her hometown, she provided intelligence information to the regular army, and when the army had driven the

A repeated couplet describes her as "A girl in an ill-fitting greatcoat, / [Our] dear battle comrade" [Девушка в шинели не по росту, / Дорогой товарищ боевой].[34]

Songs, if not life, treated the women who fought on the front lines as soldiers who happened to be female, as evident in the lines just quoted or in a song called "Soldier Girl" [Девушка-солдат], where the greatcoat appears yet again:

[Our] country's enveloped in the flames of war,	Огнем войны страна объята,
An alarm bell rings out over the Motherland,	Гремит над родиной набат,
And together with a soldier lad	И вместе с юношей-солдатом
There strides a soldier girl.	Шагает девушка-солдат.
Her greatcoat and clothing are coarse,	Ее шинель - одежда груба,
And all recognize her as a fighter;	И все бойца в ней узнают,
And only her tender lips	И только ласковые губы
Give her away everywhere.	Ее повсюду выдают.

The feminization of her image through reference to her "tender lips" notwithstanding, she serves intrepidly and proudly as a wing gunner; the refrain declares that the country is proud of her for going into battle so bravely and with such fortitude.[35] Yet that reference, which

---

invaders out of the city, she and her reserve unit left with them and were integrated into an army division. She was killed in battle outside of the village of Russkii Brod. (The biographical information is from Konovalov 2005.)

[34] The song, known from its first line as "I Remember a Snowy, Wild Night" [Помню ночь метельную, шальную], is a slightly folklorized version of a 1942 poem by Aleksei Surkov about a female military scout (See Kirdan 1995, 61, who reprints the text from Domanovskii et al. 1967, 110; see also http://a-pesni.golosa.info/ww2/folk/pomnunotch.htm, last accessed 9 June 2009).

[35] Родная девушка, подруга милая, / Страна горда, горда тобой. / С такой отвагою, с такою силою, / Родная девушка, идешь ты в бой. / [...] The song is sung by Dmitrii Dombrovskii on volume 4 of the CD series *Ships Came into Our Harbor* [В нашу гавань заходили корабли], Moscow: VOSTOKKHIM, 2001 (based on the television series of the same name conducted by Eduard Uspenskii and Eleanora Filina), which provides no information about author or composer. The text is available at http://a-pesni.golosa.info/ww2/folk/dev-soldat.htm (last accessed 9 June 2009).

unavoidably evokes the notion of "tender lips made for kissing," implies the unnaturalness of women's active participation in the lethal violence of war—a notion reinforced by the persistent identification of women with the home front in the overwhelming majority of songs, poems, and posters of the era.

An even more ambiguous perspective on the female soldier finds expression in the post-war song "Along the Wooden Sidewalk" [По мосткам тесовым 1947], which begins with the image of a former female soldier walking along the wooden village sidewalk "in fashionable heels" [на модных каблуках]. Though "even the married guys can't keep their eyes off her" [Даже все женатые ребята / Не отводят от тебя глаза], the narrator has another image of her in mind:

But I remember you differently:	Только я другой тебя запомнил –
In boots, in a military greatcoat.	В сапогах, в шинели боевой.
In our rifle battalion you	Ты у нас в стрелковом батальоне
Were listed as a private.	Числилась по спискам рядовой.

He goes on to say that in battle he was her commander, but now sooner resembles a private [Я в боях командовал тобою, / А теперь я, вроде, рядовой].[36] He is powerless in the face of her beauty: she

---

[36] The lyrics are by Aleksandr Fat'ianov and the music by Boris Mokrousov The text can be found in Lobarev and Panfilova (1994), 355. According to the official Mokrousov website, Fat'ianov was inspired to write the lyrics when he visited his cousin Nikolai Menshov and his wife Nadezhda, who had served together in the war, he as commander of a radio station, she as a radio operator. (They married after the war.) When Fat'ianov and his new wife visited them in their town of Viazniki, the Menshovs dressed up for the occasion; Nadezhda put on the high-heeled shoes she had bought in Moscow (http://mokrousov.samnet.ru/biography7.htm, last accessed 9 June 2009). The website quotes a letter from a village schoolteacher, who recalled the first time she heard the song, played over loudspeakers as veterans of the war paraded through her village. She looked admiringly at the girls, who seemed "like fairytale beauties" in their military uniforms. "And now," she wrote, "when in a formation of veterans I see our wonderful front-line women, I think about their great contributions and each time recall the words from this beautiful old song" [И когда теперь в строю ветеранов я вижу наших прекрасных женщин-фронтовичек, думаю про великие их заслуги, всякий раз вспоминаются слова из этой давней прекрасной песни].

has effectively lowered him in rank. With the war over, women's physical allure trumps their contribution to the war effort, reinstating the "natural order of things." Whereas during the years of conflict female beauty took a back seat to women's stoic resilience, armed resistance, and faithfulness to "their men," the restoration of peace meant a return to polarized gender roles.

The issue of military ranks and of what one might view as a kind of emasculation appears as well in a humorous song about a married couple that served in the army, she starting as a simple rifleman, he in a technical unit. By the end of the war, she had advanced to the rank of major, and his life is now changed:

In her presence I don't smoke, I don't drink wine,	При ней я не курю, не пью вино,
I'm afraid not to bring my pay home,	Боюсь не принести домой получку,
I'm afraid to go to the movies without my wife –	Боюсь я без жены сходить в кино –
She'll charge me with going AWOL.	Припишет самовольную отлучку.

He decides that he should rejoin the army and work his way up to his wife's rank, but he fears that by the time he achieves that, she will be a general.[37] In other words, women who had advanced through their military skills bred anxiety in their male counterparts once the war ended. Women were expected to return to their traditional roles, which by definition required subordination to the male as the nominal head of the family.

First lieutenant (старший лейтенант) was the highest rank achieved by Valeriia Khomiakova, but as the first woman to shoot down a German plane in nighttime combat she was memorialized in "The Song of Pilot Khomiakova" [Песня о летчице Хомяковой]. During the siege of Stalingrad, Khomiakova scrambled against a German Junker

---

[37] The song, called "[My] Wife, the Major" [Жена-майор] is sung by Vladimir Men'shov on volume 4 of the CD series *Ships Came into Our Harbor* (see note 35), which provides no information about author or composer. This may well be a much later song than others discussed here. See also Uspenskii, Filina and Pozina (2000), 1:126–7 and http://www.shansonprofi. ru/archiv/lyrics/narod/wJ/p1/zhena_mayor_.html (last accessed 9 June 2009).

88 bomber that had penetrated the anti-aircraft defenses surrounding a crucial Volga bridge at Saratov. As the song tells it:

The signal's given for takeoff, the steel bird flies.	Подан старт, летит стальная птица.
Everyone waits with bated breath.	Каждый, затаив дыханье ждет.
Here's the enemy—and a round's hit the Kraut;	Вот и враг—и очередь по фрицу,
Flames have enveloped the plane.	Пламя охватило самолет.
The battle's over, the pilot reports:	Бой закончен, летчик рапортует:
Everything's OK—my opponent has been shot down!	Все в порядке—мой противник сбит!
And the family of pilots is exultant:	И семья пилотов торжествует:
The accounting of heroic deeds has begun!	Счет геройским подвигам открыт!

The "family of pilots" was not just any family: it was the 586th Women's Air Fighter Regiment [586-й женский истребительный авиационный полк].[38] Notably, the song focuses less on Khomiakova as individual (she is "the pilot") than on the collective, relying on Stalin's trope of the nation as family and of the plane as a "steel bird."

Songs about women soldiers and pilots (and their stories) were fewer and less known than those about female partisans. Partisan fighting is more of an equal-opportunity enterprise than regular warfare, a manifestation in the Soviet case of the "noble fury" (ярость благородная) that, in the words of Vasilii Lebedev-Kumach, should boil up like a wave.[39] The official image of the regular army, on the other hand, was of the male кра-

---

[38] The text, by Sgt. Tat'iana Ivanchuk, together with some information about Khomiakova, can be found in Lebedev (1983).143–5. There is more information about the pilot available at http://www.airaces.narod.ru/woman/homykova.htm (last accessed 9 June 2009). Sgt. Ivanchuk's text was sung to the melody of the 1939 song "Three Tankmen" [Три танкиста], written by Daniil and Dmitrii Pokrass (words by Boris Laskin).

[39] Lebedev-Kumach's poem, published two days after the Nazi invasion of the Soviet Union and set to music by Aleksandr Aleksandrov, became "Sacred War" [Священная война], the first mass song of the war (see the text and music in Lukovnikov 9–11).

сноармеец (Red Army soldier). Among the songs about women partisans, who also appeared in posters and films, were ditties [частушки], such as:

There's a birch tree on the hill,	На горе стоит береза,
Tanks under the birch.	Под березой танки,
My darling's a partisan,	Мой миленок партизан,
And I'm a partisan.	А я партизанка.
or	
My darling and I together	Мы с миленочком вдвоем
Are going up on the mountain.	В гору поднимаемся.
Two revolvers at our sides;	Два нагана по бокам,
We're not just going for a walk.	Гулять не собираемся.
or	
The Germans shot my brother;	Немцы брата расстреляли,
I shed many tears.	Пролила я много слез.
I'll get even with you, you snakes,	Рассчитаюсь, гады, с вами,
I'll derail a train.[40]	Пущу поезд под откос.

Folksongs about women partisans also included many reworkings of "Katiusha," such as the following:

The fascists burned the apple and pear trees,	Жгли фашисты яблони и груши,
They plundered the whole village,	Всю деревню грабили подряд,
But toward evening, led by Katiusha,	А под вечер во главе с Катюшей
A partisan detachment approached.	Партизанский подошел отряд.
Katiusha surrounded the enemy headquarters	Вражий штаб Катюша окружила
And rushed forward with a hand grenade;	И с гранатой бросилась вперед;
She took out seven of them on the spot,	Семерых на месте уложила,
While the eighth one fled into the garden...	А восьмой удрал на огород...

---

[40] The first two chastushki are cited in Astaf'eva (1987), 230, and the third, in Selivanov (1990), 173.

He was a general, and Katiusha shot him with her rifle.[41] Not just a fighter, but also the head of a partisan detachment, this Katiusha (as decisive agent) differs dramatically from the one who waited patiently for her beloved to return from battle.

Women partisans also appear in songs by professional composers and songwriters, such as in the famous "Dark-Complexioned Girl" [Смуглянка]. Written by composer Anatolii Novikov and poet Iakov Shvedov in 1940 for a suite about the Civil War, it was first performed in 1944, when it fit the circumstances of the Great Patriotic War. In the song, the male narrator has fallen in love with his Moldavian neighbor, but when he invites her to go down to the river with him to watch the summer sunset, he receives an unexpected answer:

But the dark-complexioned Moldavian girl	А смуглянка-молдаванка
Answered the lad in kind:	Отвечала парню в лад:
"We're putting together	– Партизанский, молдаванский
A Moldavian partisan unit.	Собираем мы отряд.
This morning the partisans	Нынче рано партизаны
Left their homes.	Дом покинули родной.
The road into the dense forest	Ждет тебя дорога
To the partisans is waiting for you."	К партизанам в лес густой.

When she leaves for the forest, he feels hurt that she has not invited him to come along, but when he joins the partisans, she greets him warmly ("Hello, my dear handsome lad" [Здравствуй, парень мой хороший, мой родной!]). Contrary to stereotypical assumptions about women's inherent preoccupation with love and romance, the Moldavian "girl" places country above any love interest. Not the frivolousness of personal romance, but the purposefulness of a committed resistance fighter defines her. Thus while the bulk of war songs about women focused on their loving patience at home, they also portrayed, albeit infrequently, their contrasting roles as partisans and members of

---

[41] The text of this version of "Katiusha" and excerpts from several others are in Gusev (1979), 69–70. See also Rozanov 1964. There were also numerous Polish partisan songs based on Katiusha, some of which can be found in Świrko (1971), 382–90.

the Soviet fighting forces, skillful, courageous, and heroic combatants in the struggle to repel the enemy.

Russian songs largely relied on native traditions, but a few engaged ancient ideas about the relationship of war to everyday life and its institutions. An anonymous Soviet Latinist changed Cicero's "In time of war the laws fall silent" [Inter arma silent leges] to "In time of war the Muses fall silent" [Inter arma silent Musae]. During World War II, however, the Muses were far from silent, and poets and songwriters were inspired by their muses and by the women who waited as well as the women who fought at their side. Indeed, Soviet songs, posters, films, and literary works produced during and after World War II amply illustrate that under the threat of extinction the Muses tirelessly served the national cause with fervent passion. As the poet and songwriter Lebedev-Kumach wrote in "Only at the Front" [Только на фронте]:

Who said you've got to give up	Кто сказал, что надо бросить
Songs on the battlefield?	Песни на войне?
After a battle your heart asks	После боя сердце просит
For music twice as much!	Музыки вдвойне.

REFERENCES

Aleksievich, Svetlana. 1989. *U voiny – ne zhenskoe litso.* Moscow: Sovetskii pisatel'.

Ament, Suzanne. 2006. "Reflecting Individual and Collective Identities: Songs of World War II." In *Gender and National Identity in Twentieth-Century Russian Culture,* edited by Helena Goscilo and Andrea Lanoux, 115–30. DeKalb: Northern Illinois University Press.

Astaf'eva, Lidiia, ed. 1987. *Chastushki.* Moscow: Sovremennik.

Attwood, Lynne. 2001. "Rationality versus Romanticism: Representations of Women in the Stalinist Press." In *Gender in Russian History and Culture,* edited by Linda Edmondson, 158–76. Houndmills: Palgrave.

Barber, John, and Mark Harrison. 2006. "Patriotic War, 1941 to 1945." In *The Cambridge History of Russia,* Vol. 3, *The Twentieth Century,* edited by Ronald Grigor Suny, 217–42. Cambridge: Cambridge University Press.

Domanovskii, L. V. et al., eds. 1967. *Russkii sovetskii fol'klor.* Leningrad: Nauka.

Ehrenreich, Barbara, and Deirdre English. 1978. *For Her Own Good: 150 Years of the Experts' Advice to Women.* Garden City, NY: Anchor Press.

Gudoshnikov, Iakov. 1959. *Iazyk i stil' pesen Velikoi Otechestvennoi voiny.* Voronezh: Izdatel'stvo Voronezhskogo universiteta.

Gusev, Viktor, ed. 1979. *Slavianskie partizanskie pesni.* Leningrad: Nauka.

———. 1964. *Russkii fol'klor Velikoi Otechestvennoi voiny.* Moscow-Leningrad: Nauka.

Hochschild, Arlie. 1989. *The Second Shift: Working Families and the Revolution at Home*, with Anne Machung. New York: Viking Penguin.

Kirdan, Boris, ed. 1995. *"… I poet mne v zemlianke garmon'…": Fol'klor Velikoi Otechestvennoi voiny.* Moscow: Prosveshchenie.

Kolberg, Oskar. 1986. *Pieśni i melodie ludowe w opracowaniu fortepianowym*, part I. (*Dzieła wszystkie*, v. 67/I). Cracow: Polskie Wydawnictwo Muzyczne.

Konovalov, A. 2005. "Podvig pulemetchitsy." *Orlovskaia Pravda*, 26 March, 3. http://www.kompas.orel.ru/files/downloads/2005/03/26032005/3.pdf (last accessed 6 June 2009).

Lebedev, Pavel. 1986. *Pesni boevykh pokhodov: Soldatskoe pesennoe tvorchestvo Velikoi Otechestvennoi voiny.* Saratov: Privolzhskoe knizhnoe izdatel'stvo.

———, ed. 1983. *Pesni rozhdennye v ogne.* Volgograd: Nizhne-Volzhskoe knizhnoe izdatel'stvo.

Lebedeva-Kumach, Marina. 1980. *Pesni na stikhi Vasiliia Ivanovicha Lebedeva-Kumacha: Melodii i teksty.* Moscow: Muzyka.

Mlotek, Eleanor Gordon, ed. 1977. *Mir trogn a gezang!* 2nd edition. New York: Workmen's Circle Education Department.

Lobarev, Grigorii, and M. M. Panfilova, eds. 1994. *Ob ogniakh-pozharish-chakh… Pesni voiny i pobedy.* Moscow: Respublika.

Lukovnikov, A. E., ed. 1975. *Druz'ia-odnopolchane: O pesniakh, rozhdennykh voinoi.* Moscow: Voenizdat.

Medvedeva, Irina, ed. 1985. *Muzyka v bor'be s fashizmom.* Moscow: Sovetskii kompozitor.

Rothstein, Halina, and Robert A. Rothstein. 1997. "The Beginnings of Soviet Culinary Arts." In *Food in Russian History and Culture*, edited by Musya Glants and Joyce Toomre, 177–94. Bloomington: Indiana University Press.

Rothstein, Robert A. 1980. "The Quiet Rehabilitation of the Brick Factory: Early Soviet Popular Music and Its Critics." *Slavic Review* 39: 373–88.

Rozanov, Ivan. 1964. "Pesni o Katiushe kak novyi tip narodnogo tvorchestva." In *Russkii fol'klor Velikoi Otechestvennoi voiny*, edited by Viktor Gusev, 310–25. Moscow-Leningrad: Nauka.

Selivanov, Fedor, ed. 1990. *Chastushki (Biblioteka Russkogo Fol'klora*, Vol. 9). Moscow: Sovetskaia Rossiia.

Shilov, Aleksandr, ed. 1967. *Slavim pobedu Oktiabria!: Izbrannye russkie sovetskie pesni*, 1–5. Moscow: Muzyka.

Sokhor, Arnol'd. 1959. *Russkaia sovetskaia pesnia.* Leningrad: Sovetskii kompozitor.

Svitova, Klavdiia, ed. 1985. *Nezabyvaemye gody: Russkii pesennyi fol'klor Velikoi Otechestvennoi voiny.* Moscow: Sovetskii kompozitor.

Świrko, Stanisław. 1971. *Z pieśnią i karabinem: Pieśni partyzanckie i okupacyjne z lat 1939–1945.* Warsaw: Ludowa Spółdzielnia Wydawnicza.

Uspenskii, Eduard, and Eleonora Filina, eds. 2001. *V nashu gavan' zakhodili korabli* – 2. Moscow: RIPOL KLASSIK.

Uspenskii, Eduard, and Evgeniia Pozina, eds. 2000. *V nashu gavan' zakhodili korabli* – 1. Moscow: Strekoza.

Vanshenkin, Konstantin. 2000. "V moe vremia. Iz zapisei." *Znamia* 5. http://magazines.russ.ru/znamia/2000/5/vanshen.html (last accessed 8 June 2009).

RECENT WARS

CHAPTER 8

"Black Widows": Women as Political Combatants in the Chechen Conflict

Trina R. Mamoon

Acts of political violence by women always draw disproportionate attention, not only because female political aggression is still a relatively rare phenomenon, but also because most cultures traditionally perceive women as nurturers and peacemakers. Over the past decade, several such acts—specifically, suicide bombings—in the ongoing conflict between Chechnya and Russia have been attributed collectively to various women who in the course of their activities acquired the label "Black Widows."[1] Though the nomenclature implies a group united by common aspirations, the phenomenon of black widows is much more complex. My article examines the diversity of forces conditioning and motivating Chechen women's involvement in lethal activities traditionally deemed male-specific, the difficulties in determining any pattern or dominant structure to these forces, and reactions by both Russian and Western commentators to those activities.

The first suicide bombing by a Chechen woman was recorded in 2000, when Khava Baraeva, along with her partner, Luiza (Aiza) Magomadova, attacked a Russian military base. In 2002, the world

---

[1] The term "Black Widows," which hereafter I use without quotation marks or capitals, evokes several associations. The most poignant one is the association with the deadly venomous species of spiders. In the Muslim world, however, especially in the Middle East, the term conjures the image of widows in mourning who are clad in black chadors or hijabs. The third association would be the Russian use of "chernyi" (black) to identify, derogatorily, the people of the Caucasus and other peoples of color.

saw its first broadcasts of female Chechens in black hijabs alongside their male counterparts, holding hostage the audience of the
Dubrovka Theater in Moscow. It was not until 2003, however, that
the phrase became firmly established in political discourse, when a
would-be suicide bomber, Zarema Muzhikhoeva, told investigators
that she belonged to a group called the "Black Fatima" of Chechnya.
Until the armed occupation of the Dubrovka Theater, the outside
world had assumed that combatants in Chechnya were exclusively
male. Chechen women went on to gain further notoriety for their participation in the Beslan school massacre of September 2004, a siege
for which anonymous callers identifying themselves as black widows
claimed responsibility.

Thereafter, the media characterized the political violence perpetrated by black widows as "terrorism." Even if, for the moment, one
accepts this problematic term, the Chechen women's terrorist activity
in a repressive Muslim, male-dominated society raises questions about
the role of the Russian state and the relationship between militancy
and Islam that await adequate exploration. My essay attempts to identify and examine some of the underlying conditions and circumstances
that could compel Chechen women to violence. Although case studies
show that each Chechen woman who opts to end her life in the process
of causing destruction and the death of others has individual, complex,
and often highly personal reasons for such a choice—reasons that may
be impossible to identify, let alone understand—what unquestion-
ably merits discussion is how these women's social, historical, and
political environment has positioned them vis-à-vis social violence and
also how commentators have framed and interpreted the phenomenon of the black widows. For instance, Russian media and scholarship as well as Western discourse of the "war on terror" read women's
role in the Chechen conflict very differently from specialists in contemporary transnational feminism. Comparing the portrayal of black
widows in the framework of these divergent perspectives, my analysis
aims to situate the rise of Chechen female suicide bombers and their
actions within the larger political and social context to which they
belong. Neither justification nor condemnation is part of my agenda.
In what follows, I present two major discourses (of gender roles in
Russian society and of terrorist rhetoric) that frame the phenomenon
of the Chechen black widows. Then, I focus on concrete case studies

of Chechen suicide bombers against the background of social, political, religious, and individual conditions that all contribute to the motivation of the black widows.

Gendered Cultural Framework

In Russia, as elsewhere, the perception of womanhood originates in patriarchal values that equate women with maternity and therefore assume that women are by nature caring and sensitive, passive and submissive. Accordingly, national identity in Soviet/Russian historical grand narratives and political discourse rests on a binary gendered model, with the tsar (and later, Soviet leaders) as the Father of the nation and the land as Mother Russia.[2] These concepts of womanhood and nationhood, interconnected and deeply ingrained in the Russian folk imagination (Goscilo and Lanoux 2006, 3), thrive to this day.

Unthinking acceptance of this stereotypical gendered concept of women and womanliness partly accounts for the enormous and overwhelmingly negative impact made on Russians by the emergence of Chechen female combatants/black widows in the public political arena. Given the existing patriarchal expectations of "womanly" behavior, which by definition presuppose the giving, not the taking, of life, the Russian government and official media have been able to demonize the female enemy warriors as lethal black widows.[3] Articles such as "Chernye vdovy derzhat v strakhe voiska i militsiiu" ["Black Widows Terrorize the Army and the Police"] (*Diplomaticheskii mir*, 12–19 November 2003) and Andrei Sharov's "V Moskve ishchut 'chernuiu vdovu'" ["Searching for a 'Black Widow' in Moscow"] (*Rossiiskaia gazeta*, 2 September 2004) adopt this stance. These attitudes resemble the response and perception of Russian women participating in World War II, as explicated in other chapters in this volume. The French journalist Anne Nivat has aptly captured the perceptions and preju-

---

[2] For more on the cultural construction of "Mother Russia" see Hubbs (1988).

[3] Raven Healing's article "White Stockings and Black Widows: Women in Chechnya—Myths and Realities" examines the role played by the Russian army and the media in demonizing of women combatants.

dices of Russian society toward women who participate in violent, armed acts:

> The Russian public was galvanized by this major terror attack [Dubrovka hostage crisis] on innocent citizens right in the middle of their city. Most shocking of all was the fact that some of the attackers were women. Devout Muslim women, always thought of as subservient and anonymous in their long, flowing chadors, were wearing explosive belts tied with detonator cords. It was a sight that had never been seen or even imagined. The Russian media dubbed them as "black widows." (2008, 123)

Deftly manipulated by the official propaganda, gender stereotypes effectively curbed any nascent anti-war sympathy among Russian women (Russell 2007, 56–7). Gender prejudices and the government's and the media's characterization of the militant Chechen women as "mothers, monsters, and whores" (Sjoberg and Gentry 2008, 89) helped to discredit their violent behavior as utterly unnatural.[4] The use of gender stereotypes to delegitimize a cause adopted by women is not a novel strategy devised by Russians, having been employed in other conflicts around the world to sway public and international opinion against women combatants (Sharoni 1995, 32).

Conflicting Terrorism Rhetoric

Historically, the construction and definition of terrorism has never been clear-cut and unproblematic. All terrorist acts and strategies, as well as the circumstances under which they occur, are not identical, and sweeping generalizations about terrorism are likely to fall short. Whether one perceives violent aggressors as terrorists or freedom fighters depends on where one stands politically and ideologically. History has demonstrated that sometimes the moral line can

---

[4] Most of the feminist theory on female combatants and suicide bombers has been developed by Western (non-Russian) scholars. Therefore my article relies heavily on Western sources for the theoretical—feminist or otherwise—framework.

be very thin. For example, American combatants and heroes in the Revolutionary War were not viewed as freedom fighters by the British colonial powers, and similarly, what the Bolsheviks termed the Great October Socialist Revolution of 1917 was characterized as a bloody coup d'état by the White Army that fought against them. The English Enlightenment thinker Edmund Burke was one of the first writers to define terrorism. An upholder of patriarchal values and morality embedded in British colonial mores, Burke regarded French revolutionaries as "base and ambitious" individuals who espoused terrorist tactics (40). Yet to those sympathetic to the ideals of liberty, equality, and fraternity, they were, and still are today, revolutionaries. These examples help illustrate that the definition of terrorism is fluid and contentious; there is no *a priori* or universally accepted definition. As Charles Tilly puts it, "Politically speaking, it usually helps your cause to use the term 'terror' for actions which you disapprove, and to exempt actions which you approve" (2005, 18).

Terrorism has a direct link to the state, and it is no different in the case of Chechnya. Discourse about terrorism has to take into consideration the power of the state as a military-industrial complex that "typically uses inappropriate means to maintain or expand its power, domination, and profit" (Oliverio and Lauderdale 2005a, 3). The state has the means, resources, and moral justification on its side when it comes to using excessive force to suppress revolts or resistance. Enjoying the rights and privileges of a sovereign nation, and invoking national defense and security, the state can legitimize the use of terror against a minority group living on its territories. State-sponsored terror such as bombing and shelling of civilian sites can then be justified by constructing the state as the legitimate apparatus that controls society, maintains law and order, and defends its sovereignty as a nation. Subscribing to this ideology, one anti-terrorism scholar claims that terrorists "provoke governments into using such harsh and desperate measures as anti-terror activities" (Ben-Yehuda 2005, 45). The Russian state maintains its power base in a volatile and strategically located region at the expense of a minority ethnic-religious group by carrying out such "anti-terror activities."

Even though the state constructs terrorists as operating independently, in practice, terrorism and the state are mutually implicated: terrorism arises out of a direct reaction and/or resistance to state policy and control. Such is the position argued by Tilly, who asserts that "terror is a strategy" that "involves interactions among political actors, and to explain the adoption of such a strategy we have no choice but to analyze it as part of a political process" (2005, 21).

A similar position is advanced by John Reuter, who argues that the brutalities perpetrated against Chechen civilians by the Russian army since the beginning of the second Chechen War in 1999 has "engendered extremist tactics such as suicide terrorism" (2004, 2–3). Reuter bases his argument on the fact that the first incident of suicide-terrorism by Chechen rebels coincides with the gross human rights violations committed by the Russian army throughout the second Chechen War (2004, 6). Defining terrorist attacks as "secular and strategic," and not as a manifestation of religious fundamentalism, Robert Pape, a political scientist, contends that political groups employ these tactics "to compel modern democracies to withdraw military forces from territory that the terrorists consider to be their homeland" (2005, 8). It follows from these arguments that the participation of Chechen women in terrorist acts falls within the parameters of political process. Even given the limited scope of their direct political participation, Chechen women cannot help but be affected by their environment and their relations to others. In this respect they are part of the political process, and terrorism is one strategy among others (such as negotiation, subversion, open warfare, etc.) for effecting change and an intended outcome.

In stark contrast to the above positions, which hold the state responsible for violent acts by minority groups, the state's definition of terrorism is couched in moralistic, nationalistic, and self-righteous rhetoric[5] that adopts a zero tolerance policy towards the perpetrators of terrorist acts. Such is President George Bush's declaration, "You're either with us or with the terrorists" in the so-called "war against terror" campaign that started soon after 9/11 (Bush 2001). Two years prior to President Bush's now famous pronouncement, Vladimir Putin, then prime minister of Russia in President Boris Yeltsin's administration, had made headlines in Russia and around the world with his

---

[5] John Russell explores how both the West and Russia demonize and dehumanize those who stand against their interests by labeling them as "terrorists." See *Chechnya—Russia's 'War on Terror'* (2007, 54–68).

blunt anti-terrorist declaration in 1999: "V sortire popadetsia terrorist—budem mochit' v sortire"[6] [If a terrorist is found in the outhouse, we'll rub him out in the outhouse]. This controversial utterance, televised nationwide, helped establish Putin as a hardliner in all matters of state affairs, including the handling of Chechnya. The state's "anti-terrorism" discourse constructs its attack on noncombatants and civilian populations as a necessary interventional and/or retaliatory strategy that the dominant population perceives as legitimate, whereas individuals' killing of noncombatants is considered morally reprehensible. Iunna Chuprinina's article "Eto voina!..." ["This Is War!" 2004], published in *Itogi* following the Beslan tragedy, justifies anti-terrorist squads' storming of the school, which resulted in the deaths not only of terrorists, but also of many children.

Similarly, articles such as those published in *Rossiiskaia gazeta* (Borisov 2004) and *Izvestiia* (Rechkalov 2004) defend the cause of Russia's "war on terror." This kind of media discourse brings further complications. Islamic fundamentalists exploit the anti-Islamic rhetoric employed by the state, calling it a "Western and anti-Islamic" ploy in order to recruit and incite future terrorists. Islamists who plan acts of terrorism cynically rely on the anti-Islamic rhetoric adopted by some Western governments as a strategy, using human weapons to further their own political and ideological goals, while their misguided recruits themselves embrace the anti-Western rhetoric of their leaders as an expression of their faith and fidelity to Islam. Thus, the Chechen black widows appear caught in these conflicting political and anti-Islamic discourses. On the one hand, their behavior can be viewed as a legitimate form of a political process and, on the other, their activities can be condemned by the state's position as morally liable, reinforced by the anti-Islamic rhetoric of Western governments.

---

[6] Vladimir Putin made this statement on Russian national television on 24 September 1999, following the bombing of Grozny by Russian fighter planes the day before. Russian commentators have observed that "to rub out someone in the outhouse" evokes the killings of prisoners in the Gulag by guards and fellow prisoners during Stalinism. See the Vikipediia entry on "mochit' v sortire" for the origin of this phrase and commentaries on Putin's use of it (last accessed 3 July 2009, ru.wikipedia.org/wiki/Мочить_в_сортире (To Kill in the Outhouse)).

Women and Terrorism

Research on women and terrorism is negligible, "despite participation of women in terrorist groups throughout history" (Oliverio and
Lauderdale 2005b, 158), and until recently, most of the existing work
explored the issue from the standpoint of women's criminal behavior.
Alternative and feminist theories have emerged, however, that reinter-
pret violence by women during war from an angle that validates the
women combatants' actions by according agency to the women and
legitimacy to their cause. Work recently published by feminist scholars
Laura Sjoberg and Caron E. Gentry characterizes the black widows as
"revolutionaries," agents capable of making rational choices for themselves (2008, 89), even though these choices are (self-)destructive. The
authors maintain that the Russian government skillfully uses the phrase
"black widow" to inscribe the Chechen women with a "racialized,
monstrous image" (2008, 89) that divests them of personhood and
perpetuates sexist and subordinating stereotypes of women. Horrific as
acts of suicide bombings may be, some Chechen female combatants
adopt this course of action as a means to achieve their goal, which they
perceive as legitimate—a point to which I return below.[7]

Questioning the conventional notion of the term "terrorism," soci-
ologists Annemarie Oliverio and Pat Lauderdale insist that the concept
has inextricable connections to domination, hierarchy, and patriarchy
(2005b, 8). Researchers, they maintain, must dissociate terrorist action
from its politicized construction and explicate it in a more neutral,
exact, and methodical way. A less politicized treatment of the subject-
matter may be achieved by presenting the conflict from the viewpoint
of the perpetrators of political violence, as well as refraining from operating on the premise that the rebels' cause has no moral basis. The
reinterpretation and reexamination of women's violence offered by

---

[7] See works by Speckhard and Akhmedova, "Black widows and beyond:
understanding the motivations and life trajectories of Chechen female terrorists" (2008) and Iuzik *Nevesty Allakha. Litsa i sud'by zhenshchin-shakhidok, vzorvavshikhsia v Rossii* (2003) on this topic. I cite these works later in
the article.

feminist scholars opens up new lines of investigation into the phenomenon of "black widows."

Chechen Women and Violence: Conditions and Exceptions

Why do Chechen women turn to violence and terrorism? The answer to the question is fraught with complexities and contradictions. No single, straightforward explanation can illuminate the entire phenomenon. It would be safe to say that numerous causes come into play, and undoubtedly, among those, both political and personal motives rank high. Lisa Kruger sums up these motives as follows: "Women are motivated by nationalism, ideology, political agendas, revenge for personal suffering, and sense of duty" (quoted in Skaine 2006, 87). Chechen women's engagement in the conflict started a decade after their personal experience of the protracted and brutal war. Loss of family members, loss of national identity, and the fragmentation of personhood have all contributed to Chechen women's identity crisis, driving them to pursue a course of violence.

Scholars such as Speckhard and Akhmedova (2008, 101–3), Mia Bloom (2008, 3), and Kruger, who study female militancy and participation in terrorist acts, demonstrate that female combatants' motivations largely coincide with those of their male counterparts. Kruger argues that "the notion that women are differently motivated than men is largely the result of gender biased reporting" (quoted in Skaine 2006, 87). Although this particular feminist line of argument strives to reconstitute gender equality in its approach to members of violent minority groups and grants women agency in the process, it overlooks the complexities that surround black widows—complexities that I address below.

THE POLITICAL REALITY

Chechnya has been an unstable region for more than a decade: the first Chechen War "created 250,000 refugees" (Skaine 2006, 98), and the total number of Chechen deaths as a direct or indirect consequence of the two wars since 1994 is also estimated at 250,000 (Reuter 2004, 3). Apart from the casualties and the hardships of its

population, there have been reports of atrocities—torture and rape—
committed by the Russian army (Politkovskaia 2002, 130–1).[8] It does
not seem far-fetched to link the rise of militancy, especially among the
women whose age ranges from fifteen to thirty-eight (Speckhard and
Akhmedova 2008, 107), to Russia's military policy towards Chechnya
under the leadership of Yeltsin and Putin, and currently under Dmitrii
Medvedev. The first suicide bombing carried out by a Chechen woman
did not occur "until the Second Russo-Chechen war, when Russian
forces began systematically targeting Chechen civilians in so-called
cleansing operations" (Reuter 2004, 3). The above data give grounds
for attributing Chechen female militancy at least partially to political
and nationalist passions, which prompted women to participate in
Chechnya's nationalist resistance against its oppressor.

Black widows' political awareness doubtless responds to the fundamental lack of democratic process in what Chechens consider occupied territory, where their status is that of second-class citizens of the
Russian Federation. Indeed, in this respect the Chechen conflict shares
some characteristic traits with other nationalist struggles around the
world, such as the Palestinian struggle for a homeland. Although the
Russian Federation encompasses a diversity of ethnic, linguistic, and
religious populations, federal laws and statutes do not reflect this diversity. Moshe Gammer, a historian who studies Chechen-Russian relations, argues that the Russian state must become a pluralistic society
and "accept as legitimate the many faces of Russian society" (2005,
220) that it has yet to acknowledge and accommodate. Given the
political situation in which the Chechens find themselves—part of the
Russian Federation, yet treated as inferior subjects—one may reason-
ably perceive their struggle as a fight to overthrow colonialism in the
postcolonial era.

---

[8] Anna Politkovskaia was one of the first Russian journalists (working for the
newspaper *Novaia gazeta* and reporting on the Chechen War) to publicly
condemn Putin's policy towards Chechnya through her published reports,
books, and interviews in the foreign press. Among her best-known works
are *Vtoraia chechenskaia* (Moscow: Izdatel'stvo Zakharova, 2002) and *Putin's
Russia: Life in a Failing Democracy* (New York: Metropolitan Books, 2005),
where she discusses the atrocities committed by the occupying Russian army
as well as the patriarchal practices of the Chechens. Politkovskaia was mur-
dered in Moscow in October 2006.

The Chechen-Russian conflict has a long-standing history, with Chechen resistance against Russian expansionism and imperialism dating back to the late eighteenth century.[9] In the seventeenth and eighteenth centuries, Chechnya and other territories of the North Caucasus became the focus of "military and political competition for the Russian and Ottoman Empires and Persia" (Tishkov 1997, 189). A brief period of truce (1781–1785) punctuated the Tsarist military and colonial expansion in Chechnya, during which Chechens gave their allegiance to Russian rule. In 1785, however, under the leadership of Sheikh Mansur, there was a Chechen revolt against Russia, which led to Mansur's arrest and imprisonment. Ever since the first armed uprising, Russian and Chechen relations have been antagonistic.

The Russo-Chechen hostilities continued during the Soviet era. In the 1920s, the Soviet regime began forced collectivization in Chechnya and at the same time started "to persecute religion and repress those working at the mosques and Islamic schools" (Tishkov 1997, 191), causing Chechen uprisings. In 1944, following Chechen revolt against Soviet rule, massive deportations of Chechens to Siberia and the Kazakh and Kirghiz SSRs began, resulting in heavy demographic losses due to the hardships and deprivations caused by the trauma of deportation and resettlement (Tishkov 1997, 192). After the fall of the Soviet Union, the situation has only deteriorated.

In some ways, the collapse of the Soviet Union rendered the Chechen quest for self-determination even more urgent, given that all fifteen Soviet republics, some surrounding Chechnya, were able to break away from the USSR and form independent states in 1991.[10] More than a decade later, Chechnya, Russia's ethnic, religious, and linguistic "other," remains part of the Russian Federation, subject to orders from Moscow. From the viewpoint of a repressed minority, this condition is not only humiliating and shameful, but alarming as well, given the staggering number of casualties since 1994, when the first Chechen War began.

---

[9] For the historical background of Russian-Chechen relations, see Gammer (2005), Seely (2001), and Tishkov (1997).

[10] Georgia, Armenia, and Azerbaijan, neighbors of Chechnya, are three former Soviet republics that became independent in 1991.

The Russo-Chechen encounter can be traced back to nineteenth-century Russian literature. Literary depictions of the Muslim peoples of the Caucasus by Pushkin, Lermontov, and Tolstoy serve as ethnographic source books for Russian readers (Layton 1995, 7–9). Pushkin's romantic poem "Kavkazskii plennik" ["Prisoner of the Caucasus" 1822] contrasts the "savage" mountain people to the "civilized" Russians (Layton 1995, 89). Whereas Pushkin's representation shows ambivalence towards the natives of the Caucasus and questions tsarist expansion (Layton 1995, 92), Lermontov's "Kavkazskii plennik" ["Prisoner of the Caucasus" 1828] depicts the Muslim other as bloody and violent. Tolstoy's earlier attitude towards Russia's "other" (as expressed in "Kavkazskii plennik" ["Prisoner of the Caucasus" 1872]) and war in general underwent a deep spiritual change. In *Hadzhi-Murat* [*Hadji Murad*, published posthumously in 1912], Tolstoy renounces his earlier notion of Russian superiority over the peoples of the Caucasus, espousing and promoting the idea of self-determination for ethnic minorities living in the peripheries. More recently, Sergei Bodrov's critically acclaimed film *Kavkazskii plennik* [*Prisoner of the Mountains* 1996], loosely based on Tolstoy's short story with the same title, humanizes the enemy—the Chechens—and offers a complex view of the conflict. Bodrov portrays the interaction between the captive Russian soldiers and the Chechen captors with subtlety and sensitivity. In stark contrast, Aleksei Balabanov's film *Voina* [*War* 2002], in black-and-white terms, demonizes the Chechens as violent barbarians. Two other texts worthy of note that treat the topic of Russia and its Caucasian "other" are Leonid Gaidai's screen comedy *Kavkazskaia plennitsa* [*The Female Prisoner of the Caucasus* 1966] and Vladimir Makanin's "Kavkazskii plennyi" ["The Prisoner of the Caucasus," *Novyi mir* 1995]. While Gaidai's film focuses more on "gender, not ethnic minority" (Goscilo 2003, 198), Makanin's controversial text, with its overtly homoerotic slant, "echoes [...] other narratives of colonial dominion where the colonizer in the midst of his alien, 'primitive' surroundings is forced to confront himself" (Goscilo 2003, 200).

THE MILITARY CONFLICT

Examining the rise of female militancy, the political theorist Zillah Eisenstein connects it to war—in the case of Chechen women, the prolonged war with Russia—and to the failure of patriarchal institutions. Pointing out the fundamental difference between the daily living conditions of women in war and women in civilian life, Eisenstein observes:

> Patriarchal gender continues to morph according to context. Many US women looking for job training and steady-paying work continue to join the military in new numbers [...] Similarly positioned women in countries elsewhere also look to the militarized zones of their lives [...] Their lives have little space for what is usually considered private and familial, and few of them could claim civilian status in their war-torn circumstances. They suffer and struggle and die in equal numbers to their men [...] Women suicide bombers reflect similar gender bending to that in other militarized arenas. Female suicide bombers do not bespeak the demise of patriarchal relations in these countries—Lebanon, Palestine, Chechnya—but rather the new fluidity of gender roles carried out by male and female alike. (2007, 30)

Confronted with the extreme and unusual conditions in which they find themselves, Chechen women resort to extreme and unusual measures that women in civilian life normally would not adopt. In other words, their involuntary involvement in a prolonged war (and the alienation and isolation that follow) is another factor contributing to Chechen women's evolution into voluntary suicide bombers.

SOCIAL OPPRESSION

Even under normal circumstances, the life of a typical Chechen woman comes with many challenges and hardships.[11] The terrorist acts committed by black widows are the tragic consequences of patriarchy (Russian domination and Islamic oppression of women),[12] which breed dissent and ultimately lead to violence. A disturbing fact is that "a total

---

[11] For more information on Chechen family life and the role of women in the family, see Smirnova (1968).

[12] Interviews given to researchers by family members of suicide bombers (cited in this article) suggest that women's social status or lack thereof is the underlying cause of their radicalization.

of 42 percent of all Chechen suicide bombers have been women—that
is, forty-six women bombers out of 110 Chechen suicide bombers"
(Speckhard and Akhmedova 2008, 100). For Chechen women, domination comes in two different guises: the Russian state policy of prolonged war against Chechen militants and civilians alike, and Chechen
men's sexist attitude towards women. That attitude partly accounts for
the media's allegations that male terrorist groups have forced women
into the roles of black widows who carry out terrorist attacks.

An interview given by a Chechen "smertnitsa-neudachnitsa"
(unsuccessful female suicide bomber), Zarema Muzhikhoeva, helps
shed light on the circumstances surrounding black widows.[13] The
twenty-three-year-old Muzhikhoeva's story as recorded in Dmitrii
Bykov's article "Ne vezet mne v smerti" ["I'm unlucky in death"
2004], published in *Ogonek*, speaks of grim adversities experienced by
Muzhikhoeva in her native village and of her subsequent recruitment
by a female follower of the guerilla leader Shamil Basaev. A widow who
had run away from her deceased husband's family and lacked friends,
money, and support, Muzhikhoeva was an easy target for Basaev's
recruiters. The counter-terrorism analyst Clara Beyler has observed
that recruiters often prey upon disenfranchised women when the latter
are psychologically weaker, targeting them as potential suicide bombers
(Beyler 2004). While coercion may have figured in Muzhikhoeva's
recruitment, there were objective factors, such as her social marginalization and destitution, that made her an easy target.

Whether she enlisted in Basaev's army under pressure or not, as
a black widow Muzhikhoeva did not carry out her mission of deto-
nating a bomb in a Moscow restaurant in July 2003. One of the few
black widows to defy the terrorist leaders, she was "pervaia shakhidka,
kotoraia ne to chto ne smogla, a ne zakhotela vzryvat' moskvichei. I
dobrovol'no sdalas'" [the first *shakhidka* [Muslim female martyr] who
not so much wasn't able to, as didn't want to, blow up Muscovites.
And she surrendered willingly] (Bykov 2004).

Muzhikhoeva's interview/testimony, given while in police custody,
raises several issues. First, she could hardly be considered representa-

---

[13] Muzhikhoeva's interview is available in the form of a journal article, as nar-
rated by the well-known journalist Dmitrii Bykov (2004). No direct tran-
script of her interview is available to the general public.

tive of the approximately forty female suicide bombers, since, unlike the rest, she did not carry out the operation. Whereas her testimony is available, the black widows who fulfilled their mission have not survived to tell their story. And if her assertion—that she had been forced to undertake her operation—is accurate, it opens up yet another alarming aspect: that militant Chechen men (and women) pressure women into performing violent deeds. While the research available on female suicide bombers does not confirm such a hypothesis, it does validate the theory that "the men in these women's lives play an important role in mobilizing them to terrorism" (Bloom 2008, 1).

Subordination in another guise lies behind the seventeen-year-old Khava Baraeva's decision to become the first Chechen female suicide bomber. According to journalist Iuliia Iuzik, Baraeva became a *shakhidka* because she fell in love with her militant cousin, Arbi Baraev, the leader of the Dubrovka hostage-takers (Iuzik 2003, 18). Iuzik reconstructs Baraeva's last months before the suicide mission, showing how the lonely teenager was fatefully attracted to her handsome cousin, and subsequently lured into Wahhabism—a radical sect of Islam:

> She fell in love with Arbi. He was devilishly handsome: all women fell in love with him as soon as they set eyes on him.
> [Ona vliubilas' v Arbi. On zhe byl krasiv kak d'iavol: v nego vliublialis' vse zenshchiny, tol'ko uvidevshie ego.] (2003, 18)

In Baraeva's case, falling in love had dire consequences. It caused the motherless young woman to subscribe to radical views—views espoused by the man she fell in love with—inciting her to carry out her suicide mission. Another hypothesis for this interpretation of Baraeva's case suggests that perhaps media and society at large are more eager to express sympathy for a "vulnerable" and "deceived" young woman rather than to entertain the possibility of her independent will and agency. This reaction reflects longstanding gender biases, considering women as emotional, vulnerable, and often weak.

The image of a servile, emotional black widow differs from the impression of the Chechen female captors conveyed by the hostages at the Dubrovka Theater. In interviews, freed hostages noted that subservient and deferential as the black widows were to their male counterparts, some of them focused on the hardships they faced as a result of the war Russia waged against their nation (Politkovskaia 2005, 186–229; Skaine 2006, 111–12). "Skilled in trauma bonding" (Skaine 2006, 112), the black widows connected with their hostages. By describing the human dimension of their plight, the black widows were able to elicit a sympathetic response from some of the hostages, who later expressed regret that the women had been killed (Skaine 2006, 112).[14] This sympathetic response, however, is different from the pity that Baraeva's case provoked.

THE PSYCHOLOGICAL REALM

Whatever the rationalized motivations for becoming a suicide bomber may be, in some cases a kind of pathology or disorder may shape the consciousness of marginalized Chechen women, prompting them to step outside their traditional roles. The very fact that many of the female combatants are war widows or related to men who have died at the hands of Russian troops (Speckhard and Akhmedova 2008, 114) suggests that they have suffered trauma. Their resort to violence and self-destructive behavior lends itself to the Freudian psychoanalysis of "melancholia."

Freud's 1917 essay "Mourning and Melancholia" identifies melancholia as a type of psychological disorder that springs from bereavement and mourning. In his study of bereaved women afflicted with melancholia, Freud found such patients prone to low self-esteem, which in turn expressed itself in masochism and/or sadism (1959, 164). Freud's case studies and subsequent analyses suggest that the murderous impulse is actually a suicidal drive redirected against others. The extreme and violent response of the black widows to their personal loss[15] and social and political conditions seems compatible with this psychoanalytic framework. One such case of the murderous/suicidal impulse would be the twenty-year-old widow Luiza (Aiza)

---

[14] Hostages' sympathetic response may have been the result of the Stockholm Syndrome, whereby the hostages identify with their captors.

[15] Data collected by Anne Speckhard and Khapta Akhmedova show that one or more family member of 87 percent of Chechen suicide bombers were killed, tortured, or raped by Russian military forces. See Speckard and Akhmedova (2008, 114).

Gazueva, who in November 2001 exploded herself in order to kill the commanding officer Geidar Gadzhiev, who had ordered her husband's torture and subsequent execution.[16] The Russian army killed not only Aiza's young husband, but also her brother (Iuzik 2003, 30). There are limits to this kind of explanation, however. While it would be reasonable to suppose that some Chechen black widows do indeed suffer from melancholia as defined by Freud and act out of irrational impulses, to ascribe this motivation to all of the black widows does not seem warranted by the research available on them, research that has been presented elsewhere in this essay.

RELIGION, TRADITION, AND MEDIA MANIPULATION

The oppressive authority and patriarchal power structure of Islam play a large part in Chechen widows' engagement in terrorist activities. Since scholars investigating the Chechen conflict maintain that few suicide bombers were religious prior to their involvement with recruiters from militant groups (Speckhard and Akhmedova 2008, 109; Russell 2007, xi; Smith 2001, 54–5), these widows clearly do not view Islam as calling the faithful to holy war. Interviews given to Akhmedova, Iuzik, Nivat, Politkovskaia, and Speckhard by friends and relatives of black widows identify alienation and desperation as the motivating factors leading these women to militancy. According to Yassita and Madni—mothers, respectively, of the suicide bombers Gazueva and Zareta Baikarova—trauma and a sense of hopelessness were the underlying causes of their daughters' turn to suicidal behavior. Both mothers maintain that their daughters were reacting to the deaths of close family members who had been killed by Russian troops (Nivat 2008, 124–5). While the sister of another suicide bomber, Aminat, explained the latter's militancy as rooted in her alienation from the rest of the community when she became religious (Nivat 2008, 125–6), Aminat, too, had lost a family member to the conflict.

Islam radicalizes women in Chechnya by being a force of gendered oppression. Traditional Islamic law, to which many in Chechnya

---

[16] See Gazueva's biography in Iuzik (2003, 27–30).

adhere, emphasizes strict, ancient gender divisions that do not accord women the same rights and privileges as men. Even though Chechens did not practice their Sufi brand of Islam for some seventy years from the inception of the Soviet Union until its fall in 1991, during those decades Chechen identity and social practices continued to reflect their Islamic heritage. Today individual families' interpretations of Islamic laws vary, but observance of traditional Muslim values is generally expected by, and of, all members of the community. Islamic religious tradition relegates women to a role largely limited to the domestic sphere. As Muslims, Chechen women are socialized to be private individuals—mothers, wives, daughters, and sisters—within the family that is the core social unit defining and shaping individual identity.

The primacy of the family has considerable explanatory power in accounting for the emergence and underlying causes of the Chechen black widows' activities. Islamic societies and states privilege the family in all spheres of life: social, religious, economic, and political (Joseph 2001, 1). The familial structure in Chechnya, as in the rest of the Islamic world, is "shaped by and works through the institutions of patriarchy [,] which affect much of the social order" (Joseph 2001, 2). Consequently, a woman's identity, status in her community, sense of self-worth, and her very personhood are constituted by, and embedded within, her family. As noted earlier, many of the Chechen women who took part in suicide bombings were widows or women who had lost multiple family members in the war. Since a married woman's identity and status are validated by and tied to her husband's, for Chechen women the loss of a spouse means marginalization and loss of personhood and identity.

While female combatants are engaged in a nationalist movement, they may be conflating their two oppressors: the state and their religious institution. Discriminated against as women on the social level, they also suffer discrimination on the national, political level as Chechens. Desperation, familial loyalty, and lack of political voice all contribute to their frustration, and consequently, their turn to violence, which can also be interpreted as their attempt to take control of their lives, albeit in death.

Unlike Russian widows whose husbands have been killed in combat, Chechen widows do not have the comfort of taking part in the national commemorative rituals normally accessible to spouses

of soldiers and even well-known noncombatants. Though their husbands also perish in combat, Chechen widows are not accorded the
traditional war widows' rights to public mourning and commemoration
of the dead.[17] Not unlike Sophocles' Antigone, Chechen war widows
find themselves in a tragic situation, torn between two laws: that of the
(Russian) state, which forbids honoring its enemies, and their ethnic
culture's law, which demands burial of, and honor for, the dead.

Examining the actions of the black widows, the psychologist
Leonid Kitaev-Smyk in an interview with *Ogonek* titled "Shakhidskoe
schast'e" ["Happiness à la Shahid" 2003] offers an original analysis
of their motivations. He claims that black widows preparing to meet
their death are in a state of ecstasy—a state of mind achieved by going
into a trance induced by Sufi meditation and dancing. Basing his argument on the fact that the traditional form of Islam practiced in pre-
Soviet Chechnya was Sufism, Kitaev-Smyk asserts that the recruiters
of suicide bombers exploit an indigenous spiritual practice to further
their own murderous agenda. His explanation is more concerned with
how black widows are able to carry out suicide missions rather than
with why they do so.

While Islam as a culture and tradition undoubtedly affects the
life of Chechen women and their involvement in the violent conflict,
the Russian state and media excessively focus on the black widows'
religious background. This is not to say that Islamists do not play a
role in the Chechen conflict; they manipulate, recruit, enlist, and
politicize Chechen women in order to accomplish their own goals.
The Russian state, however, too quickly and willingly adopts anti-
Islamic rhetoric, which relies on primitive fears and stirs nationalist passions. For instance, in his essay "Zapiski na poliakh tragedii"
["Notes on the Margins of Tragedy" 2005] Vladimir Pastukhov connects Chechen terrorists, and even leaders such as Aslan Maskhadov
and Shamil Basaev, to al-Qaeda and to criminal activities, particularly
human and drug trafficking. He declares, "[T]oday we [Russians] are
doomed to continue this war" [segodnia my obrecheny prodolzhat'

---

[17] Serguei Oushakine's article "The Politics of Pity: Domesticating Loss in
a Russian Province" (2006) examines the practice of commemorating the
dead in Siberian villages. Oushakine shows how this practice helps bereaved
mothers of fallen Russian soldiers to deal with their loss and grief.

etu voinu], justifying his pronouncement by pointing out that Russian children are being held hostage by "bandits" (Pastukhov 2005, 11). The well-known scholar Valerii Tishkov, writing on the Chechen conflict, expresses moral indignation at the "apathetic" attitude adopted by Western governments, media, and public opinion, which all fail to realize the links between the Beslan tragedy and global jihad (2005, 13).

Religious misconceptions and mischaracterizations abound in the Russian media's sensationalization of these acts and in the state's references to female terrorists as "brides" or "the betrothed" of Allah. Even if the phrase *nevesty allakha*[18] is used metaphorically, for Muslims it represents a mistake in ontological category that betrays Russians' ignorance of Islam. Since Allah is a transcendent being devoid of human likeness and attributes, no one can be married or betrothed to Allah. In an interview titled "Nevesty Allakha" ["The Betrothed of Allah" 2004] in *Ogonek* (36:11), the Russian journalist Natal'ia Radulova expresses her views on why Chechen women turn to terrorism. In a seemingly feminist fashion, she maintains that there should be nothing surprising in acts of violence perpetrated by women, but she proceeds to place the blame for such acts unproblematically on the way Chechen women are treated in their communities. While no one would deny the inequitable conditions under which Chechen women live in their national community, Radulova fails to acknowledge that the Russian state shares responsibility for the bloody conflict and for the destinies of Chechen women.

THE UNKNOWN

The motivations behind the eighteen black widows' participation in the siege of the Moscow Dubrovka Theater in October 2002 cannot be determined with certainty because none of them survived the attack. What little is known about them comes from information supplied by their relatives and friends as well as the hostages. All but one of

---

[18] This phrase was coined by Iuliia Iuzik (2003). Iuzik's portrayal of black widows is generally sympathetic, even though her analysis may be somewhat simplistic, revealing her unfamiliarity with, and lack of understanding of, Chechen culture.

the forty-one rebels who held about 850 people hostage in the theater were killed when Russian *spetsnatsovy* (Special Forces) pumped in an unknown chemical agent through the theater ventilation system. Ironically, the 129 hostages who were killed during the siege died not at the hands of the black widows and the hostage-takers, but as a result of the anti-terrorist operation carried out by government forces.[19]

Two black widows who participated in the Beslan school hostage takeover were also killed during the "rescue." Conflicting testimony makes it impossible to ascertain whether they were killed by their male comrades or whether they themselves detonated their explosives before Russian Special Forces raided the school (Speckhard and Akhmedova 2008, 103). According to one eyewitness report, two female terrorists who openly disagreed with their leader in taking children hostage were killed by remote detonation (Skaine 2006, 108). This testimony actually credits these two black widows with agency, since they had the independence and courage to disagree with their leaders by refusing to take children hostage.

Conclusion

As mentioned earlier, research has shown that no single factor or motivation prompts Chechen women to become suicide bombers. A combination of circumstances and personal motives—"the lethal mix" (Speckhard and Akhmedova 2008, 113)—is instrumental in their decisions to blow up their targets and themselves. To varying degrees their actions are rooted in political conflict, nationalist ideology, patriotism, trauma, coercion, and personal revenge, but it is impossible to determine which cause predominates. Most discourses frame them as victims, and although existent social, political, and religious factors create certain conditions that marginalize these women, one ought to acknowledge their agency as well. It is difficult, if not impossible, to determine to what degree their independent willpower drives them

---

[19] Anna Politkovskaia describes the plight of one of the hostages, Irina Fadeeva, whose son Yaroslav was killed during the siege. In Fadeeva's case, the suffering was made worse by the Russian police, who gave her no information about the circumstances of her son's death (2005, 188–91).

to such acts but, undoubtedly, their subjectivity can be detected in their choices. In other words, whereas Muzhikhoeva may be coerced, and while Baraeva falls in love, both live in a society that allows their objectification and deprives them of individuality and will in everyday life. To this picture, however, one can add the cases of the two female rebels from the Beslan school act, rebels who disagreed and objected to their male leader, behavior that points to agency and will under extreme conditions.

The specific examples I have analyzed indicate that gender likely plays a role in some of the black widows' decisions: factors such as social oppression and their double marginalization (political and familial) contradict Kruger's claim that the motivations of female terrorists are no different from those of their male counterparts. As the various approaches to the phenomenon of black widows reveal, however, a single explanation for their choices (whether implicating the Russian state for the emergence of political brutality or granting black widows agency to control their destinies, if not in life then in death) only partially accounts for female violence.

The concept of alterity is central to explicating Chechen women's adoption of terrorist methods with the goal of affecting change. Chechen women represent "the other" in multiple ways. In the domain of social and religious group identity, they belong to the "second sex"; in the context of the state and nationality, they are second-class citizens of Russia. Subjected to a secondary status in all spheres of life, Chechen women struggle to survive in a hostile environment that in large measure helps to account for their actions, while in certain cases drives them to assert their agency in acts that can only be called desperate.

NOTES

Unless otherwise indicated, translations from Russian into English are mine.

REFERENCES

Balabanov, Alexei. 2002. *Voina*. Moscow : Kinokompaniia STV.

Ben-Yehuda, Nachman. 2005. "Terror, Media, and Moral Boundaries." *International Journal of Comparative Sociology* 45, no 153: 33–53.

Beyler, Clara. 2004. "Messengers of Death—Female Suicide Bombers." *International Institute of Counter-Terrorism*. 3 July. http:www.ict.org/ (last accessed March 30, 2009).

Bloom, Mia. 2008. "Women as Victims and Victimizers." *US Department of State*. 11 April. http:www.america.gov/st/peacesec-english (last accessed 27 March 2009).

Bodrov, Sergei. 1996. *Kavkazskii plennik*. Russia/Kazakhstan: Karavan.

Borisov, Timofei. 2004. "Na rasstoianii priamogo vystrela. Beslan: tri dnia v operativnom shtabe." *Rossiiskaia gazeta*, 7 September.

———. 2003. "Smertnitsa Dudueva." *Rossiiskaia gazeta*, 10 July.

Burke, Edmund. 2003. *Reflections on the revolution in France*. New Haven: Yale University Press.

Bush, George W. 2001. *Address to a Joint Session of Congress and the American People*. 20 September.

Bykov, Dmitrii. 2004. "Ne vezet mne v smerti." *Ogonek* 4830, 3: 12–16.

Chuprinina, Iunna. 2004. "Eto voina!..." *Itogi* 36: 430.

Eisenstein, Zillah. 2007. *Sexual Decoys: Gender, Race, and War in Imperial Democracy*. London: Zed Books.

Freud, Sigmund. 1959. "Mourning and Melancholia." In *Collected Papers*, Vol. 4, translated by Joan Riviere, 152–70. New York: Basic Books Inc. Publishers.

Gaidai, Leonid. 1966. *Kavkazskaia plennitsa, ili novye prikliucheniia Shurika*. Moscow: Mosfilm.

Gammer, Moshe. 2005. *The Lone Wolf and the Bear: Three Centuries of Chechen Defiance of Russian Rule*. Pittsburgh: University of Pittsburgh Press.

Goscilo, Helena. 2003. "Casting and Recasting the Caucasian Captive." In *Two Hundred Years of Pushkin*, Vol. 1, edited by Joe Andrew and Robert Reid, 195–207. Amsterdam and New York: Rodopi.

Goscilo, Helena, and Andrea Lanoux, eds. 2006. *Gender and National Identity in Twentieth Century Russian Culture*. DeKalb: Northern Illinois University Press.

Healing, Raven. 2005. "White Stockings and Black Widows: Women in Chechnya—Myths and Realities." *Off Our Backs*, 1 March.

Hubbs, Joanna. 1988. *Mother Russia: the Feminine Myth in Russian Culture*. Bloomington: Indiana University Press.

Iuzik, Iuliia. 2003. *Nevesty Allakha. Litsa i sud'by zhenshchin-shakhidok, vzor-vavshikhsia v Rossii*. Moscow: Ul'tra Kul'tura.

Joseph, Suad, and Susan Slyomovics, eds. 2001. *Women and Power in the Middle East*. Philadelphia: University of Pennsylvania Press.

Karaganov, Sergei. 2002. "Govorit' o chechentsakh pravdu — znachit oskor-
bliat' tselyi narod." *Ogonek* 4773, 45: 14–15.
Kitaev-Smyk, Leonid. 2003. "Shakhidskoe schast'e." *Ogonek* 4807, 28: 14–16.
Kruger, Lisa. 2005. *Gender and Terrorism: Motivations of Female Terrorists.*
Master of Science, Strategic Intelligence Thesis, Joint Military Intelligence
College.
Layton, Susan, and Catriona Kelly, eds. 1995. *Russian Literature and Empire:
Conquest of the Caucasus from Pushkin to Tolstoy.* Cambridge: Studies in
Russian Literature.
Lermontov, M. Iu. 1964. "Kavkazskii plennik." In *Sobranie sochinenii* vol. 4,
127–58. Moscow: Khudlit.
Makanin, Vladimir. 1995. "Kavkazskii plennyi." *Novyi mir* IV: 3–19.
Nivat, Anne. 2008. "The black widows: Chechen women join the fight for
independence—and Allah." In *Female Terrorism and Militancy: Agency,
Utility, and Organization,* edited by Cindy Ness, 122–30. London:
Routledge.
Oliverio, Annamarie, and Pat Lauderdale. 2005a. "Terrorism as Deviance or
Social Control: Suggestions for Future Research." *International Journal of
Comparative Sociology* 45, no. 153: 153–69.
———. 2005b. "Introduction: Critical Perspectives on Terrorism." *International
Journal of Comparative Sociology* 45, no. 153: 3–9.
Oushakine, Serguei. 2005. "The Politics of Pity: Domesticating Loss in a
Russian Province." *American Anthropologist* 108, no. 2: 297–311.
Pape, Robert A. 2005. *Dying to Win: The Strategic logic of Suicide Terrorism.*
New York: Random House.
Pastukhov, Vladimir. 2005. "Zapiski na poliakh tragedii." In *Posle Beslana:
Diskussiia rossiiskikh i amerikanskikh ekspertov,* 4–11. Moscow: Rossiiskaia
Akademiia Nauk. Institut etnologii i antropologii 176.
Politkovskaia, Anna. 2005. *Putin's Russia: Life in a Failing Democracy.*
Translated by Arch Tait. New York: Metropolitan Books.
———. 2002. *Vtoraia chechenskaia.* Moscow: Izdatel'stvo Zakharova.
Pushkin, A. S. 1959. "Kavkazskii plennik." In *Sobranie sochinenii* vol.10,
87–120. Moscow: Khudlit.
Putin, Vladimir. 1999. "Address on Russian National Television." 24
September.
Radulova, Natal'ia. 2004. "Nevesty allakha." *Ogonek* 4836, 36: 11.
Rechkalov, Vadim. 2004. "Privet Mama! Ia uchu arabskii." *Izvestiia,* 9
February.
Reuter, John. 2004. "Chechnya's Suicide Bombers: Desperate, Devout, or
Deceived?" *American Committee for Peace in Chechnya.*
Russell, John. 2007. *Chechnya—Russia's 'War on Terror.'* London: Routledge.
Sanin, Grigorii. 2004. "Chernyi den' kalendaria." *Itogi* 36: 430.
Seely, Robert. 2001. *Russo-Chechen Conflict 1800–2000: A Deadly Embrace.*
London: Frank Cass.
Sharoni, Simona. 1995. *Gender and the Israeli-Palestinian Conflict: The Politics of
Women's Resistance.* Syracuse: Syracuse University Press.

Sharov, Andrei. 2004. "V Moskve ishchut 'chernuiu vdovu.'" *Rossiskaia Gazeta*, 2 September.

Sjoberg, Laura and Caron E. Gentry. 2008. *Mothers, Monsters, Whores: Women's Violence in Global Politics*. London: Zed Books.

Skaine, Rosemarie. 2006. *Female Suicide Bombers*. Jefferson, North Carolina: McFarland.

Smirnova, Ia. S. 1968. "Sem'ia i semeinyi byt." In *Kul'tura i byt narodov Severnogo Kavkaza*, edited by V. K. Gardanov, 185–273. Moscow: Nauka.

Smith, Sebastian. 2001. *Allah's Mountains: The Battle for Chechnya*. London: Tauris.

Speckhard, Anne, and Khapta Akhmedova. 2008. "Black widows and beyond: understanding the motivations and life trajectories of Chechen female terrorists." In *Female Terrorism and Militancy: Agency, Utility, and Organization*, edited by Cindy Ness, 100–21. London: Routledge.

Tilly, Charles. 2005. "Terror as Strategy and Relational Process." *International Journal of Comparative Sociology* 46, 153: 11–32.

Tishkov, Valerii. 2005. "Terror i ego obozrevateli." In *Posle Beslana: Diskussiia rossiiskikh i amerikanskikh ekspertov*, 11–15. Moscow: Rossiiskaia Akademiia Nauk. Institut etnologii i antropologii 176.

———. 1997. *Ethnicity, Nationalism and Conflict in and after the Soviet Union: The Mind Aflame*. London: Sage.

Tolstoi, L. N. 1959. "Hadzhi-Murat." In *Sobranie sochinenii* vol. 12, 234–50. Moscow: Khudlit.

CHAPTER 9

War Rape: (Re)defining Motherhood, Fatherhood, and Nationhood

Yana Hashamova

> "You will have a Serbian child.
> You'll have to give birth to a Chetnik."[1]
>
> Rape victims' reports

Conservative estimates of the rapes committed during the Bosnian war (1991–1995) range from twenty thousand to fifty thousand (Boose 2002, 71). Unlike the Nuremberg Charter, which did not include special provisions for rape, in 2001, The Hague International War Crimes Tribunal for Yugoslavia identified rape and sexual enslavement as "crimes against humanity" (Fischer 1996). Since the early 1990s, a lot has been reported and written about rapes in the Yugoslav wars. These atrocities have been examined from various perspectives: from analyzing the traumatic consequences for individuals, families, and society to probing the international legal system that defines crimes against humanity and genocide.[2] Emphasizing male-on-female sexual

---

[1] Fighters for the Serbian nationalist cause during the break-up of Yugoslavia assumed the name Chetniks, inherited from Serbian partisans during World War II.

[2] For books that have become standard reference texts on the Yugoslav war rapes, see Stiglmayer (1994) and Allen (1996). Although Lumsden's article does not focus on war rapes, it offers an interesting framework for studying the psychological consequences of war violence on individual and societal levels (Lumsden 1977). In "The Trauma of War Rapes: A Comparative View on the Bosnian War Conflict and the Greek Civil War,"

violence, which demanded attention and activism, feminist scholarship
had both a direct and indirect impact on the changes in international
criminal law. As a result, the predominant Western scholarship on war
rapes explores the victimization of women. Only a few voices of dis-
content emerged, "attending to the trauma [violated women] might
have experienced without allowing that trauma to define them and
their communities in an overdetermined manner" (Eagle 2005, 816).[3]

Serbian soldiers' violation of Muslim women (mostly Bosniak)
intensified their longstanding subjugation. Rape generated not only the
trauma of bodily abuse but also social rejection and marginalization
enforced by family members and society. According to the traditions
of many Muslim families in rural Bosnia and Kosovo, a raped female
member dishonors and shames her husband, father, and brother(s).
Cases of rape victims testify that violated women were expelled from
their communities or killed by their husbands; some committed suicide
after the rape (Folnegovic-Smalc 1994). A story of a Kosovar Albanian
girl reports that after witnessing her repeated rape, her father sent her
to join the Kosovo Liberation Army, where she would seek revenge
against her abusers, and her likely death would redeem his honor
(Boose 2002, 73).

All these excruciating consequences of the rapes during the
Yugoslav wars prompted many scholars to view them as ethnic
cleansing and genocide. Surveying numerous cases of Serbian soldiers raping Bosniak women while screaming at them, "You will bear
Serbian Chetniks!", Siobhan Fischer contends that the war rapes were
actually forceful impregnation, which under international law ought to
be considered genocide. The author notes:

> It may seem counterintuitive that impregnation, the creation of
> new life, can in fact be an instrument of genocide. But forced
> impregnation—interference with autonomous reproduction—can
> destroy a group. This interference in the group's reproduction

---

Van Boeschoten explores the practice and the political context of war rapes
in the two neighboring countries (Van Boeschoten 2003).

[3] In various venues, some scholars from the Balkans such as Vesna Kesić,
Lepa Mladjenović, Maja Korac, and Žarana Papić also appealed for looking
beyond women's victimization.

may take a number of forms. First, women may be psychologically traumatized by the pregnancy and unable to have normal sexual or childbearing experiences with members of their own group. Second, women who are raped and bear the children of the aggressors may no longer be marriageable in their society. Third, the women, simply because they are pregnant with the children of the aggressors, cannot bear their own children during this time—their wombs are "occupied." Interference with the reproductive capacity of a group has severe implications for the psychological, religious and ethnic identity of the group. (Fischer 1996, 93)

All these arguments notwithstanding, two particular statements strike the reader more than the rest: first, the belief in (and insistence on) "pure" ethnic identity at a time when the very notion of identity is challenged, and second, the notion of woman as solely a means of reproduction, as a vessel in the reproductive process. No doubt, this is how perpetrators viewed women and how some women understood themselves. More interestingly, if perhaps surprisingly, most scholarship has also focused on women's helplessness and oppression, denying them both agency and a future.

I contend that two fictional works by women, Slavenka Drakulić's *S. A Novel about the Balkans* [*Kao da me nema* 1999] and Jasmila Žbanić's film *Grbavica: The Land of my Dreams* [*Grbavica* 2006],[4] counter this tendency. They open space for imagining victimized women's possible transformation and future—a possibility envisioned when raped women who for various reasons decide (or are forced) to carry the pregnancy to term raise their children and attempt to take control over their lives, however difficult and painful these processes may be. This possibility leads to (manic) defenses that enable these women to become mothers and bring up children—their own and not their own, children of the self and the other (the enemy). My essay focuses precisely on this possibility, on the unwanted and yet accepted experience of motherhood. As Julia Kristeva asserts, within this hor-

---

[4] The film was distributed in the West with two different English titles: *Grbavica: The Land of my Dreams* and *Esma's Secret*. The latter introduces melodramatic nuances and I opt for the former in my essay.

rifying mother-child dyad, "each strives to fill the impossible lack in/ of the other. The *I* truly is an other" (Kristeva 1993a, 93). There is no separation between mother and child, and thus none between self and other.

I advance the hypothesis that the two female authors, Drakulić and Žbanić, although from different generations and national and cultural backgrounds, have a similar outlook on the subjectivity of raped women, an outlook that differs from the overall Western perspective on Balkan rape-victims as powerless objects of male oppression and brutality. Drakulić, born in 1949, grew up in Tito's Yugoslavia. She studied at the University of Zagreb and graduated with specialties in literature and sociology. Despite the close affiliation of her Croatian parents with the Communist Party, as a journalist she developed an acutely critical view of communism. After World War II, Tito's Yugoslavia stressed the unity and brotherhood of all peoples of the federation, ignoring cultural, religious, and historical differences. This ideology guided cultural policies until the early 1970s, when cultural, linguistic, and religious identities slowly became recognized, as long as the political unity of the federation in general (and the Serbian central role in it, in particular) remained unchallenged (Wachtel 1998). Resulting from such political and ideological inconsistencies and maneuvers (among other historical and political causes), the disintegration of Yugoslavia came as no surprise. During the Croatian-Serbian war, Drakulić's daughter (from her first husband, a Serb) left the country; persecuted by Franjo Tudjman; Drakulić also departed shortly afterwards. Today, the author lives in Sweden.

In her fiction and non-fiction, Drakulić explores the problems of communism—especially its Yugoslav variant—as well as the consequences of the Yugoslav wars.[5] Often critical of her home country, the writer/journalist and her works appear to have better reception in the West than in Croatia. Pertinent to the discussion of this article is the

---

[5] Her fiction includes *Holograms of Fear* (1992), *Marble Skin* (1995), *The Taste of a Man* (1997), *S. A Novel about the Balkans* (2001), while the titles of her most significant non-fictional works are *How We Survived Communism and even Laughed* (1991), *Balkan Express: Fragments from the Other Side of the War* (1992), *Café Europa: Life after Communism* (1996), *They Would Never Hurt a Fly: War Criminals on Trial in the Hague* (2005).

criticism of some scholars describing her as an "uninformed outsider" whose comments on national identity are "ambiguous, flat, and will disturb no browser at Brentano's" (Banac 1993–4, 177). Ivo Banac vehemently asserts that she caters to Western feminism and understands little of Croatian history, culture, and politics (1993/4, 177).[6] My goal is not to dispute such claims, but to point out how similar Drakulić's observations on raped women are to those of Žbanić, a much younger Bosniak, who was seventeen years old when Yugoslavia collapsed.

Born in Sarajevo, Žbanić graduated from the Sarajevo Academy of Fine Arts. Apart from a short period when she worked in a Vermont-based puppet-theater company, she has lived and continues to live in Sarajevo, Bosnia-Herzegovina. She belongs to a generation of young Bosnian artists who began creating films while the war was still going on. Her debut feature film, *Grbavica*, received international acclaim and the Golden Bear prize for best film at the Berlin Film Festival in 2006. Her second film, *On the Path* [*Na putu* 2010], also explores postwar realties in Bosnia: wounded personal identities, issues of relationships, and the role of Islam in the healing process. The director calls her debut film "a story about love" (Žbanić [no date]). One remains tempted, however, to draw broader cultural conclusions while analyzing the film.

Only a closer analysis of the two works of fiction (literary and cinematic) can show the similarities in the views of these two very different female creators. Drakulić's novel narrates the traumatic destiny of a young Bosnian teacher who suddenly finds herself imprisoned in the so-called "women's rooms," in which Bosnian women were repeatedly violated by Serbian soldiers. The female protagonist becomes known to the reader as S., and her story opens in a Stockholm hospital, where she has delivered a boy. Within a few pages and without many details, the author describes S.'s animosity towards her baby and her recollection of the cruelty and abuse she experienced a few months earlier. The next chapter transports the reader to Bosnia, where it all began

---

[6] Banac indulges in the following salvo: "The interest in Drakulić is the interest in East European ingenues—in the sort of deprived provincial girls who do laundry without household appliances and delight in soft, pink rolls of toilet paper as badges of civilized living" (Banac 1993/4, 176–7).

with "the smell of dust," "the taste of coffee with too much sugar," and "the image of women quietly climbing on to the bus" (11). S.'s bewilderment and her total unpreparedness for all the horror that will engulf her life is conveyed in the first sentence, which portrays the spirit of an ordinary morning for the Bosnian teacher. Only the image of women in a remote village lining up to enter a bus (not from the regular bus-line to town) hints at the looming horror. The next stage of S.'s war experience entails the sound of pleading voices in neighboring houses, followed by a Serbian soldier's kicking open the door of her kitchen. S. has only a few minutes to collect the most necessary belongings and leave. She is stunned: how can this be happening to her, a daughter of a Muslim father and a Serbian mother? With the mixed religious and ethnic background of S., Drakulić unambiguously strips away the legitimacy of Serbian nationalistic ideology, which exploits ethnic purity.

In this analysis, I forgo the psychological description of S.'s humiliation and suffering, to focus on her reaction to the discovery of her pregnancy and on the ways in which she deals with the consequences. After grim depictions of women's violation during months of imprisonment, Drakulić introduces the theme of forced pregnancy as the women's probable fate: "Not one of them was unconcerned about whether they would leave the camp with a swelling stomach" (129). In terms similar to Fischer's and others' arguments about the fatal outcome of such a possibility, the author continues: "There was no way to terminate a pregnancy, yet they could not imagine having a child conceived in this way. [...] To give birth to a child conceived by rape would be more disgraceful than betrayal for them, a fate worse than death" (129). To convey the lethal effects of such a pregnancy, Drakulić spends considerable narrative time dwelling on characters who believe that they will strangle "the child with [their] own hands" if such is the outcome of the rapes. S. witnesses the murder of a baby "who had done nothing wrong" and "had met its death before even taking a breath" (130). The author emphasizes the "natural" impulse of these women to kill their children, but also opens space for imagining that one has a choice. S. wonders whether women who kill their babies could be human again and how they could live outside the camp. She poses the poignant question: "If everyone has the same excuse, that they are forced to kill because there is a war on [...] is one really utterly deprived of all choice in war?" (132).

The imagined possibility of keeping a baby resulting from rape, however, is quickly erased when S. discovers that she herself is pregnant. By effectively combining a third-person narration with S.'s first-person reflections (inserted in the text in italics like passages from a diary), the novel evocatively conveys S's emotions and, at the same time, provides a distance in laying out the facts and constructing reality. From an omniscient narrative statement, "Only now does S. understand that a woman's body never really belongs to the woman. It belongs to the others—to the man, the children, the family. And in wartime to soldiers" (143), Drakulić transports the reader to S.'s mind: "I renounced the child in advance. As if I were a mere receptacle, temporarily housing it, like a rent-a-womb" (145). The narrative transition from omniscient third person to the private first person helps readers to understand her self-objectification and her decision that the child is not hers.

This (self-)denial of the mother as subject paradoxically and perversely echoes the Christian discourse of maternity as an "impossible elsewhere, a sacred beyond, a vessel of divinity" (Kristeva 1993b, 237). Or, to transform the sublime into the ridiculous, I evoke popular culture and, more specifically, the actor Benjamin Bratt, who before marrying his present wife (Talisa Soto), announced that he was looking "to make her the mother of [his] children" (Benjamin Bratt 2001).

Attempting to question this phallocentric view of motherhood and rejecting the understanding that deprives women of will and individuality, at the very end of the novel Drakulić reinstates the mother as subject, as an autonomous agent with power over her own life. Critically viewing the ending, Valerie Jablow contends: "The novel's dénouement, in Sweden, is both heartrending and the weakest part of the book. But that apparent contradiction is not entirely Drakulić's fault: after all, what resolution can there possibly be to losing one's identity and family, one's home?" (Jablow 2000, 3). In my view, however, this "apparent contradiction" deserves further analysis.

Although in a psychoanalytic paradigm that has proclaimed the ultimate desire for motherhood as the woman's desire to bear a child of the father, Kristeva strongly argues for the power of maternity. She theorizes two positions for the woman-mother: one, "under the sway of the paternal function," is the ultimate guarantee of symbolic coherence; the other, distant from the Freudian/Lacanian postulates, is the reunion and identification of the woman-mother with her mother (Kristeva 1993b, 239). Thus, "a woman is simultaneously closer to her instinctual memory, more open to her own psychosis, and consequently, more negatory of the social, symbolic bond" (Kristeva 1993b, 239). In other words, according to Kristeva, the woman-mother is subject to a form of split between maintaining the paternal function and negating that function by identifying with her own mother. This is "Motherhood's impossible syllogism" (Kristeva 1993b, 237).

Under much more traumatic circumstances, S. consciously faces a similar dilemma: denying her baby the function of the father (denying the existence of the father) and identifying with her own mother and sister in the image of her baby. Jablow claims that there cannot be a resolution to the loss of one's identity after the abuse of the male Symbolic order, but Kristeva sees such a resolution in the power of woman's instinctual memory. The woman-mother negates the violations of the Symbolic, though in doing so she opens herself up to psychosis.

At novel's end Drakulić convincingly depicts the circumstances in such a way as to constitute S. as a subject and an agent of motherhood rather than as a vessel. After S. resettles in Sweden as a refugee, she delivers a male baby in a Stockholm hospital, determined to give up the child for adoption. It happens, however, that for a couple of days the baby is in the same room with her and despite her vehement rejection of him, one night she reaches over to pull the blanket over the boy, who has uncovered himself. It is this gesture that keeps S. awake, but it is not this instinct that makes her decide to keep the baby. She looks at the boy and "begins to remember a forgotten image" (197). It is the "look" and the "image" that suggest not so much maternal instincts as memory, mediation, and subjectivity. Browsing through a family photo album, S. looks at a picture of her sister. "This new-born baby has the face of her sister. S. stares at the photograph, then at his face: the pronounced cheekbones and chin which is already showing a dimple, the pouting lips, the shape of the ears, the big dark eyes, the frown [...] even their hands are similar" (197). This shocking and joyful discovery (identification) propels S. to assume the agency of maternity. Her decision is driven by the "image" and the memory of her sister and, by extension, their mother. She, however, is immediately confronted by the inevitable question of the father. Her first response is a lie—"his

father had a heroic death." In a few moments, however, she comes to a
more drastic denial of the paternal function. "One day she will tell him
that he is her child, hers alone. That he has no father—because this is
the truth" (199). Manic defenses settle in to aid S. in her impossible
role of a mother loving her child—the child of her violator (the ultimate Other). When asked whether the novel's ending should be interpreted as hopeful, Drakulić responded, "I did not consider alternative
endings and I am not convinced that this ending is so hopeful. The
consequences of accepting a child conceived by rape are grave. The
child will have, in a way, a completely false identity and the mother
will be responsible for it."[7] That overwhelming responsibility receives a
full-blown exploration in *Grbavica*. Even though (according to Lacan)
denying the existence of the father challenges the symbolic coherence
of mother and child, after making a decision to keep the baby and deny
him paternity, S. "is for the first time overwhelmed by a feeling of utter
tranquility" (199).

In a sense, *Grbavica* takes up where Drakulić's novel leaves off,
for Žbanić's film makes clear just how difficult (or impossible) it is to
sustain this tranquility.[8] Interestingly, it explores the same theme—
impossible motherhood—but fourteen years later and back in Sarajevo.
Whereas *S. A Novel about the Balkans* imagines a future for S. only
abroad and does not elaborate on the consequences of her trauma,
Grbavica chooses to probe precisely the cost of the tragedy and, moreover, in the environment of the woman's home country. The pan of
the opening scene, slowly and attentively depicting local carpet motifs
and women's hands and faces, paired with the mournful vocals of a
traditional Islamic song, *ilahija*, effectively sets the tone of melancholy and hardship for the rest of the film. An abrupt cut shifts the
viewer to a Sarajevo nightclub, where the aggressive turbo-folk music
is deafening. The stark contrast of the two scenes suggests not only the
clash of tradition and modernity, but also the disharmony of private
sorrow and public enjoyment. The viewer learns that Esma, a middle-
aged Bosnian woman, on whose face the camera dwells in the opening
scene, lives with her teenage daughter, Sara, in Grbavica, a Sarajevo

---

[7] "A Conversation with Slavenka Drakulić," published as a Guide at the end
of the Penguin edition.
[8] For a more detailed review of *Grbavica*, see Brooke (2007).

suburb and a site of Serbian rape camps during the war. After several
signs of Esma's awkwardness around men, the viewer realizes the
secret behind Sara's parentage, and the climactic scene, when the truth
comes out, is a revelation only for Sara.

Esma's life could hardly be further from the tranquility that over-
whelms S. after her decision to keep her baby and to deny him a father.
As Drakulić points out, the ending of her novel suggests that S.'s experience of motherhood will be burdened with hardship and impossible
responsibility—precisely Esma's situation. As a single mother, Esma
maintains two jobs to make the most basic ends meet, but when Sara
tells her that a school trip will cost two hundred euros, desperation
overcomes her. Esma's permanent exhaustion and her anxiety are powerfully projected by the excellent performance of Mirjana Karanović;
her body language and sorrowful facial expressions are more eloquent
than the sparse dialogue. Material privation is only one of Esma's difficulties, as she is under daily pressure from her daughter to prove that
Sara's father was *shaheed*, a hero who died defending Bosnia. Žbanić
replaces S.'s denial of the father with a myth of the father-hero, which
likewise denies the real father. More importantly, Sara herself is bullied
by her classmates and coerced by society at large to maintain the myth.
Children of *shaheeds* have a discount on the school trip, and inclusion in the list of such children provides not only financial assistance,
but also socially and culturally elevates their status. When her mother
fails to produce a certificate of her father's heroic past, Sara physically
fights with her classmates in order to maintain the story of her *shaheed*-
father. That fight represents her struggle to be included in a society
where alliance with *shaheeds* determines identity.

Only one sequence modifies this presentation of Sara's complete
submission to the mythic construction of her identity, closely tied to
the heroic national identity of resistance against the Serbian aggressor.
At home, she rehearses the lyrics of a song about Bosnia's might and
beauty—a song that she ought to know by heart as part of her school
assignments. The camera shows Sara lying on the sofa, her head hanging
upside down over the edge of the sofa [Plate 9.1]. The reversed shot
of her face, coupled with the difficulty she has remembering the lyrics,
hints at Sara's unconscious doubts about her identity as well as the
official construction of Bosnia's national ideology. Frustrated by her
inability to memorize the lyrics, Sara calls the poem "stupid." A single

scene does not overturn the overall impression of Sara as someone struggling to insert herself in the "accepted" ideology, but it does sound a dissonant note—however faint—in the homogeneous ideological discourse.

Whereas S. rejects the existence of the father, in *Grbavica* society invents a father: the father-hero who died for Bosnia's independence— a different reaction to children of rape but also a similarly manic defense aids this community in its (re)construction of past and present. The image of the male teacher, who functions as the students' surrogate father and acts as their protector, serves to reaffirm the impression of an orphaned country. Fatherhood colludes with nationhood, exposing the anxieties and challenges of an elaborated monolithic national identity. The fact that both mother and daughter befriend men who have lost their fathers reinforces the sense of an orphaned country that seeks to resurrect a heroic past through fathers-warriors.

Ostensibly casual asides reveal much about the country's post-war devastation—material and moral—and its attempts to rebuild people's relationships and recover their humanity. For instance, the nightclub is a place for gambling and sexual abuse. A brief scene also reveals how the club's owner can easily lose the loyalty of his henchman, approached for competitive illegal deals by a former war fellow. At the same time, Esma's friend Sabina is a source of constant support and solace: when Esma is on the verge of a breakdown, distraught at her inability to pay for her daughter's trip, Sabina comes to the rescue by collecting the money from her co-workers at the factory. The bond of female friendship, in other words, responds to lived experience, in contrast to the masculine ethos of military glory, which operates in the realm of coercive myth.

Although it offers no revelation, the film's climactic scene nonetheless is striking in its intensity. A rebellious teenager and tomboy, the daughter brutally offends her mother, questioning her morality and integrity as at gunpoint she demands to know the truth about her father [Plate 9.2]. And the mother's powerful, emotional response addresses not just Sara, but the society that substitutes macho myths for reality: "You want to know the truth? Here's the truth! I was raped in the war camps and you're the bastard of a Chetnik!" Esma's outburst challenges the public construction of national identity, for personal trauma and dilemmas of identity cannot be separated from the society's anxieties about national identity.

Though painful, the truth about Sara's parenthood, once articulated, is also liberating. By admitting and accepting the horrific reality,
Esma (and, potentially, the community) acknowledges the past, with
all its harrowing consequences. The moment marks a dramatic moral
and psychological turn as Esma renounces the lies of her culture's
dominant myth and abandons her manic defenses. The cathartic and,
at the same time, burdening moment allows the Real to enter the two
females' lives. The scene ends as Esma, leaving Sara crying on the sofa,
sits on a chair with her back to the camera, as if ignoring the specta-
tor's inquisitive gaze. Sara's diegetic sob is gradually transformed into
the intra-diegetic female vocals of an *ilahija*. After this sound transition, the camera cuts to a close-up of the woman singing the song
before shifting to an all-female group therapy meeting. Panning slowly
across the faces of the women—all of them engulfed in their own pain
and sorrow—the camera finally settles on Esma's face as she softly
sobs. In a following cross-cut the viewer observes Sara shaving her
head; Esma's voice, saying how she originally had wanted to kill her,
effects a transition back to the group therapy. This montage, relying
on both vocal and visual transitions, powerfully connects mother and
daughter at the most critical and conflictive moment of their lives.
Again, image and sound reinforce the bond between mother and
daughter.

Enduring the catharsis of voicing the truth, Esma for the first time
is able to narrate her devastating experience, to recuperate her memories, to give expression to the trauma. According to Judith Herman,
clinical professor of psychiatry, the second stage for a victim of trauma
who has established safety is telling the story of the trauma. In the
process, Herman points out, "She tells it completely, in depth and in
detail. This work of reconstruction actually transforms the traumatic
memory, so that it can be integrated into the survivor's life story"
(Herman 1997, 175). Esma not only admits the truth to her daughter,
but also shares the memory of her violation with other women in the
social therapy group [Plate 9.3]. This liberating, though long-delayed
and excruciating, "opening-up" is symbolically significant for Esma's
life. It is the first step toward her psychological recovery and healthy,
albeit difficult, future.

"I pounded my belly with my fists to make her fall out of me. It
was no use. My belly grew with her inside. Even then they came. In

twos, threes, every day. In the hospital when I gave birth to her, I said: 'I don't want her. Take her away.'" When she hears the baby crying behind the wall, however, her milk gushes from her breast and she decides to feed the infant, just once. If up to that point it is the biological-maternal instinct that prompts Esma to have contact with her newborn, the decisive moment comes when Esma sees her, so small and beautiful, and decides to keep her daughter. As in the episode of S. looking at the baby and recognizing her sister, so in the film Esma's response to the sight of her infant entails a long-forgotten aesthetic recognition: "I had already forgotten that there was anything beautiful in this world." The scene implies that not only maternal instincts but also a symbolic mediation, expressed through her aesthetic choice, determines her decision.

I argue that both Drakulić and Žbanić show the raped women's conscious resolve to become mothers despite the violation that led to their babies' conception and the dramatic consequences for them and their offspring. Their choices are not reduced to their maternal instincts, for agency plays a key role in their decisions. In other words, Kristeva's insistence on woman's closeness to her instinctual memory (that is, identification with the mother) is negotiated through woman's active subjectivity. Although instinctual memory à la Kristeva is directly revealed only in the case of S., both Drakulić's heroine and Esma surpass biological instincts and make conscious decisions for the future of their children.

Various aspects of S.'s and Esma's behavior construct them as independent and active women. S. is a teacher when the war breaks, and Esma studies medicine. Under the extreme conditions of the war camp, S. finds subversive ways to feel liberated: "When she realised that the make-up enabled her to don a mask, she discovered that it was a way to gain power. Yes, she would look pretty for the boys, play with them and thus perhaps deprive them of the chance to humiliate her" (86). S. attempts to turn her own self-objectification in her favor. Later on, she employs the same tactics to seduce and manipulate the camp's captain, who, in fact, does release her.

Esma, too, is portrayed as a woman of will and determination. A scene in which she unexpectedly encounters her aunt, Safija, in a mall illustrates Esma's marginalization by the family. With insincere pity that fails to disguise nastiness, the aunt recalls how Esma's mother hoped that her daughter would become a doctor, and concludes that it is better that she never lived to witness what happened. A hypocritical elderly woman who wears a fur coat but complains that her pension is too small for her to lend Esma money for Sara's school trip, the aunt, especially in her remark about the shame Esma brought on the family, reflects society's discrimination against raped women. The highly unpleasant encounter with a family member, from whom one might expect understanding and support, however, leaves Esma unshaken, and she proceeds to seek and secure the funds elsewhere. An episode similarly evidencing Esma's will power involves her nightclub-owning boss, who physically attacks her and his bouncer, Pelda (who has developed a romantic relationship with Esma), knocks the man down, and drags Esma out of the nightclub. When he insists that Esma join him in the car, she resolutely refuses and walks away, disgusted by the violent scene. Despite the abuse and subjugation that she has experienced, Esma has taken control of her life. These examples from the two works testify to both heroines' strong sense of self and exercise of agency—which account for their conscious, albeit complex and controversial, choice to give birth to and raise their children.

Whereas hatred for the enemy wins out with other raped women and they murder the babies conceived in the violence of war, love for a part of one's self and one's female family members leads Esma and S. to a difficult but empowering alternative. Sparked by love, their desire to keep their offspring surpasses the common hatred of war that contaminates other women. In words that recall Drakulić's remark about her novel's ending, Žbanić notes:

> *Grbavica* is first of all a story about LOVE. About love that is not pure, because it has been mixed with hate, disgust, trauma, despair. It's also about VICTIMS who, though they did not commit any crime, they are still not entirely innocent in relation to future generations. GRBAVICA is also about TRUTH, a cosmic power necessary to progress, and very much needed by society in Bosnia and Herzegovina, which must strive to reach maturity. (no date)

Clear-sighted about the responsibilities of mothers like Esma to the next generation, Žbanić nonetheless suggests that their controversial decisions and their acceptance represent a step toward their society's maturity. Given the appalling circumstances in which such choices are made, Esma's may be the best possible decision, however loaded with repercussions.

Esma's honesty, however, does not help Sara, who wishes to belong in a society that reveres only children of *shaheeds*. In a symbolic response to the trauma of learning about her origins, Sara shaves her head—an act that suggests multiple psychological motivations: since earlier in the film Esma tells her that she has her father's hair, the act symbolizes dissociation from any resemblance to her real father. At the same time, in ridding herself of what traditionally is seen as "a woman's glory," Sara disavows her femininity. Furthermore, a shaven head evokes camp prisoners. Finally, on a more general level, the dramatic gesture may be interpreted as Sara's protest against social codes and expectations.

The film's concluding sequence, of the students' departure for the trip, testifies to the difficulties that mother and daughter need to overcome in order to re-establish their bond. Distressed and distant from each other, they walk quietly side by side to the bus, beside which Esma embraces her daughter, who remains cold and remote. Once inside the bus, Sara appears at the rear window, gazes impassively her mother, then after a few moments hesitantly extends her hand, placing it palm-up against the window in a traditional gesture of peace and as if to wave to her mother. The camera cuts to a close-up of Esma's face, which lights up, and she begins to wave energetically to her daughter as the bus moves off.

In a review of the film, Meta Mazaj observed, "As the school bus pulls away, we see an affectionate moment between mother and daughter, a gesture certainly hopeful and forward looking, yet where this gesture might lead is unclear" (2007, 61). Though the gesture certainly cannot and should not be read as a clear sign of Esma and Sara's future harmony and closeness, the song "Sarajevo, lubavi moe" ["Sarajevo, my love"], which the students sing and which prompts Sara to join in with a smile, encourages a cautiously optimistic interpretation of the ending [Plate 9.4]. Popular from the Yugoslav period, the song is not about Bosnia but about Sarajevo. It would be misguided, I believe, to read this ending as a nostalgic reference to Yugoslavia. Rather, it is a reminder of the spirit of Sarajevo as a multi-ethnic, multi-religious, and multi-cultural city, as a locus of the "cosmic power necessary to progress" so essential to Bosnia and Herzegovina's maturity.

The scene of the mother and daughter's hesitant, ambivalent reunion through the final reciprocal gaze in Žbanić's film (not unlike S.'s gaze at her baby) unveils a space of recovery and of possibility for a future; or, in Lacanian terms, a space of identification temporarily removed but not utterly disconnected from the paternal function, which secures symbolic coherence and escapes psychosis. Herman contends that after the survivor comes to terms with her traumatic past, she "faces the task of creating a future" (1997, 196). Having acknowledged the painful truth of the rapist father, a truth that has settled between mother and daughter, *Grbavica*'s final scene evokes neither manic defenses nor maternal psychosis. Instead, it invites imagining a female locus where (to return to Kristeva) "alterity becomes nuance, contradiction becomes a variant, tension becomes passage, and discharge becomes peace" (Kristeva 1980, 240).[9] This imaginative space (which uncannily parallels the city of Sarajevo) promises life to raped women, life that is burden rather than privilege, for it entails a motherhood that needs reconciliation with the past to empower the future. The film's title, "grbavica," is the name of a Sarajevo neighborhood, but it also means a hunchback. Motherhood has marked Esma as if with a hump, and her ability, as well as Sara's, to cope with that "deformation" will determine the nature of their shared and individual future life. S.'s and Esma's conscious choice affirms their subjectivity, although their past experience is full of hardship and fraught with contradictions, and the nature of their future with their offspring remains a question mark.

Drakulić's novel and Žbanić's film focus on the challenge and potential of maternity under the grimmest of circumstances, presenting it as possibly the sole empowering practice of oppressed and violated women. I contend that these two women-"authored" gynocentric texts urge us to look beyond the usual discussion of war rape victims as crea-

---

[9] Kristeva further complicates her argument by insisting that motherhood is a special nature/culture threshold, which is representable only in art, as long as there is language-symbolism-paternity. Even this extended proposition allows for a similar interpretation of the two fictional works discussed here.

tures devoid of will and power. Although this debate was helpful for the time, when the war rapes were internationally recognized as genocide, it further victimizes raped women by denying them the possibility of agency in their own lives. Forcefully impregnated, S. and Esma do not give birth to Chetniks, but to babies whom they raise as their loved children. The greatest danger to the children is that a militarized society could turn them into fighters against their Serbian fathers. As Lacan points out, the "sender [always] receives his own message back from the receiver in an inverted form" (1977, 85).[10] Both Drakulić and Žbanić propose, however, that maternal love has the potential to thwart the anticipated outcome of military violence and hatred.

My essay opened with Western feminist scholarship on war rape victims, scholarship that actively contributed to the decision of The Hague International War Crimes Tribunal to decree war rapes a crime against humanity. The importance of this scholarship notwithstanding, I argue that it is time to move beyond the much-discussed victimization of raped women so as to take into account their subjectivity and future (or presence today). To illustrate what such a perspective entails, I have analyzed two fictional works by Balkan women whose views, regardless of their different backgrounds, converge and expand (or challenge) Western feminist approaches. Such a methodology begs the question of authenticity of experience and representation, since both Drakulić and Žbanić witnessed the war atrocities and their consequences, but never experienced them directly.[11]

The issue of authenticity, however, is equally, if not more, pertinent as regards Western scholars who engage problems of Balkan women raped during the wars; they are even further removed from the traumatic experience. If we are to learn in less mediated form about the atrocities, we need to hear raped women tell their stories. Yet many of them remain silent, and those who decide to speak do so with hesitation or resistance, not only because of fear, but also because they have no strength to relive their trauma and subsequent social ostra-

---

[10] See also Žižek, who offers a similar argument about post-communist relations between the West and the former socialist countries (Žižek 1993, 208).

[11] For calling attention to this aspect of the argument, I am grateful to my colleague Dorothy Noyes and her response as a discussant to papers at the Women in War conference in Columbus, Ohio.

cism. A third option for scholars and artists committed to socio-political engagement is to acknowledge raped women's agency and power in works that do not downplay the violated women's brutalization. To the objection that a creative work constitutes a representation that inadequately substitutes for real agency and, in fact, may explore the trauma of rape merely to reproduce the spectacle of trauma and thus erase the materiality of the suffering, one can respond in several ways. Depending on their aesthetic and psychological power and integrity, at one extreme, such works can collude in the construction of readers/ spectators as voyeurs who enjoy a secret pleasure in exploiting the victims; or, at the other end of the spectrum, they can enable readers/ spectators to attain "the position of being a witness"—an effect that can open a space for "transformation of the viewer through empathic identification." The latter, obviously, is not only the humane, but also the most politically useful position (Kaplan and Wang 2004, 9–10).

Ultimately, any representation and study of trauma is an inherently political act because it calls attention to human suffering. Remembrance and mourning are essential for communities recovering from war and violence, which is why a public forum or a symbolic space for discussion and debate of the traumatic past is paramount for restoring a sense of social community. Otherwise, all social relationships remain tainted by the corrupt practice of denial. Drakulić's novel and Žbanić's film not only grant agency to raped women and challenge homogeneous national ideology, but also, and more importantly, afford precisely such a space for the reflection, recollection, and mourning that drive the cosmic power of progress.

<h1 style="text-align:center">REFERENCES</h1>

Allen, Beverly. 1996. *Rape Warfare: The Hidden Genocide in Bosnia-Herzegovina and Croatia.* Minneapolis: University of Minnesota Press.
Banac, Ivo. 1993/4. "Review." *Foreign Policy* 93 (Winter): 176–7.
Boose, Lynda. 2002. "Crossing the River Drina: Bosnian Rape Camps, Turkish Impalement, and Serbian Cultural Memory." *Signs* 28 (Autumn): 71–96.
Bratt, Benjamin. 2001. "Benjamin Bratt Searches for Mother of His Children." http://www.imdb.com/news/wenn/2001-10-30#celeb2 (last accessed 13 February 2012).

Brooke, Michael. 2007. "Esma's Secret." *Sight & Sound* (February): 53.

Eagle, Karen. 2005. "Feminism and Its (Dis)Contents: Criminalizing Wartime Rape in Bosnia and Herzegovina." *The American Journal of International Law* 99, no. 4 (October): 778–816.

Fischer, Siobhan. 1996. "The Occupation of the Womb: Forced Impregnation as Genocide." *Duke Law Journal* 46, no. 1 (October): 91–133.

Folnegovic-Smalc, Vera. 1994. "Psychiatric Aspects of the Rapes in the War against the Republics of Croatia and Bosnia-Herzegovina." In *Mass Rape*, edited by Alexandra Stiglmayer, 174–80. Lincoln: University of Nebraska Press.

Herman, Judith. 1997. *Trauma and Recovery: The Aftermath of Violence: From Domestic Abuse to Political Terror.* New York: Basic Books.

Jablow, Valerie. 2000. "No Place like Home." *The Women's Review of Books* 17, no 6 (March): 1–4.

Kaplan, E. Ann, and Ban Wang, eds. 2004. *Trauma and Cinema: Cross-Cultural Explorations.* Aberdeen: Hong Kong University Press.

Kristeva, Julia. 1993a. "Revolution in Poetic Language." In *The Kristeva Reader*, edited by Toril Moi, 89–136. Oxford: Blackwell Publishers.

———. 1993b. "Motherhood according to Giovanni Bellini." In *Desire in Language*, edited by Leon Roudiez, translated by Thomas Gora, Alice Jardine, and Leon Roudiez, 237–71. New York: Columbia University Press.

———. 1980. *Desire in Language: A Semiotic Approach to Literature and Art.* Translated by T. Gora, A. Jardine, and L.S. Roudiez. New York: Columbia University Press.

Lacan, Jacques. 1997. *Ecrits. A Selection.* New York: W. W. Norton & Co.

Lumsden, Malvern. 1997. "Breaking the Cycle of Violence." *Journal of Peace Research* 34, no. 4: 377–83.

Mazaj, Meta. 2007. "Review: *Grbavica*." *Cineaste* 32, no. 3 (Summer): 60–1.

Stiglmayer, Alexandra, ed. 1994. *Mass Rape.* Lincoln: University of Nebraska Press.

Van Boeschoten, Riki. 2003. "The Trauma of War Rapes: A Comparative View on the Bosnian War Conflict and the Greek Civil War." *History and Anthropology* 14, no. 1: 41–54.

Wachtel, Andrew. 1998. *Making a Nation, Breaking a Nation: Literature and Cultural Politics of Yugoslavia.* Palo Alto: Stanford University Press.

Žbanić, Jasmila. No date. "Interview with Jasmila Žbanić." http://www.coop99.at/grbavica_website/regie_bio_en.htm (last accessed 13 February 2012).

Žižek, Slavoj. 1993. *Tarrying With the Negative.* Durham: Duke University Press.

CHAPTER 10

Dubravka Ugrešić's War Museum: Approaching the "Point of Pain"

Jessica Wienhold-Brokish

The war in Yugoslavia during the 1990s, which resulted in the deaths of hundreds of thousands of people and an estimated two million displaced persons, prompted considerable commentary on the traumatic loss of life in the bloody conflict. In a related vein, Croatian author Dubravka Ugrešić in her text *The Museum of Unconditional Surrender* [*Musej bezuvjetne predaje* 1994] explores the symbolic loss of life experienced by her and other people displaced by the conflict. Her fragmented narrative collates the memories of country, identity, friends, and family torn apart by war. The resulting collection of narratives (observations, short vignettes, and references to other writers) creates a war museum that through a disjointed and borrowed framework commemorates and recalls the displaced people, identities, and objects of the war, focusing primarily on women.

After the dissolution of Yugoslavia in 1991, many historians and scholars viewed the country as an "artificial creature" (Lampe 1996, 4). However, Ugrešić and others of like mind challenged such a dismissal of the country as hollow and insincere, noting the genuine suffering of individuals at the loss and destruction of their country, their identities, and their friendships. Ugrešić's text builds a war museum that pays attention to the "point of pain" generated by the loss of physical and personal life due to the war in Yugoslavia.

Ugrešić wrote *The Museum of Unconditional Surrender* while in self-imposed exile in Berlin during the war.[1] The text that resulted from

---

[1] *The Museum of Unconditional Surrender* was first published in Dutch in 1997 and in English the following year. Although written in Croatian, the book was not published in the original until 2002 owing to the author's strained

her loss of home, family, and friends defies both plot and genre. The disjointed narrative mirrors the fragmented wartime experiences of a displaced person attempting to memorialize that, which has been lost. The work's narrator is in exile in Berlin compiling a collection of short vignettes, quotations, diary entries, short stories, essays, and observations on myriad topics ranging from Berlin to art installations that she frequents while in the city of her Yugoslav childhood.

The fragmented pastiche that fashions the text consists of seven sections. Four of them recount the narrator's present impressions in Germany and have German titles: "Ich bin müde" (I'm tired), "Guten Tag" (Good day), "Was ist Kunst" (What is art), and "Wo bin ich?" (Where am I?). These "German" sections are numbered segments that introduce direct quotations from various exiled writers, haphazard remarks from people in Berlin (ranging from her neighbors to the mailman), and the narrator's own sparse observations. The impressions of the narrator's life in Germany follow no narrative organization. The remaining three parts of the text, inserted between the narratives by Germans and in contrast to them, focus on the past, have Croatian titles, and contain longer vignettes. Bits of stories, diary entries, and soup recipes comprise the vignette "Family Museum," while "Archive: Six stories with the discreet motif of a departing angel" tells about friends and acquaintances, and "Group Photograph" relies on tarot card readings to reveal the characteristics of the narrator's Croatian girlfriends. As reviewer Jasmina Lukić notes, *The Museum of Unconditional Surrender* is nothing short of "a series of discontinuities" (2000, 391). The narrator's montage mirrors her exilic position by creating a disorganized series of sketches and observations tenuously held together by leitmotifs, recurrent images, and interlocking cross references.

Ugrešić's juxtaposition creates a textual war museum where the lost homeland and new "home" mirror the fragmented experiences of war. The title of the text refers to a war museum in Berlin commemorating the 1945 German capitulation ending World War II. The museum had been maintained by the Soviet Union in East Berlin, but now, following the elimination of the wall, it commemorates a Germany

---

relationship with the Croatian government. In this article I cite from the original Croatian, *Musej bezuvjetne predaje* (2002).

that no longer exists. Like the Berlin museum now visited only by refugees and émigrés, Ugrešić's war museum is a personal tribute and memorial. The war has isolated the narrator from her country, her family, and her friends, and the text emulates this inaccessibility through fragmentation and borrowing. She is unable to create a sustained narrative and at times even adopts the memories and literature of others to access the point of pain, the loss of her former way of life.

Ugrešić's text resists a unified reading precisely because her project purposely avoids identification with a traditional narrative or genre, above all the familiar structures of autobiography and war testimony. The reader is told that the fragments and pieces in the text should be considered an "arheolosk[a] iskopin[a]" [archeological excavation],[2] with the chance objects that have been uncovered and displayed forming a connection based upon their proximity to one another. As the title of the book suggests, the text is a negotiation of two competing, paradoxical actions. On the one hand, the narrator undertakes a project of collecting and exhibiting her life's experiences, prompted by a desire to extract a narrative outlining both the life of the narrator and her former country. In its collection of fragments, the imaginary museum strives to give order to uncertainty. On the other hand, the narrator's parallel project is that of unconditional surrender. Instead of creating a museum exhibit that provides a sustained narrative around the objects in the collection, the project of surrender purposely avoids maintaining one.

Simply by glancing at the title readers confront the competing, paradoxical claims of the text, which mix agency (order and collection) with submission and surrender. The narrator's contradictory agenda produces an unlikely text that resists both assertions of ideological truth and narrative closure. In the context of the war in Yugoslavia and the newly found nationalisms in the areas of the former federation, the

---

[2] Unless noted otherwise, I use Celia Hawkesworth's translation of the Croatian text, *The Museum of Unconditional Surrender* (London: Phoenix House, 1999). In the passage cited here, however, "archeological excavation" seems to me a more accurate translation than the English edition's "archeological exhibit" (1), since it suggests a recuperation of something, rather than a display.

narrator resists simplified or official narratives that explain the war, create it as a spectacle, or take a particular political stance.

The war rhetoric and the extreme nationalism in Croatia at the height of the war were nothing short of habitual, automated propaganda, all-encompassing and thoroughly gendered. Discounted as a "witch" and driven into self-imposed exile, Ugrešić herself was a victim of the war discourse.[3] At the time, scholar Djurdja Knezevic stated, "Women are not considered as 'only women' but as the personification of and symbol for the nation. When this is the case, women are not human beings and individuals. Male discourse denotes women as a group imbued with (imagined) characteristics similar to those of the nation" (1997, 65).[4] In this constrictive, dangerous environment, there is little room for voices challenging the readymade rhetoric of war. The female narrator seeks a method of writing that neither replicates nor feeds into the official national narrative. Thus she unsettles her text in an attempt to create and inhabit an aesthetic space that not only resists official narratives and war rhetoric, but also enables her to address the traumatic loss of her homeland. Ugrešić creates that space by giving a dream logic to her text.

The narrator illuminates her approach when she associates the fragmented structure of the text with that of the structure of dreams:

[A]n exile feels that the state of exile has the structure of a dream. All at once, as in a dream, faces appear that he had forgotten, or perhaps had never met, places that he is undoubtedly seeing for the first time, but he feels that he knows them from

---

[3] On 11 December 1992, an anonymous article titled "Witches from Rio, Croatia's Feminists Rape Croatia," published in the Croatian nationalist newspaper *Globus*, accused Ugrešić and four other women of being unpatriotic in their anti-war attitude by focusing generally on the sufferings of women in war, instead of specifically on the sufferings of Croatian and Muslim women at the hands of Serbian men. Ugrešić was called a "witch" and driven into self-imposed exile. She left her position in Comparative Literature, specializing in Russian literature, at the University of Zagreb. For further scholarship on the "witches" of Croatia, see Kesić (1997, 2000).

[4] To explore the topic of post-communist national rhetoric and gender in greater detail, see Scott, Kaplan, and Keates (1997); Corrin (1999); and Renne (1997).

somewhere. The dream is a magnetic field that attracts images from the past, present, and future. [...] [T]he exile begins to decipher signs, crosses and knots, and all at once it seems as though he were beginning to read in it all a secret harmony. (12, 246; translation adjusted)[5]

By connecting dream and exile, the passage positions the narrator and the reader in a space of uncertainty, where everyday life must be interpreted and translated, just as in the dream world. The underlying structure of dream, thus also of Ugrešić's text, lacks a master narrative to support its inner logic. What holds the dream together is a personal universe with a secret unity. Therefore, interpretation plays a prominent role in translating the dreamlike textual fragments (such as leitmotifs, repeated images, and cross references) into a unified text that submits to a neat hermeneutical reading. The reader attempts to translate the dreamlike structure, yet always falls short because of the endless references and possibilities. However, since the recurring motifs and images are strewn throughout the text, the reader feels compelled to interpret them—a task encouraged by the narrator, who advises the reader to "tr[y] to establish semantic coordinates" (1) [pokuša[ti] uspostaviti neke značenjske koordinate (11)]. "Try" is the key word here, as the incoherent form of the text hinders any exhaustive effort to interpret the narrator's dream world.

Slavoj Žižek at the beginning of his book *Tarrying With the Negative* discusses a similar displacement when he describes the political changes in Eastern Europe. During the overthrow of the Romanian government, the Communist symbol was cut out of the national flag, leaving a hole.[6] According to Žižek, the appearance of the hole made visible the hole in the official narrative. The dreamlike position of the

---

[5] "Egxilantu se čini da stanje egzila ima strukturu sna. Najednom se, kao u snu, pojavljuju neka lica koja je bio zaboravio, koja možda nikada nije sreo, neki prostori koje pouzdano prvi put vidi, ali mu se čini da ih odnekud zna. San je magnetsko polje koje privlači slike iz prošlosti, sadašnjosti i budućnosti. [...] [E]gzilant počinje odgonetati smušene znakove, križiće i čvoriće i najednom mu se čini da u svemu čita tajni sklad" (24, 299–300).

[6] Similar symbolic act took place during the 1956 Hungarian Revolution: the Communist emblem was cut out of the Hungarian flag by revolutionaries.

exile in Ugrešić's text makes visible that same hole. Unlike the new national narratives and war rhetoric that desperately strove to fill the post-communist vacuum, Ugrešić's text not only distances itself from such narratives, but also eludes completion. Although part of her museum endeavor longs for a strong, unifying narrative to organize and construct her newly found post-communist position, Ugrešić also realizes the danger of a museum project that would erase or rewrite her memories of Yugoslavia with such a newly created post-communist "story." On the one hand, she refuses to join in the excision of communist memory promoted by the new Croatian state. On the other, she resists the simplified, official narratives of wartime Croatia. She chooses to keep the hole in her flag, neither allowing complete access to her feelings of loss nor reconstructing them. The issue is not an inability to access traumatic memory, but an attempt to preserve by surrendering and vice versa.

Ugrešić describes the war in Yugoslavia—the hole in her flag—as a point of pain ["točka boli"]. The war in Croatia is the epicenter out of which all the leitmotifs, recurrent images, and cross references are temporarily pulled together. A character in the text claims, "I always write my poems about something else, so as not to write about the first thing" (175) [Ja pišem svoje pjesme uvijek o nečem drugom de ne bih morala o onom prvom (218)], and the narrator surmises, "It seems that we can only easily express pain, and curses, in a language that is not our own (35) [Čini se da bol, kao i psovku, s lakoćom možemo izreći samo na jeziku koji nije naš (50)]. In one of the text's brief stories, the narrator recounts trying to comfort a schoolmate at the university who attempted to commit suicide after her affair with a married man ended. The woman was able to speak about the affair only in English. The narrator notes, "She told her pain in a foreign language and at the same time preserved it by not destroying its nucleus" (35) [Ona ispričala bol na stranom jeziku [...] i istodobno bol sačuvala ne uništivši njezinu jezgru (50)]. In other words, like the narrator of Ugrešić's text, the young woman surrenders her story, yet preserves its "nucleus."

That recollection functions as a key to Ugrešić's dominant device in the work, though whereas the woman speaks on the point of pain in another language, Ugrešić via her narrator substitutes other topics and other people's stories for her own point of pain. Thus *The Museum of Unconditional Surrender* sidesteps the point of pain, the loss of country, and the war through surrogacy. Unable to explain the position of exile and the pain at the core of the text without erasing it or creating another master narrative, Ugrešić solves the dilemma with a replacement—by writing about something and someone else. Her weaving of voices and literary adaptations simultaneously negotiates between the contrary modes of preservation and surrender, absence and presence, enabling her to address the war indirectly.

The invitation to interpret the text as a dream and to protect the traumatic point of loss calls for a Freudian reading. Freud argues that in dreams displacement is one of the ways to express what has been repressed. For Ugrešić's narrator, this means that her emotions about the war are transferred elsewhere. Though Ugrešić's war museum, ironically, avoids most references to war, the fragments of the text all point back to it. Freud notes, "What was the essence of the dream-thoughts finds only passing and indistinct representation in the dream" (1989, 25). This strategy, whereby war gains only "indistinct representation," can be viewed as a means to commemorate what the Croatian post-communist war narrative overshadows. In this case, Ugrešić uses dream displacement as a literary technique. The method is not a sign of repression, but a strategy of resistance and agency. Ugrešić refuses to allow her narrative to be subsumed by official narratives.

Through this literary dream displacement, Ugrešić's narrative intimates a technique that the exiled Russian theorist Viktor Shklovsky calls *ostranenie* (defamiliarization).[7] Developing his theory of defamiliarization after World War I, Shklovsky posited the concept as a literary tactic that would disrupt perception, which war had automated. According to Shklovsky, "Automatization eats away at things, at clothes, at furniture, at our wives, and at our fear of war" (1990, 5). Shklovsky credits defamiliarization with the capacity to deter war by

---

[7] According to Shklovsky, the purpose of art is to "return sensation to our limbs" (1990, 6). Shklovsky advised that in a world where the everyday had become habitual, literature should make strange the world that we inhabit and generate new methods of perception. Shklovsky advocates the use of complex literary techniques, such as impeded form, baring the device, contrasts in tone, an estranged narrator, chronological displacement, and digressions, to make perception of the habitual difficult.

forcing one to see "things out of their usual context" (1990, 9). It is no wonder, then, that during the war in Yugoslavia Ugrešić directly references Shklovsky through quotations from his books and through her use of defamiliarization via displacement and substitution. Through her narrative strategy, Ugrešić forces the reader to actively create the text's connections in the process of reading. Any semblance of a traditional war narrative or genre is disrupted, for everything is out of context and nothing can be read "automatically."

The citations within the text function as dream displacement, whereby the narrator "speaks" through the words of others. Either directly or indirectly the narrator references the following: Walter Benjamin's notions of angels, snow, and archeology; Milan Kundera's angels, ice, and oblivion; Christa Wolf's Christa T.; the Berlin of Miroslav Krežla, Shklovsky, and Vladimir Nabokov; Marguerite Duras' semi-autobiographical fiction; Irena Vrkljan's numbered vignettes; Daniil Kharms' absurdism; Nikolai Gogol's humor; and Isaak Babel's gestures toward magic realism. All of these writers at some point in their careers experienced difficulties with their respective state governments and many of these contentious relationships ended in exile for the writer. Ugrešić uses the words and figures from their works as a museum project that points back to her own wartime experience of attempting to write under perilous political conditions. The category of writers with whom Ugrešić feels camaraderie occupies the same in-between position that she does as a displaced writer creating a space to write when her connection to home has been lost.

These direct and indirect references create a literary home for Ugrešić while allowing her to tell her story of loss without destroying its epicenter. She keeps the memory of her loss fresh by refusing to discuss it outright and at the same time reveals her disaccord with the Croatian government and its attempts to rewrite or erase the past. In this way, she aesthetically resists the official narratives of the new Croatian state and keeps alive the pain and loss that these narratives attempt to ignore or efface.

In this fragmented compilation of others' voices and stories, an inner logic emerges in the narrator's relationship to the fragments and in the reader's active construction of meaning among the fragments. The numerous quotations from other writers and stories about other people are haunting reminders of the silence at the heart of the narrative, as well as of the desire to find a way to voice that silence in a caustic environment that has prescribed the position of women and Croats. What appears to be an absence of personal narrative and voice in the proliferation of mimicry and imitation actually facilitates a space for the voice of Ugrešić's narrator.

Imitation and direct reproduction of other writers' works function as a metonymy whereby the connection between Ugrešić's silence about the war and the substituted story or quotation is an association between concepts.[8] Meaning derives from the play between and the interpretation of the two. Whereas in a metaphor two referents are connected by a transfer of similar quality traits, the contiguity of referents is what fashions metonymy. Consequently, Ugrešić does not present herself as a replica of the writers she emulates, but as a unique voice that arises in the interplay between the "point of pain" in the text and the substitute reference.

For instance, the text teems with associations encompassing angels, as in the description of Berlin, with its Victory Column—a monument to wartime victory topped by an angel. Besides the physical landmark, angels appear as textual reproduction, including a quote from Kundera's novel *The Book of Laughter and Forgetting* and a dialogue from Wim Wenders's film *Wings of Desire* (1987*)*—in the original German, *Der Himmel über Berlin* [*The Sky over Berlin*]—where two angels roam the city in an attempt to capture its reality. Furthermore, various characters in the text are described as angel-like or as having wings, an angel materializes in one of the stories, and Benjamin's angel of death and Kundera's angel of oblivion become developed ideas. The impressions of war, forgetting, and memorializing pull all of these associations together, just as the references to Nabokov, Shklovsky, and Krežla evoke exile, Berlin, and war (in the last two cases). Even the city of Berlin, which functions as a main character in the text, displaces the city of Zagreb and calls to mind division, war, and refugees. Ugrešić hints at her literary techniques by providing quotations from

---

[8] See Jacques Lacan's 1957 lecture, "The Agency of the Letter in the Unconscious or Reason since Freud," in which he transforms Freud's concept of "displacement" into "metonymy" (1977, 146–79). Instead of metaphor, where the signified occupies the place of the signifier, metonymy is a perpetual deferral.

writers and then scattering leitmotifs throughout the text that remind readers of their works: Babel's magical realism in "The Sin of Jesus," where a visiting angel appears from heaven (also associated with the angels in *Wings of Desire*); the absurd and comic elements of Kharms and Gogol, evident in the text's black humor; the structure of works by Benjamin and Vrkljan, both in-between writers of exile who used numbered vignettes, and of Kharms, known for his brief snippets, sometimes only a few paragraphs long, in which the realities of deprivation alternate with dreamlike occurrences. Duras' "autobiographical" works, where autobiography and fiction meet and mingle, are layered upon Ugrešić's own literary attempts. Autobiographical issues emerge again as the East German character Christa in Ugrešić's text appears to duplicate Wolf's *Christa T.* The search for a narrator, for a self, pulls these references together. A detached narrator displaces what on first glance may seem an autobiographical text.[9]

The key to Ugrešić's literary metonymy is that it is only as good as her reader's literary knowledge. Because the reader creates it, it emerges anew each time it is read, depending upon the reader's historical, political, and literary knowledge or lack thereof. It is in this interplay between text and reader, dream and interpretation that Ugrešić's agency arises. This technique provides her with an aesthetic space of survival and resistance in an embattled environment where war rhetoric has become totalizing and habitual.[10]

The work of reading Ugrešić thus relies upon a tenacious attention to interpretation and to literary and political history. Ugrešić achieves defamiliarization by never adopting a stable position. Her text avoids the familiar binary of "us" versus "them," the polarization of nationalism and war, in an effort to find an independent, shifting perspective from which to quilt her narratives as it addresses Croatia's gendered

---

[9] Christa Wolf's concept of "subjective authenticity" applies well here as a method of maintaining realism yet including the subjective experience of the author as an important perspective from which to tell the story. Wolf's text *Kindheitsmuster* applies her concept of "subjective authenticity" by detailing an autobiographical journey from a detached third-person perspective. Both Wolf and Ugrešić defer the question of autobiography and truth.

[10] Svetlana Boym also notes that defamiliarization functions as an aesthetic of exile and as a technique of survival and resistance for Shklovsky (1998, 241–63).

wartime discourse. Some critics dismiss the historical and political context of Ugrešić's text. Ellen Handler Spitz, for instance, reads the text as simply a mirror of the human experience of loss (2000, *passim*). She diminishes the nuances and complexity of the text by reducing it to a commonplace experience. Similarly, those critics who deem Ugrešić's work a postmodern play with identity miss the political wartime constraints under which she, as a female writer, functioned. Others, like Renata Jambrešić Kirin, argue that Ugrešić proposes a "mutant identity" that denies the voices of refugees and victims of war and proposes an unsuitable identification (1999, 75).

Similarly, Jambrešić Kirin worries that war narratives by writers like Ugrešić, whose experience of war is mediated, will come to stand as representative of war experience in general, thus effacing the immediate experiences and trauma of others.[11] She also suggests that the hybrid subject-position of Croatian mediated wartime narratives like Ugrešić's—both "insider" and "outsider"—encourages a postmodern identification of "'the mutant' with hybrid cultural identity and of *no fixed* abode" (1999, 81; emphasis in the original). A "mutant" subject-position whose agency is located in its instability may be acceptable for mediated narrators of wartime trauma who choose their situations. Acceptance of such an unstable identification, however, is complicated by unmediated narrators who may not find an unstable, hybrid identity empowering. Jambrešić Kirin fears that the narratives of Ugrešić and other mediated war narrators propose a "homogenous community of immigrants and individuals in Diaspora" that bypasses the experiences of those who do not choose their positions (1999, 82).

In light of this viewpoint, it is germane to note that in discussing the war and the "right" to tell the story, Ugrešić maintains that "[s]ome have found an identity, others have lost one. To speak about identity at a time when many people are losing their lives, the roof over their heads and those closest to them seems inappropriate. Or else the only thing possible; everything began with that question, with that question like an unfortunate noose everything ends" (1998, 45). Although Ugrešić's

---

[11] Jambrešić Kirin asserts that Croatian ethnographers who study personal war narratives "insist on the distance between mediated and immediate lived war experiences (of being expelled, bombarded, tortured or drafted)" (1999, 75).

text definitely addresses the war in Yugoslavia, she is not interested in representing anyone or in writing a war documentary.

As Monica Popescu perceptively argues, "Ugrešić casts her novel into a fragmented form not to celebrate postmodern disenchantment with truth but to counter nationalist reification of memory" (2007, 354). Ugrešić is concerned with formulating a method of writing from within the political context of the early nineties in Croatia. She is interested neither in postmodern identity nor in documenting wartime trauma, but in modes of reclamation. In fact, *The Museum of Unconditional Surrender* is not only about recovering memory, but also about finding a literary form and voice in a highly political, nationalized, and fractured context. The epigraph Ugrešić chose for her volume provides insight into its major concerns: it states that when analyzing the contents of the stomach of a dead walrus in the Berlin Zoo, we should keep in mind that he died in 1961 on the day construction began on the Berlin Wall. Context, in short, is critical, even when the pieces of Ugrešić's text seem disjointed and unassociated with her narrator. It is the date and historical context that endow the contents of the walrus' stomach with "some subtler, secret connections" (1) [sobom uspostavili tananije veze (11)], just as the Yugoslav war orients the segments of Ugrešić's text.

The specific context of hyper-nationalism and war in Croatia is both the basis of the loss at the heart of the text and the difficulty with finding a method of writing in this highly prescribed and guarded arena. To combat this restricted space and speak of her pain, Ugrešić's war museum focuses on her personal experiences and on women. She takes great care to register the past as the narrator experienced it—a past filled with female figures. These female personae appear as radically different from the women in official post-communist narratives. They prevent an erasure of memories of a time when multiethnic peoples lived peacefully side by side. The post-socialist moral majority, especially in Croatia, played a large role in the imagining of a new independent Croatia in relation to gender constructions. Renata Salecl describes the moral majority as a patriarchal construction that imagines the nation in such a way as to subsume gender and religion within nationalism. Thus, objections to social issues such as abortion are not made on religious grounds, but on the claim that it is a threat to the nation. Salecl writes, "Thus emerges the hypothesis that to be a good Slovene or a good Croat means primarily being a good Christian, since the national menace can only be averted by adhering to Christian morals" (1994, 27). Women within this construction feel the brunt of a national imagined community in which religion serves the nation and women are expected to serve both.

Insisting that above all the nation must be protected from the threat of its demise, especially in wartime Croatia, the moral majority blames women, abortion, and pornography for the nation's problems. According to its discourse, "This trinity murders, or rather hinders, the birth of little Croats, that 'sacred thing which God has given society and the homeland'" (quoted in Salecl 1994, 28). The Croatian moral majority regards women who have not given birth to at least four children as "'female exhibitionists,' since they have not fulfilled 'their unique sacred duty'" (Salecl 1994, 28). The shifting notions of nationalism in Croatia that abandoned the individual to national identification emerged in the eighties and nineties, when Yugoslavia dissolved and the new republic was created. In the process, women in Croatia became subject to gender impositions based on a traditional identification of women with marriage and motherhood. Anyone deviating from these goals earned the label of traitor to her nation.

Ugrešić's avoids such sweeping generalizations based on patriarchal customs and writes a text that honors the women of her past. The majority of stories told in the text are about women, who are identified not as intrinsically linked to their national identity, but to shared experiences of life in Yugoslavia or to displacement. The female characters in the short vignettes include the narrator's childhood seamstress, who sews bits and pieces of scraps together to create modern clothes for her customers, much as Ugrešić sews together her text; her mother, who left her war-torn homeland of Bulgaria after World War II and learned to speak a new language and live in a new country; her ever-knitting Bulgarian grandmother, to whom the narrator feels a connection despite having met her only a few times and having no common language to communicate in; her lesbian friend Vida, who after moving to the United States tried to fill her life with memorabilia; the over-emotional Polish-American Lucy, who searches for a way to understand her half-American, half-Polish existence; the aloof Indian student Uma, the narrator's roommate; the East German wanderer Christa, who after leaving East Germany is unable to find a satisfactory "home" and thus keeps roaming across Europe, and so forth. While eschewing self-representation as a spectacle of war that many readers expect from her, the wartime narrator maintains her sense of sadness and of loss for her former country. As a poignantly tangible silence at the heart of the text, the war in Yugoslavia becomes more haunting and unapproachable than any gruesome media clip. The writer's voice emerges only in its superimposition upon the voices of others.

Like intertextuality and citationality, the stories of others in Ugrešić's text function as a metonymy for her own autobiography. As part of her strategy of defamiliarization, she employs, in addition to literary appropriations, women's life-stories and photographs. Quoting and emulating writers is a type of mimetic art, as is the text's incorporation of photography and autobiography. While the latter two are snapshots of an event or someone's life, the quotations are a snapshot of a writer. The standard expectation of a mimetic art is that it shows "the truth," reports "reality." As part of the war museum, these modes of replicating a happening, a person, or a text become memorial acts that preserve something of importance.[12] The narrator writes: "There is something that both genres [photography and autobiography] can count on [...] and that is the blind chance that they will hit upon the point of pain" (28) [Jedino na što oba žanra mogu računati [...] jest slijepa slučajnost da će napipati točku boli (46)]. The superimposition of others' voices and images on Ugrešić's absent voice and image sustains the memorial act that she strives for, while acknowledging the impossibility of capturing the "truth" in its entirety.

---

[12] Current scholarship has put to rest any former belief that any of these genres or strategies of representation could be created without authorial intervention of some kind. Philippe Lejeune notes, "Telling the truth about the self, constituting the self as complete subject—it is a fantasy. In spite of the fact that autobiography is impossible, this in no way prevents it from existing" (1989, 131–2). The desire to achieve the impossible is a potent force. In a similar vein, intertextuality as a meaningful replication has also lost much of its weight as homage to a particular writer and fallen into a postmodern act of endless signification. Lastly, Susan Sontag's discussion of photography is also quick to point out the desire to simply report through photographs cannot truly be achieved, noting, "the camera's rendering of reality must always hide more than it discloses" (1977, 23).

Susan Sontag's *On Photography* observes that mimetic art, like photography, is double-sided: "A photograph is both a pseudo-presence and a token of absence" (1977, 16). Likewise, Ugrešić's narrator reminds us that "It is concerned with what once was, and the trouble is that what once was, is being recorded by someone who is now" (28) [Ona se bavi onim što je jednom bilo, a to što je jednom bilo ispisuje netko koji *sada* jest (46)]. The passage of time works against immediacy, which cannot be re/captured, and Ugrešić fully understands this weakness in her choice of genre. At the same time, she recognizes its potential to access a different form of knowledge—what Sontag calls "understanding."[13] Sontag defines "understanding" as the realization that mimetic art cannot be accepted as a true record, but that narrative enables us to access some elements of the object or happening. The narrative that Ugrešić presents is a mix of autobiography, citationality, and photography—a mix remote from the sort of streamlined narrative that potentially could unify these modes.[14] Her palimpsest of multiple genres results in a partial rendering of her point of pain and is rife with gaps that leave unusually generous room for readers' interpretation.

Nowhere is reader explication more necessary than in the narrator's layering of biography (the story of the other) and autobiography (the story of the self). The story of Lucy, a woman who interviews the narrator, richly conveys this contested and shared space between narrator and character. Lucy feels bonded to the narrator (a feeling unreciprocated by the latter) and credits her with the ability to write what

---

[13] This "understanding" does not mean that the reader or viewer has reached the "truth" of the mimetic art, but that, as Ugrešić suggests, they access the point of pain.

[14] Akin to Walter Benjamin's arcades project focusing on Paris in the late nineteenth century, Ugrešić's series of observations, notes, commentaries, analyses, quotations from books, excerpts, random aphorisms, and references can be arranged and rearranged in any number of different constellations. In his file on methodology, Benjamin states, "Method of this project: literary montage. I needn't say anything. Merely show. I shall purloin no valuables, appropriate no ingenious formulations. But the rags, the refuse—these I will not inventory but allow, in the only way possible, to come into their own: by making use of them" (1999, 460). Ugrešić mirrors Benjamin's methodology in which fragments and leitmotifs begin to make sense in their relationship to each other. Like Benjamin, she furnishes no narrative connections for the reader.

she herself feels but is unable to express: "That is why she had so liked my book. As though she had written it herself. As though I had taken down her thoughts" (120) [Zato joj se, uostalom, toliko svidjela moja knjiga. Kao da ju je sama napisala. Kao da sam skinula njezine misli (148)]. Ugrešić herself resorts to the same substitution of other for self when she borrows quotations from other writers' works. She even appears to co-opt Wolf's character Christa T. as a woman whom her narrator meets. In all such examples, the reader must parse through the blurred lines between self and other.

Implementing this strategy of assorted viewpoints and voices, Ugrešić leaves room for her readers' subjectivity even while presenting perspective as shifting and multiple. In the last section of the text, the narrator describes her friends' using tarot cards. She maintains: "Tarot was nothing other than a kind of alternate literature in which the strength of the text depended on the power of the interpreter and the imagination of the reader" (187). [Tarot je bio alternativna književnost, gdje je snaga teksta ovisila o moći interpretator i imaginaciji čitatelja (232)]. It remains for the reader to build the associations between the stories and provide the neat narrative that Ugrešić refuses to supply. Ugrešić's method counters the technique of establishing master narratives characteristic of traditional male texts and of the rigid ideology of Croatian patriarchal discourse. In many ways, Ugrešić's text parallels Virginia Woolf's works, such as *Mrs. Dalloway* and *To the Lighthouse*. While *The Museum of Unconditional Surrender* is a wartime text, Woolf's *Mrs. Dalloway* is set in post-World War I England and *To the Lighthouse* encapsulates 1910–1920. The patriarchal discourse of war influences all of these gendered texts. In each, plot is secondary and prose is often meandering and difficult to follow. Like Woolf, Ugrešić investigates the means of perception by unfolding the text through shifting perspectives. Because both Woolf's and Ugrešić's texts lack an omniscient narrator, there is no apparent guide to lead us and we must rely upon our own formulation of impressions and conclusions. As such, their texts are morally ambiguous and avoid the master narratives or singular authorial perspectives often attributed to traditional male texts.

The use of photography in Ugrešić's text as war museum likewise becomes an act of translation and interpretation when what should be stable boundaries constituted in photographs emerge as fluid and shared. Looking at some photographs, the narrator believes that she recognizes a snapshot of herself: "[O]ne of me, taken on the beach. I could have been about thirteen. On the back of the picture I discovered a text in Bulgarian written in my distant cousin's unskilled hand: 'This is me, taken on a beach, in my new swimsuit.' Under the text was her equally clumsy signature" (26–7).[15] In this scene, which dramatizes competing claims, the narratives of self and other combine, and the physical body itself becomes contested (or shared) through its indistinguishability. This fusion and confusion raise the question of individual identity and one's self-image as well as implying a kinship through gendered experiences. This stratagem counters the dominant male construction of womanhood as monolithic by substituting sharing for perceived sameness.

In a parallel scene, gazing at a photograph leads to the narrator's realization of a similarity between her mother's face and her own. She detects the same "two lines around my mouth. They pointed downward, making on either side of my mouth a small, barely noticeable pouch" (35) [dvije male bore oko ustiju. Spuštale su se nadolje, stvarajući sa svake strane lica posve mali, jedva primjetni mješčić (51)]. Earlier in the text, the narrator describes a picture of her mother in identical words: "Sometimes I catch in my voice something of her cracked voice, sometimes her voice breaks in under mine, I speak in duet (61–2) [Ponekad lovim u svome glasu njezin napukli glas, ponekad ispod moga glasa probija njezin, govorim u dvoglasu (83)], and "I know all her gestures, movements, expressions, the tone of her voice. I recognize them in myself" (61) [Poznajem tek njezine geste, pokrete, izraze lica, boju glasa. Prepoznajem ih u sebi (82)]. Apart from inscribing generational continuity, such passages show that for the narrator, women's bodies and their stories may be understood only in connection to one another. In fact, the narrator cannot tell her story without telling the story of other women. And in that sense she may be said to represent a gendered perspective that transcends her

---

[15] "[J]e bila jedna moja, snimljena na plaži. Mogla sam imati trinaestak godina. Na poleđini fotografije otrila sam tekst na bugarskom jeziku ispisan nevještom rukom moje daleke sestrične: *To sam ja, snimljena na plaži, u svom movom kupaćem kostimu.* Ispod teksta bio je njezin jednako nevješt potpies" (41).

own. Later, when recounting her monthly baking exploits, the narrator remarks, "[T]he spirit of my grandmother [...] is settling in me and obliging me once a month to follow her pattern" (136) [useljava duh moje bake [...] i primorava me da jednom mjesečno ponovim njezin slučaj (169)]. Thus, whatever the fragmentation of her text, Ugrešić posits links with other women as the basis for understanding the self. Such connections form the basis of a museum where objects acquire additional meaning through "cohabitation" with other objects, just as the narrator and, presumably, Ugrešić find their identity shaped by gendered ties and parallels over time.

In his *Theory of Prose* Shklovsky says of Laurence Sterne: "In the very place where we expect to find a landing, we find instead a gaping hole" (1990, 156)—an image partially reprised in Žižek's remark about the national flag. This same gaping hole appears in Ugrešić's text as the place of loss, but also of possibility. Her narrator carries with her two photographs: one shows three unknown women bathing in the Pakra River in northern Croatia at the beginning of the century; the other is an overexposed "reject photograph" (181) [škart foto-grafija (225)]. The all-white "reject" is of the narrator's last dinner with a group of girlfriends in Croatia, which subsequently disbanded owing to rifts caused by the war and its ethnic politics. While time has transformed the first photo of the women in the river into a museum piece, a part of history, the war in Yugoslavia has done the same to the second photo. The narrator situates this blank photograph of herself and her friends alongside the anonymous photo of the women bathers,[16] with the explanation, "The yellowed photograph from the beginning of the century is like a lamp lit in a murky window, a heartening secret gesture with which I draw pictures out of the indifferent whiteness" (181) [Požutjela fotografija s početka stoljeća je poput upaljene svijetiljke na mrklu prozoru, udobrovoljavajuća tajna gesta s kojom izvlačim slike iz ravnodušne bjeline (225)]. Though the English translation uses the verb "to draw," a more accurate equivalent for "izvući" is "to pull out," "to extract," or "to save," reflecting the nuance of the original.

---

[16] This snapshot appears on the cover of most English-language editions of *The Museum of Unconditional Surrender.*

Throughout *The Museum of Unconditional Surrender*, layering and superimposing others' stories and styles fleetingly enable access to the point of pain through a mediated form of association, which simultaneously denies access to the heart of loss. That which is lost—in this case, the group picture and subsequently the narrator's former Yugoslavia—can be saved and extracted in an unsettling act of translation and appropriation from one image to another. While the photo of the bathers has no accompanying narrative to explain the tableau, the second photo has only narrative to attest to the "captured" occasion, for the photo is ruined. These photos therefore epitomize Ugrešić's project of preservation and surrender.

The memorial arts employed in Ugrešić's textual war museum convey a sense of both presence and absence. Mimetic arts (citationality, autobiography, and photography) provide Ugrešić with a method of recording and honoring her past while evading wartime discourse. The loss of Yugoslavia, the narrator's sense of self, as well as her friends and memories, may have become a gaping hole due to the war, but through a mediated extraction of superimposed photographs and of others' words and stories, she was able to accomplish a dreamlike translation with women at its very heart.

REFERENCES

Benjamin, Walter. 1999. *The Arcades Project*, translated by Howard Eiland and Kevin McLaughlin. Cambridge, Massachusetts: Belknap Press of Harvard University Press.

Boym, Svetlana. 1998. "Estrangement as a Lifestyle: Shklovsky and Brodsky." In *Exile and Creativity: Signposts, Travelers, Outsiders, Backward Glances*, edited by Susan Rubin Suleiman, 241–63. Durham: Duke University Press.

Corrin, Chris. 1999. *Gender and Identity in Central and Eastern Europe*. Portland, OR: Frank Cass.

Freud, Sigmund. 1989. *New Introductory Lectures on Psycho-Analysis*, translated by James Strachey. New York: W. W. Norton & Co.

Jambrešić Kirin, Renata. 1999. "Personal Narratives on War: A Challenge to Women's Essays and Ethnography in Croatia." *Estudos de Literatura Oral* 5: 73–98.

Kesić, Vesna. 2000. "From Reverence to Rape: An Anthropology of Ethnic and Genderized Violence." In *Frontline Feminisms: Women, War, and*

Resistance, edited by Marguerite R. Waller and Jennifer Rycenga, 23–39. New York: Garland Publishing.

———. 1997. "Confessions of a 'Yugo-Nostalgic' Witch." In *Anna's Land: Sisterhood in Eastern Europe*, edited by Tanya Renne, 195–200. Boulder: Westview Press.

Knezevic, Djurdja. 1997. "Affective Nationalism." In *Transitions, Environments, Translations: Feminism in International Politics*, edited by Joan W. Scott, Cora Kaplan, and Debra Keates, 65–71. New York: Routledge.

Lacan, Jacques. 1977. *Écrits: A Selection*, translated by Alan Sheridan. New York: W. W. Norton & Co.

Lampe, John R. 1996. *Yugoslavia as History: Twice There Was a Country*. New York: Cambridge University Press.

Lejeune, Philippe. 1989. "The Autobiographical Pact (bis)." In *On Autobiography*, edited by Paul John Eakin, translated by Katherine Leary, 119–37. Minneapolis: University of Minnesota Press.

Lukić, Jasmina. 2000. "Witches Fly High: The Sweeping Broom of Dubravka Ugrešić." *European Journal of Women's Studies* 7: 383–96.

Popescu, Monica. 2007. "Imagining the Past: Cultural Memory in Dubravka Ugrešić's *The Museum of Unconditional Surrender*." *Studies in the Novel* 39, no. 3 (Fall): 336–56.

Renne, Tanya. 1997. *Anna's Land: Sisterhood in Eastern Europe*. Boulder: Westview Press.

Salecl, Renata. 1994. *The Spoils of Freedom: Psychoanalysis and Feminism after the Fall of Socialism*. New York: Routledge.

Scott, Joan W., Cora Kaplan, and Debra Keates, eds. 1997. *Transitions, Environments, Translations: Feminism in International Politics*. New York: Routledge.

Shklovsky, Viktor. 1990. *Theory of Prose*, translated by Benjamin Sher. Elmwood Park, Illinois: Dalkey Archive Press.

Sontag, Susan. 1977. *On Photography*. New York: Picador.

Spitz, Ellen Handler. 2000. "Lost and Found: Reflections on Exile and Empathy." *American Imago: a Psychoanalytic Journal for Culture, Science, & the Arts* 57, no. 2 (Summer): 141–55.

Ugrešić, Dubravka. 2002. *Musej bezuvjetne predaje*. Zagreb: Konzor & Samizdat B92.

———. 1999. *The Museum of Unconditional Surrender*, translated by Celia Hawkesworth. London: Phoenix House.

———. 1998. *The Culture of Lies: Antipolitical Essays*, translated by Celia Hawkesworth. University Park, Pennsylvania: The Pennsylvania State University Press.

Žižek, Slavoj. 1993. *Tarrying With the Negative: Kant, Hegel, and the Critique of Ideology*. Durham: Duke University Press.

List of Contributors

HELENA GOSCILO is Professor and Chair of the Department of Slavic & East European Languages and Cultures at The Ohio State University.

YANA HASHAMOVA is Associate Professor in the Department of Slavic & East European Languages and Cultures and the Director of the Center for Slavic and East European Studies at The Ohio State University.

MARK LIPOVETSKY is Professor of Russian Studies at the University of Colorado-Boulder.

TRINA R. MAMOON is Associate Professor of Foreign Languages at the University of Alaska Fairbanks.

TATIANA MIKHAILOVA is Senior Instructor of Russian Studies at the University of Colorado-Boulder.

Dr. ELZBIETA OSTROWSKA teaches in the Department of English and Film Studies at the University of Alberta.

ALEXANDER PROKHOROV is Associate Professor of Russian and Film at College of William and Mary.

ELENA PROKHOROVA is Associate Professor of Russian and Film at College of William and Mary.

ROBERT A. ROTHSTEIN is Professor of Slavic and Judaic Studies and Amesbury Professor of Polish Language, Literature and Culture at the University of Massachusetts Amherst.

IRINA SANDOMIRSKAJA is Professor of Cultural Studies at the Baltic and East European Graduate School of the University College of South Stockholm, Sweden, at University College Södertörn.

JESSICA WIENHOLD-BROKISH is an independent scholar of comparative literature.

Index

Page numbers in Italics refer to illustrations.

A

E

Ehrenreich, Barbara, 181
Eisenstein, Sergei, 86
Eisenstein, Zillah, 218–19
Elusive Avengers, The [*Neulovimye mstiteli*] (Keosaian film, 1966), 109
"Enemies Have Burned [His] House Down, The" ["Vragi sozhgli rodnuiu khatu"] (song), 180, 190
Engel, Barbara, 83, 85, 89
English, Deirdre, 181
Ennis, Garth, 8n18
Eremina, 162n22
Ermler, Fridrikh, 5, 11, 60, 83; criticized by party censors, 71–72, 75; moral occult and, 64
Erokhin, Aleksei, 108–9, 127
essentialism, 112, 163, 180–81
ethnic cleansing, 234
Euripides, 1
Europe, Eastern, 114, 121n21, 127, 257
Everyday Life in Early Soviet Russia (Kiaer and Naiman, eds.), 81
Ezhov, Valentin, 82, 87, 88

F

Fadeev, Aleksandr, 82, 83
Fadeeva, Irina, 227n19
fairy tales, 111n12, 115n18
Fall of Berlin, The [*Padenie Berlina*] (film, 1949), 75
Famous Five series (Blyton), 13
Fate of a Man [*Sud'ba cheloveka*] (Bondarchuk film, 1959), 165, 190
Fat'ianov, Aleksandr, 196n36
Female Prisoner of the Caucasus, The [*Kavkazskaia plennitsa*] (Gaidai film, 1966), 218
femininity, 20, 30n2, 41, 84, 98; avoidance of stereotypes in Soviet poster art, 170–71; disavowal of, 247; embodied in motherhood, 32; essentialization of, 15; everlasting and indestructible, 33, 34, 44, 54, 56; external markers of, 13; ideal, 44; identified with nature, 46; in *Kanal*, 42; in Leningrad siege, 144–46; Soviet femininity and Thanatos, 98–102; in Soviet propaganda, 63, 163; stereotyped as emotionally governed, 37; traditional archetypes of, 82; as universal myth, 31; "warrior" identity and, 96
feminism, 15, 112, 161, 181, 210n4; Chechen female combatants and, 208, 226; rise of, 19; Soviet culture and, 87; on violence by women, 214–15; Western, 237, 249; World War I and, 2–3
Filipowicz, Halina, 45
Filipowski, Tadeusz, 108n5
Finland, 4
First Circle, The [*V kruge pervom*] (Solzhenitsyn), 103
First World War [*I wojna światowa*] (Rapacki), 34n3
Fischer, Lucy, 61
Fischer, Siobhan, 234–35, 238
Fitzpatrick, Sheila, 81
Five-Year Plan, first, 182
folk culture/folklore, 60, 62, 98, 126
Forefathers' Eve [*Dziady*] (Mickiewicz), 32, 35n5
Foucault, Michel, 103
Four Cabmen and a Dog (Popov, 2004), 108n7
Four Tank Men and a Dog [*Czterej pancerni i pies*] (Nałęcki, Polish TV series), 12–13, 111–13; background of, 113; characters, 113–15; end of series as growing up/settling down, 125–27; humor in, 114, 117, 119, 122–24; male

Index

of, 70; Soviet propaganda posters and, 160, 171, 172, 173; technology and, 66; women in Soviet air force and, 8, 9, 19
NEP (New Economic Policy), 104
Netherlands, 4
Nevskii, Aleksandr, 157
Night Witches (*Nachthexen*), 8, 12, 19
Nikonenko, Sergei, 97
900 Days, The (Salisbury), 168n35
Nivat, Anne, 209–10, 223
NKVD (Soviet secret police), 134n7, 137, 138n12
nostalgia, 127, 247
"Notes on the Margins of Tragedy" ["Zapiski na poliakh tragedii"] (Pastukhov), 225–26
novels, nineteenth-century Russian, 14
Novikov, Anatolii, 179n1, 187n19, 200
Nowell-Smith, Geoffrey, 74
nuclear family, 62, 63
nurses, 6, 112, 164; in poster art, 14, 163; in post-Soviet Russian military, 20; songs about, 180, 183, 190–93; supporting role of, 20, 112

O

October (1917) Revolution, 76, 211
Odes (Horace), 2
"Ogonek" (song), 167
Oktiabr'skaia, Mariia, 156n8
Oliverio, Annemarie, 214
On Photography (Sontag), 267
On the Path [*Na putu*] (Žbanić film, 2010), 237
"Only at the Front" ["Tol'ko na fronte"] (song), 201
orphans, after World War II, 9
Orthodoxy, Russian, 59, 64, 161
Ostrowska, Elżbieta, 10

"Our Girl" ["Nasha devushka"] (song), 193
Oushakine, Serguei, 225n17
Over Her Dead Body (Bronfen), 51–52

P

paganism, 59, 60, 62
Pape, Robert, 212
Paret, Peter, 155n7
Parker, Paul, 157
partisans, 4, 9, 163; number of women serving as, 83; songs about female partisans, 198–200; in Soviet films, 11, 63, 72
Pasternak, Boris, 161n20
Pastukhov, Vladimir, 225–26
patriarchy, 37, 66, 96, 115, 119; in Chechnya, 16, 218–19, 223; in Croatia, 268; Hollywood cinema and, 75; murder professionally performed by women and, 86–87; Russian national identity and, 209; terrorism and, 214; in Thaw period, 89
patriotism, 2, 4; Chechen, 17, 227; feminism and, 3; Polish, 39, 121; propaganda and, 155; Russian, 21; Soviet, 11, 156
Peasant Woman [*Krest'ianka*] magazine, 182
Pennington, Reina, 163n24
Penthesilea, 1
Petersburski, Jerzy, 126n24
Petrova, Sof'ia Nikolaevna, *134*
Petrukhina, Nadezhda (fictional character), 88–89, *92–94, 97*, 103–4; implied suicide of, 90–91, 101–2; love associated with war, 98, 101; "mobilized" or "military" personality of, 91–92, 95, 100; "normal" femininity and, 98–101; split subjectivity of, 93–94, 97

Y